Reprints of Economic Classics

MORAL VIEWS OF COMMERCE,
SOCIETY AND POLITICS

MORAL VIEWS

OF

COMMERCE, SOCIETY AND POLITICS

IN TWELVE DISCOURSES

BY

ORVILLE DEWEY

[1838]

REPRINTS OF ECONOMIC CLASSICS

Augustus M. Kelley · Publishers
NEW YORK 1969

First Edition 1838
(New York: David Felt & Co., *Stationers' Hall*, 1838)

Reprinted 1969 by
Augustus M. Kelley • Publishers
New York New York 10010

SBN 678 00527 3

Library of Congress Catalogue Card Number
68-27851

PRINTED IN THE UNITED STATES OF AMERICA
by SENTRY PRESS, NEW YORK, N. Y. 10019

MORAL VIEWS

OF

COMMERCE, SOCIETY AND POLITICS,

IN TWELVE DISCOURSES,

BY

ORVILLE DEWEY.

NEW-YORK:
DAVID FELT & CO. STATIONERS' HALL.

1838.

Entered according to an Act of Congress, in the year 1838, by Orville Dewey, in the Clerk's office of the District Court of the Southern District of New-York.

CONTENTS.

	Page
DISCOURSE I. On the Moral Laws of Trade, ...	9
DISCOURSE II. On the Moral Law of Contracts, ...	48
DISCOURSE III. On the Uses of Labor, and a Passion for a Fortune,	74
DISCOURSE IV. On the Moral Limits of Accumulation, . . .	99
DISCOURSE V. On the Natural and Artificial Relations of Society,	117
DISCOURSE VI. On the Moral Evils to which American Society is exposed, ...	145
DISCOURSE VII. On Associations, ...	170
DISCOURSE VIII. On Social Ambition, ...	190
DISCOURSE IX. On the Place which Education and Religion must have in the Improvement of Society, ...	210

DISCOURSE X.
On War, ... 235

DISCOURSE XI.
On Political Morality, ... 257

DISCOURSE XII.
The Blessing of Freedom, ... 280

PREFACE.

THE character of some of the following Discourses will, doubtless, be thought unusual for the pulpit. The subjects themselves, indeed, are out of the ordinary course of preaching. I might say in their defence, that such topics have been sometimes admitted into occasional Sermons; and that Commercial Morality, in particular, has been made the subject of, at least, one entire volume of Religious Discourses, which has not offended the popular taste. But this defence, I must confess, does not satisfy me. In justice to my own convictions, I must be allowed to place the following discussions on a broader ground than that of exception. If I deserve blame, I cannot fairly escape on such a plea. For I am persuaded, not only that such discussions are entirely proper for the pulpit, but that it is the bounden duty of the pulpit to entertain them.

If, indeed, I have violated the proper decorum of religious discourse, such an error is capable of no defence. But I must be allowed to say, that when I had determined that it was my duty as a preacher, to discuss certain subjects, I could not allow any formality or fastidiousness of the pulpit, to prevent me from doing so with as much thoroughness and detail, as were compatible with the gravity of the place. Thus, with regard to the first discourse—on the Moral Law of Contracts—knowing, as I did know, that the consciences of men around me, were deeply involved in the questions that arose, I could not hesitate about going into the necessary specifications, however unusual, in preaching;—the serious business of such a discourse, would not allow me to stand on pulpit ceremony, as to terms and phrases and instances. I could not well be understood without them; and as the object of speaking is to be understood, I knew of no sanctity of time or place, that was to contravene the laws of that very instrument, speech, which I was using.

I am not ignorant, at the same time, in what manner any thing unusual in the subjects or style of religious discourses is likely to be received. I know that there will be some readers, as there have been hearers of these discourses, to say, that a part of them would be more suitable for the Lyceum and lecture-room. Nay, I will confess, that in delivering them, I have had certain feelings of reluctance to contend with, in my own mind; so powerful are old prepossessions against new or singular views of duty. Since I understand the feeling of objection, therefore, will the kind reader who may entertain the same feeling, permit me to reason the matter a little with him and with myself, in the remainder of this preface?

Let me ask, in the first place, if our ideas of propriety in this case, are not very much matters of convention and usage? If we had always been accustomed to hear discussions in our churches, on such subjects as the Morals of Traffic, of Politics, and of our social well-being as a nation—if the terms and phrases appropriate to such subjects had found a place in the pulpit, should we ever have doubted their propriety? It is observable, indeed, that certain topics have forced their way into the pulpit, within the last quarter of a century, which, it is probable, sounded as questionably and strangely in ears accustomed only to the old scholastic preaching, as any grave moral topics can now. I allude to discussions on War and Peace, on Temperance, Abolition, and the various religious enterprises of the day.

The question then is—what is the proper range of the pulpit? What is the appropriate business of preaching? The answer is plain—to address the public mind on its moral and religious duties and dangers. But what are its duties and dangers, and where are they to be found? Are they not to be found wherever men are acting their part in life? Are human responsibility and exposure limited to any one sphere of action—to the church or to the domestic circle—or to the range of the gross and sensual passions? Are not men daily making shipwreck of their consciences in trade and politics? And wheresoever conscience goes to work out its perilous problem, shall not the preacher follow it? It is not very material, whether a man's integrity forsakes him at the polls in an election, or at the board of merchandise; or at the house of rioting, or the gates whose way leadeth to destruction. Outwardly it may be different, but inwardly it is the same. In either case, the fall of the victim is the most deplorable of all things on earth ; and most fit, therefore, for the consideration of the pulpit. I must confess, I cannot understand, by what process of enlightened reasoning and conscience, the preacher can come to the conclusion, that there are wide regions of moral action and peril around him, into which he may not enter, because such unusual words as, Commerce, Society, Politics, are written over the threshold.

Nay more ; is not the greatest possible disservice done to the highest interests of mankind, by this limitation as to subjects, under which the pulpit has laid itself. The confined and technical character which belongs to the common administration of religion, does more than any thing else, in my apprehension, to disarm it of its power. I am not insensible, when I say this, to the greatness of those obstacles in the human heart and in human life, with which it has to contend. I am not, now, measuring the strength of those obstacles, but simply considering the force that is brought to bear upon them. That force is moral, spiritual force ; and the leading form of it, in the public estimation, is preaching. The pulpit is the authorised expositor to men, of their duties. Those duties, it will not be denied, press upon every action and instant of human life. But what now, is the consideration which the pulpit generally, gives to this wide and busy field of duty ? Are not whole spheres of human action left out of the account ? With the exception of some occasional and wholesale denunciations, are not business, politics, amusements and fashionable society, passed by entirely ? Are not men *left* to say, when engaged in those scenes—" religion has nothing to do with us here ?" Do they not, naturally enough, feel that these engagements are, in a manner, set apart from all sense of duty ? Is it strange, then, that the public conscience is lax in these matters ? It seems to me, I must confess, rather a hard measure that the pulpit deals out to these departments of life. It never recognizes them as spheres of duty : it does nothing for the correction or culture of men's minds in them ; and yet, every now and then, it comes down upon their aberrations with cold, bitter and unsparing censure.

Let me not be supposed to forget, that the pulpit has to deal with topics and questions of duty, that go down into the depths of the human heart—with faith, and repentance, and love, and self-denial, and disinterestedness—and that its principal business is thus to make the fountain pure. But religion has an outward form, as well as an inward spirit. That form is the whole lawful action of life. And to cut off half of that action from all public and positive recognition—what is it but to consign it over to irreligion, to unprincipled license, and worldly vanity?

There is time enough in the pulpit for all things. Nay, it *wants* variety. It is made dull by the restriction and reiteration of its topics. It would gain strength by a freer and fuller grasp of its proper objects. What it can do, I believe, yet remains to be seen. We complain of the corruptions of fashion and amusement, of business and politics. The calm, considerate, concentrated, universal attention of the pulpit, to these things, would, in one year, I believe, produce a decided and manifest effect.

But the great evil, I am sensible, lies deeper—too deep for any sufficient consideration, within the narrow limits of a preface. The pulpit not only fails in this matter, but it fails *on principle*, and on a principle almost universally adopted. The evil is, that sermons, pulpits, priests—all the active agents that are laboring in the service of religion—are, by the public judgment as well as by their own choice, severed from the great mass of human actions and interests

DISCOURSE I.

ON THE MORAL LAW OF CONTRACTS.

I THESSALONIANS IV. 6. THAT NO MAN GO BEYOND AND DEFRAUD HIS BROTHER IN ANY MATTER.

I PROPOSE to invite your attention in a series of three or four Sabbath evening discourses, to the moral laws of trade, the moral end of business, and to the moral principles which are to govern the accumulation of property. The first of these subjects, is proposed for your consideration this evening; and it is one, as I conceive, of the highest interest and importance.

This country presents a spectacle of active, absorbing, and prosperous business, which strikes the eye of every stranger, as its leading characteristic. We are said to be, and we *are* a people, beyond all others, devoted to business and accumulation. This, though it is often brought against us as a reproach, is really an inevitable result of our political condition. I trust that it is but the *first* development, and that many better ones are to follow. It does, however, spring from our institutions; and I hold, moreover, that it is honorable to them. If half of us were slaves, that half could have nothing to do with traffic. If half of us were in the condition of the peasantry of Europe, the business transactions of that half would be restricted within a narrow sphere, and would labor under a heavy pressure. But where liberty is given to each one to act freely for himself, and by all lawful means to better his condition, the consequence is inevitably what we see—an universal and unprecedented activity among all the classes of society, in all the departments of human industry. The moral principles then, applicable to the transaction of business have strong claims upon our attention ; and seem to me, very proper subjects of discussion in our pulpits.

There are moral questions too, as we very well know, which actually do interest all reflecting and conscientious men who are engaged in trade. They are very frequently discussed in conversation ; and very different grounds are taken by the disputants. Some say that one principle is altogether right, and others, that another and totally different one is the only right principle. In such circumstances, it seems to me not only proper but requisite, for those whose office it is to speak to men of their duties, that they should take up the discussion of these as they would any other moral questions. I am obliged to confess that we are liable, scholastic and retired men as we are, to give some ground to men of business, for anticipating that our reasonings and conclusions will not be very practical or satisfactory. I can only say, for myself, that I have, for some time, given patient and careful attention to the moral principles of trade ; that I have often conversed with men of business that I might understand the practical bearings and difficulties of the subject ; that I have also read some of the books in which the morality of contracts is discussed ;

and although a clergyman, I shall venture, with some confidence as well as modesty, to offer you my thoughts on the points in question. I say the points in question; and I have intimated that there are points in debate, questions of conscience in business, which are brought into the most serious controversy. I have even known conscientious and sensible men, themselves engaged in trade, to go to the length of asserting, not only that the principles of trade are immoral and unchristian, but that no man can acquire a property in this commerce without sacrificing a good conscience; that no prosperous merchant can be a good Christian. I certainly think that such casuists are wrong; but whether or not they are so, the principles which bring them to a conclusion so extraordinary, evidently demand investigation.

In preparing to examine this opinion, and indeed to discuss the whole subject, it will not be improper to observe in the outset, that trade in some form, is the inevitable result of the human condition. Better, it has been said, on the supposition already stated—better that commerce should perish than Christianity; but let it be considered whether commerce can perish. Nothing can be more evident than that the earth was formed to be the theatre of trade. Not only does the ocean facilitate commerce, but the diversity of soils, climes, and products, requires it. So long as one district of country produces cotton, and another corn; so long as one man lives by an ore-bed which produces iron, and another, on pasture-lands which grow wool, there must be commerce. In addition to this, let it be considered that all human industry inevitably tends to what is called "the division of labor."

The savage who roams through the wilderness, may possibly, in the lowest state of barbarism, procure with his own hand all that suffices for his miserable accommodation,—the coat of skins that clothes, the food that sustains, and the hut that shelters him. But the moment that society departs from that state, there necessarily arise the different occupations of shepherd, agriculturist, mechanic, and manufacturer; the products of whose industry are to be exchanged; and this exchange is trade. If a single individual were to perform all the operations necessary to produce a piece of cloth, and yet more a garment of that cloth, the process would be exceedingly slow and expensive. Human intelligence necessarily avails itself of the facility, the dexterity, and the advantage every way, which are to be obtained by a division of labor. The very progress of society is indicated by the gradual and growing development of this tendency.

Besides, it has been justly observed by a celebrated writer on this subject,* that "there is a certain propensity in human nature to truck, barter, and exchange one thing for another. It is common to all men," he says, "and to be found in no other race of animals, which seem to know neither this nor any other species of contracts. Nobody," he observes, "ever saw a dog make a fair and deliberate exchange of one bone for another, with another dog. Nobody ever saw one animal by its gestures and natural cries signify to another, this is mine, that yours; I am willing to give this for that."

Trade, then, being a part of the inevitable lot of cultivated humanity, the question is, not about abolish-

* Adam Smith.

ing, but about the moral principles that are to regulate it. And the grand question which I propose now to examine is, the only one that presses upon the conscience, and therefore proper for discussion in the pulpit; and one, too, of daily recurrence—the question, that is, about the moral law of contracts. The question, to state it more definitely, is, whether, in making contracts, it is right for one party to take any advantage, or to make any use, and if any, what, of his superior sagacity, information, or power of any kind?

Let us first inquire, how we are to settle this question? What is the process of mind by which we are to ascertain and establish the moral laws of trade?

Does the natural conscience declare them? Is there any instinctive prompting of conscience, that can properly decide each case as it arises in the course of business? Is there any voice within, that says clearly and with authority, "thou shalt do thus, and so?" I think not. The cases are not many, in any department of action, where conscience thus reveals itself. But in business they are peculiarly rare, because the questions there, are unusually complicated. You offer to sell to your neighbor an article of merchandise. You are entitled of course—i. e. in ordinary circumstances—to some advance upon what it cost you. But what that is, depends on many circumstances. Conscience will hardly mark down the just price in your account-book. Conscience, indeed, commands us to do right; but the question is, what *is* right? This is to be decided by views far more various and comprehensive, than the simple sense of right and wrong.

The Scriptures, like conscience, are a general directory. They do not lay down any specific moral laws of trade. They command us to be upright and honest; but they leave us to consider what particular actions are required by those principles. They command us to do unto others as we would have them do to us; but still this is not specific. A man may unreasonably wish that another should sell him a piece of goods at half its value. Does it follow that he himself ought to sell on those terms? The truth is, that the golden rule, like every other in Scripture, is a general maxim. It simply requires us to desire the welfare of others, as we would have them desire ours. But the specific actions answering to that rule, it leaves us to determine by a wise discretion. The dictates of that discretion, under the governance of the moral law, are the principles that we seek to discover.

Neither, on this subject, can I accept without question the teachings of the common law; because, I find, that its ablest expounders acknowledge that its decisions are sometimes at variance with strict moral principle. I do not think it follows from this, that the general principles of the common law, are wrong, or abet wrong. Nay, I conceive that they may approach as near to rectitude as is possible in the circumstances, and yet necessarily involve some practical injustice in their operation. This results, in fact, from their very utility, their very perfection, as a body of laws. For it is requisite to their utility, that they should be general, that they should be derived from precedents and formed into rules; else, men will not know what to depend upon, nor how to govern themselves; and there would neither be confidence, nor order, nor society. But general rules must sometimes bear hard upon individuals; the very law which secures justice in a thousand cases, may, and perhaps must, from the very nature of human affairs and relationships, do injustice in one. Indeed, the law of chancery, or of equity, has been devised on purpose to give relief. But oven chancery has its rules which sometimes press injuriously upon individual interests; and no human laws can attain to a perfect and unerring administration of justice. For this perfect justice, however, we seek. We are asking what it is to do no wrong to our fellow-man, whether the law permits it or not. We are asking how we shall stand acquitted, not merely at the bar of our country, but at the bar of conscience and of God.

I must add, in fine, that questions about right and wrong in the contracts of trade, are not to be decided by any hasty impulses of feeling, or suggestions of a generous temper. I have often found men, in conversation on this subject, appealing to their feelings; but however much I have respected those feelings, it has seemed to me, that they were not the proper tribunal. Nay, they have often appeared to me to mistake the point at issue. If a merchant has a large store of provisions in a time of scarcity, would it not be a very noble and praise-worthy thing, it is said, for him to dispose of his stock, without enhancing the price? But the proper question is not, what is generous, but what is just. And besides, he cannot be generous, or what is the same thing in effect, he cannot establish a generous principle in the distribution of his store. For if he sells in large quantities, selling, that is, at a low rate, it will avail nothing, because the subordinate dealers will raise the price. Or, if he undertakes to sell to each family what it wants; any one of them may take the article to the next warehouse, and dispose of it at the enhanced price. On the contrary, there are circumstances, undoubtedly, in which a man may take undue advantage of a monopoly; but this will be a case for future consideration. For the present, it is sufficient to observe, what I think must be obvious, that the great question before us is to be decided, not by any enactments of law, nor any immediate dictate of conscience, or specific teaching of Scripture, or single impulse of good feeling, but by broad and large views of the whole subject. Conscience, and Scripture, and right feeling are to govern us; but it is only under the guidance of sound reasoning.

Let me beg your indulgence to one or two further preliminary observations. The questions to be discussed are of great importance, and scarcely of less difficulty. It is hardly possible to overrate the importance of a high, and at the same time, just tone of commercial morality. I am addressing merchants and young men, who are to be the future merchants of this city and country. I am addressing them on the morality of their daily lives, on the principles that are to form their character for time, and eternity; and while I task myself to speak with the utmost care and deliberation, I shall not be thought unreasonable, I trust, if I invite the patient attention of those who hear me, to share in the task.

There is then, on this subject, a distinction to be made between principles and rules. Principles, the principles that is to say of truth, justice and beneficence, are clear and immutable; the only difficulty is about the application of them—i. e. about rules. Principles, I say, are to be set apart, at once and entirely, from all doubt and uncertainty. They hold their place on high, like unchanging lights in the heavens. The only question is, how, in obedience to their direction, we are faithfully and surely to work our traverse across the troubled ocean of business. Here, I say, is all the difficulty. Rules, I repeat, result from the application of principles to human conduct, and they must be affected by the circumstances to which they relate. Thus, it is an immutable principle in morals, that I should love my neighbor, my fellow-being, and desire to promote his happiness. This principle admits of no qualification; it can suffer no abatement in any circumstances. But when I come to consider what I shall *do* in obedience to this principle ; what I shall do for the poor, the sick, or the distressed ; by what acts I shall show my kindness to my neighbor, or my interest in the welfare of the world,—when, in other words, I come to consider the *rules* of my conduct, I am obliged at once to admit doubts and difficulties. The abstract principle cannot be my law, without any regard to circumstances, though some moral reformers would make it such. I must go on the right line of conduct, it is true, but where that line shall lead me, is to be determined by a fair consideration of the cases that come before me. If it is not, I shall contravene the very principle on which I am acting. If, for instance, I do nothing but give, give to the poor, I shall be doing them an injury, not a kindness. The great law of benevolence, in fact, as truly requires discretion as it enforces action.

This distinction fully applies to the subject we are about to examine. Rectitude, justice, benevolence, truth-telling, are immutable laws of trade, as they are of all human conduct. There is no *certain extent* to which they go; they apply without limit to every department and every transaction in business; they are never to be contravened. But in laying down practical rules for traffic, we immediately meet with difficulties, and are obliged to leave a great deal to the honest judgment of the trader. He must do right, indeed; that is the great law; but what *is* right? Let us now more nearly approach this question, having narrowed it down to a question about rules, and more closely apply ourselves to the difficulties involved in it.

And here, I must ask you to consider as a further and final preliminary topic, the language of the legal writers on this subject. It is common with those writers to make a distinction between moral and legal justice; or, in other words, between the demands of conscience and the decisions of their courts. Conscience, for instance, demands that a certain contract shall be annulled, because there was some concealment or deception, but the courts will not annul it, unless the injury be very great. In short, it is a matter of degrees. Up to a certain extent, the law will, in fact, protect a man in doing what is wrong, in doing that which violates his conscience; beyond a certain extent, it will not protect him. This distinction is founded on the policy of the law, and the policy of trade. "In law," says Pothier, "a party will not be permitted to complain of slight offences, which he, with whom a contract is made, has committed against good faith; otherwise there would be too many contracts to be rescinded; which would open the way for too much litigation, and would derange commerce."* And again, "the

---
* Traité des Obligations, Part. I. ch. 1. Sec. 1. Art. 3. § 3.

interests of commerce will not easily permit parties to escape from bargains which they have concluded; they must lay the blame to their not having been better informed concerning the defects of the article sold."* And again he says, "this rule is wisely established for the security and freedom of commerce, which demand that no one should easily be off from his bargains; otherwise men would not dare to make contracts, for fear that he with whom they had bargained, should imagine that he was injured, and upon that ground (of mere imagination or pretence) should commence an action." Hence, Pothier says, that the wrong of which the courts will take cognizance, must be an enormous wrong.†

Now there is, doubtless, a certain expediency here; a certain policy of trade, a certain policy of the law. It is expedient that a fair field be opened in business for ingenuity, sagacity and attention; and that ignorance, indolence and neglect, should meet with loss. "The common law," says Chancellor Kent, "affords to every one, reasonable protection against fraud in dealing; but it does not go the romantic length of giving indemnity against the consequences of indolence and folly, or a careless indifference to the ordinary and accessible means of information."‡

What is the nature, and what is the amount of this concession to expediency? Let us carefully consider this question, for much depends upon it.

Legal expediency, then, is not to be so construed as to warrant the supposition, that it lends a sanction to

---

* Traité du Contrat de vente, Part. II. ch. 2. Art. 2.
† Traité des Obligations, Part. I. ch. 1. Sec. 1. Art. 3. § 4.
‡ Commentaries.

what is wrong. It may, from necessity, permit or protect fraud, but does not abet it. A man is not to consider himself an honest man, simply because the law gives him deliverance. For the law *cannot* take cognizance of the secret intentions, nor of slight deviations from truth. If every man who says he has got a bad bargain, and who thinks he has been cheated, could be heard in court, our tribunals would be overwhelmed with business. No human tribunal can descend to the minutiæ of injustice. But the law, I repeat, does not sanction what it does not undertake to prevent, any more than the infinite providence sanctions those abuses which arise from its great law of freedom.

This being the nature of the concession to expediency—no principle being compromised—we may say, that the extent of the concession must be considerable. It is certainly expedient that every man be put upon his own discretion, sagacity and attention, for success. In business, as in every thing else, a premium is set upon these qualities by the hand of providence. It is expedient, in other words, that every man should take care of himself. Others are not to step forward at every turn to rescue him from the consequences of his indolence or inattention. The seller is not required to give his *opinion* to the buyer. If he *knows* of any defect in his merchandise, not apparent to the buyer, he is bound to state it; but he is not required to give his opinion. The buyer has no business to ask it of him; he is to form an opinion for himself. If he is relieved from doing this, he will always remain in a sort of mercantile childhood.

Nor do I know that there is any thing in Scripture, or in the laws of human brotherhood, that forbids this honest, not fraudulent, but honest competition between men's exertions, faculties and wits. We are indeed to do to others as we would have them do to us; but we ought not to wish them to do any thing to us, which is inconsistent with the general welfare of the community, with the lawful and necessary stimulants to action. We may have unreasonable desires: we would, perhaps, that our rich neighbor should present us with half of his fortune; but unreasonable desires are not the measure of our duties. Not *whatever* we wish, but what we *lawfully* wish from others, should we do to them. And lawfully, we can no more wish that they should give to our indolence and negligence, the benefit of their sagacity and alertness in making a contract, than that they would give to our poverty the half of that wealth, which their superior industry or talent had earned for them. Thus, too, when it is said that we ought to treat all men as brethren; it is true, indeed, so far as that relation is expressive of the general relationships of society. But while there should be a brotherly community of feeling, there cannot be a brotherly identity of interests between the members of society; and, therefore, they are not bound to deal with one another as if they belonged to a community of Shakers, or of New Harmony men. We are not to break down the principle of individuality, of individual interests, of individual aims; while at the same time, we are to hold it in subjection to the laws of sacred honesty, and of a wise philanthropy.

Besides, it is not only expedient and right, but it is inevitable, that individual power and talent should come into play in business. A man's sagacity, it is obvious, he must use—that is to say, his mind he must use—for he has nothing else to go by. He may use it unjustly, to the heinous injury of his weaker neighbor; but still he must use it. So also with regard to the power acquired by a large property, or by a monopoly, it is inevitable that it should be used. To some extent, the possessor cannot help using it. Wealth has credit; and monopoly, usually implying scarcity, carries an enhanced price with it; and such results are unavoidable. Finally, superior actual knowledge, may, and must be used, to some extent. In every department of business, superior knowledge is gained by attention, and it may and must be acted upon; albeit to the hurt or injury of those who know less, or have devoted less time and thought to the subject. A man has made an improvement in some machinery or manufacture, and he is entitled to some reward for the attention he has given to it; the government will give him a patent. A man has been to India or to South America, to acquaint himself with a certain branch of business, and he comes home and acts upon his knowledge, and he has a perfect right to do so. He is not bound to communicate his knowledge to his brother merchants who are engaged in the same trade; and, perhaps, his knowledge so much depends upon actual observation and experience, that he cannot communicate it. In like manner, a trader may obtain a superior knowledge of business and of the facts on which it depends, by a close observation of things immediately around him, and he must act upon it; he cannot employ himself in going about to see whether other men have got the same enlarged views. Nor have other men any right to complain of this. The unskilful painter or sculptor, the ignorant lawyer or physician might as well complain, that their more distinguished brethren were injuring their business, and taking all the prizes out of their hands.

I have thus attempted to set forth the claims of individual enterprise, as having a useful, a beneficent tendency. These claims, I have all along implied, are subject to certain limitations. And these limitations are set by the laws of honesty and philanthropy. That is to say, a man may pursue his own interest; he may use his endeavor, sagacity, ability; but, in the first place, he shall not pursue any traffic or make any contract to the injury of his neighbor; unless that injury is one that inevitably results from a general and good principle—that is to say, from the healthful action of business; and, in the next place, he shall not pursue his own ends to the extent of committing any fraud.

This last limitation is the one of the most palpable importance, and demands that we should dwell upon it a moment. What then is a fraud in contracts? In order to answer the question, let us ask what is a contract? A contract is a mutual engagement, to exchange certain goods for other goods, or certain goods for money, and the essence of the engagement lies in the supposed equivalency of the things that are exchanged. This results from the very nature of the case and of the human mind. For it is not the part of a rational being to give more for less. If you bargain away any thing to your neighbour, you, of course, seek from him what to you is equivalent. But how are you to judge of this equivalency; of the value, that is to say, of the article offered to you? There are two grounds on which you may judge. You may know the article as well as the seller, you may know as much about it; every way, as he does. This is ordinarily the case between trader and trader. But between the merchant and the rest of the world, this is usually not the case. And here the ground on which you proceed is, that of confidence in the good faith of the seller. You could make up no satisfactory opinion on the value of the article offered to you, if you did believe that it is what it purports to be, what it appears to be, what the price indicates it to be. If, then, there is any secret defect in the article not apparent to you, or if there is any circumstance unknown to you, materially affecting its value, or if the price set upon it is any other than the market price, *there* is fraud. Wherever the contracting parties stand in totally different relations to the matter in hand, the one knowing something—some secret, which the other does not and cannot know, *there* is fraud. The contract is morally vitiated. The obvious conditions of a contract are not complied with. It is well known by one of the parties that the grand condition—that of equivalency—does not exist in the case.

Let us now look back, for a moment, upon the ground which we have passed over in this preliminary discussion. I have, in the first place, attempted to show that no single suggestion or dictate of conscience, or scripture, or of generous feeling, or of the law, is sufficient to solve the moral questions that arise in trade. In the next place, I have said that there is a distinction to be made between principles and rules; the principles of moral conduct being clear and certain; the rules only, the specific actions under these principles, that is to say—being liable to doubt. I thus wished to set one department of this subject above all question. In the third place, I applied myself to the consideration of rules. And here I attempted to show that while, on the one hand, it is expedient that ample scope be given to human ingenuity, sagacity and alertness in business, yet, on the other hand, that they are never to transgress the bounds of philanthropy, honesty and justice.

Let us now proceed to examine some of the cases to which these general reasonings apply.

I. The first is the ordinary case of buying and selling, i. e. under ordinary circumstances.

And here, it is expedient and necessary, that men in their dealings with one another should be put to the use of their senses and faculties. There is a discretion and there is a duty proper, respectively, to the seller and to the buyer. Each of them has his part to act, his business to attend to, and neither of them is bound to assume the duty of the other. In ordinary cases there is no difficulty with this maxim, no temptation to dishonesty, no possibility of deception. The article is open to inspection; its qualities are as obvious to the buyer as to the seller. The buyer is supposed to know his own business, his own occasions; the *buyer* is fairly supposed best to know what the article is worth to him, not the seller; and it is for him to decide, whether he will purchase, and what he will give. The seller cannot be expected to enter into the circumstances of the buyer, and to ascertain by inquiry what he intends to do with the article he purchases; whether he can turn it to good account; or whether he could not buy more advantageously somewhere else; all this belongs to the province of the buyer; it is his business to settle all these questions. And he is not only best able to decide them, but he is as competent to judge of the quality of the goods which are offered him, as the seller, for they are alike open to the inspection of both.

This free action, this competition, we have already said, is to be restrained in trade as in every thing else, by perfect fairness and honesty. At that point in our preliminary discussion, the theoretical question about the nature of a contract presented itself; in our present inquiry, the natural and practical question is about price. What is the just price of an article? A man has something to sell; he wishes to deal honestly; the question then is, what shall he ask for it? If he can settle this question, all is plain. How shall he settle it? What is it that determines a price to be just? Evidently, not any abstract consideration of value. There can be no such thing as abstract value. The worth of a thing depends on the want of it. Originally, it is true; i. e. in the first rude state of society, men, in exchanging the products of their labor, would naturally estimate the value of each article by the labour required to produce it. But even this estimate, though approaching nearest to it, would not present us with an abstract and absolute value; and it would soon be disturbed by circumstances, effectually and beyond recovery. Labor would not be an accurate measure of value, because one man's labor, through its energy and ingenuity, would be worth far more than another man's. That primitive rule, too, inaccurate as it is, would soon, I repeat, be disturbed by circumstances. For, suppose that one man had manufactured axes and another, shoes; circumstances would inevitably arise that would give one or another of these articles, a factitious value. In the winter season when protection was needed for the person, and in the summer which was favorable to the felling of timber, the value of those articles must be constantly fluctuating; it would be factitious; it could not be determined by the amount of labor. And as we depart farther from those primitive exchanges, we find circumstances, numerous, complicated and very artificial, which affect value. The wants, fancies and fashions of society; the state of crops and markets, and of trade all over the world; the variations of the seasons; the success or failure of fisheries; improvements in machinery; discoveries in art; and the regulations of governments—all these things and many more, conspire alternately to fix and disturb from day to day, that ever fluctuating thing called price. It is not any one man's judgment or conscience that can ascertain the value of any thing, but millions of individual judgments go to make up the decision. It is in vain to say that such and such things are worth little or nothing; that they are unnecessary or useless, or that they confer no advantage proportionate to their cost—that is not the question. What will they fetch? is the question. You may, in a fit of generosity, or a scruple of conscience, sell them for less; but the moment they are out of your hands, they will rise to the level of the market; you have lost the difference, and gained nothing for your generous principle. In fine, *the value of a thing is the market price of it.* This is the only intelligible idea of value; and the only reasonable adjustment of price. It is certainly most likely to be reasonable ; for a multitude of judgments have been employed upon it, and have settled it. It is the legislative voice of the whole world ; and it would be as unjust and inexpedient as it is impossible, to resist it.

The way of honesty, then, in the ordinary course of traffic, seems to be very clear. The terms on which we are to buy and sell, are established for us by a very obvious rule. In a general view, we may say, that conscience has nothing to do with affixing a price. That is determined by a thousand circumstances and a million voices. The trader must *buy* at the market price, and he must sell accordingly. He does not determine the price, but the suffrage of a whole city or of twenty cities, determines it. All that conscience has to do with price therefore is, not to go beyond the usage of the market. And for the rest, the rule is, to make no false representation, and to conceal no latent defect.

In this view, the moral course in almost the entire business of trade, seems to be exceedingly plain ; and certainly it is most grateful to reflect that it is so. He that runs may read. No man needs to carry with him, in regard to most of the transactions of business, a disturbed or a doubtful conscience.

But still cases will arise for a nicer casuistry. The market price is indeed the rule ; but there is monopoly that makes a market price, and there is superior information that takes undue advantage of it. These are the cases that remain to be examined.

II. The next case, then, to be considered in the morals of business, is monopoly. This may arise in two ways : intentionally, from combination on the part of several traders, or a plan on the part of one ; and unintentionally, where it falls out in the natural and unforced course of trade. It is from confounding these two cases together, perhaps, that a peculiar prejudice is felt in the community against monopoly. That a man should set himself by dexterous management to get into his possession all the corn in market, in order to extort an enormous price for it, is felt to be oppressive and wrong. But there is often a monopoly, to a greater or less degree, resulting from simple scarcity; and in this case, that enhancement of price which is so odious, is perfectly inevitable. Nay, it may be even beneficial. For high prices lessen consumption, and may prevent famine. But at any rate, high prices in a time of scarcity are inevitable. Even if all the corn, or all the coal were in the hands of one man; and he should sell the half of his stock to the wholesale dealers at a moderate rate, and hold the remainder at the same rate to keep the price down, still, I say, the moment the article left his hands, the law of scarcity would prevail and raise the price. Monopoly, therefore, compels, and of course, justifies an enhanced price. The same principle which applies to every other commodity, applies to that commodity called money. And it is only from the habit of considering money not as a commodity, but as a possession of some peculiar and magical value, that any prejudice can exist against what is called usurious interest; saving and excepting when that interest goes beyond all bounds of reason and humanity. The practice of usury has acquired a bad name from former and still occasional abuses of it. But the principle must still be a just one, that money, in common with every thing else, is worth what it will fetch.

This, I know, is denied. It is denied, especially, that money is, or is to be regarded, like other commodities in trade. It is said that money is the creature of the government; that the mint, when stamping it with the government impress, stamps it with a peculiar character, and separates it entirely from the general condition of a commodity. It is said, too, that the common representative of money—that the banknote—that credit, in other words—is exposed to such expansion and contraction, and management and conspiracy, that it is peculiarly liable to be used for the injury of the necessitous and unwary.

Let us separate this last allegation from our discussion for a moment, and consider the question alone, as it affects the use of money in the form of bullion. And I know of no better way of considering questions of this sort, than to resolve them into their simple forms, by going back to the origin of society, or taking for example, a small and isolated community. At least, we come to the theory of the questions by this means, and can then consider what modifications are required by more artificial and complicated interests.

Suppose then a community of an hundred families, cut off from the rest of the world, engaged in the various callings of life, accustomed to barter, but not accustomed to the use of money. Suppose, now, that a gold-mine were discovered. The metal is found to be very valuable for various purposes; and, like every thing else, it takes its value in the market; an ounce of it is exchanged for so many bushels of corn or yards of cloth. But the permanent and universal value of this metal, and its being so portable and indestructible, would, ere long, very naturally bring it into use as a circulating medium; the farmer would know that if he sold corn for it, he could buy cloth with it in another part of the district, and would be glad thus to be saved the trouble and expense of transporting the produce of his farm to the distant manufactory. In this exchange, the lumps of gold of course would be weighed, and it would be natural to stamp the weight upon each lump. But another step would follow from all this. As there would be the trouble of constantly weighing this circulating medium, and the danger of mistake and deception, the community would appoint a committee, or depute its government, if it had one, to do this very thing; and the metal would be cast into various quantities, bearing distinct denominations, to answer more fully the purposes of a convenient circulating medium. Here, then, we have a mint, and here we have money. Nobody will deny that it was a commodity when each man dug it from the earth, and exchanged it at his pleasure. But the action of the government confers no peculiar character on it. The government simply weighs the metal, and affixes, as it were, a label to it; i. e., stamps it as coin, to tell what it is worth. It does not create this value, but simply indicates it.

I am sensible that many questions may still be asked, but I have not space here, if I had ability, to enter into them; and besides, if this is just theory of the value of the specie currency, it may itself suggest the necessary answers. But the great practical difficulties arise from the use of a paper currency. If the paper were strictly the representative of gold and silver—if the issue of bank-notes did not exceed the specie actually in vault, and thus were used only for convenience, the same principles would apply as before. All other paper does not represent money but credit; i. e., it represents the presumed ability of a man to pay what he promises; not his known and ascertained property. And the question is, may credit be bought and sold in the market like any commodity?

Let us again attempt to simplify the question. You want money, let us suppose, and you go to a money-lender, and ask for it. He says, "I have not the money, but I shall have it a month hence, and I will give my note, payable at that time." This may answer the purpose with your creditor, and the question now is, what interest shall you pay? Shall credit take its place in the market like money, or like a commodity? Shall we say that the government has no business to interfere in this matter, with its usury laws, obliging a man to sell his paper for seven per cent.? Shall we say that all this ought to be left to regulate itself, and that every man shall be left free to act according to his pleasure?

I certainly feel some hesitation, from deference for the opinions of some able men who are more studious in these matters than I am, about answering this question in the affirmative. There are relations and bearings of that immense and complicated subject, the monetary system, which I may not understand, and usury, perhaps, is connected with that system in ways that are beyond my comprehension. But looking at the question now, in the light of simple justice, separating all unlawful combination and conspiracy from the case, and all deception and dishonesty—I cannot see why a man has not a right to sell his credit for what another is willing to give for it. If a lawyer has so elevated himself above his brethren, that his opinion is worth not twenty but five hundred per cent more than theirs, he takes that advance for his counsel. Why then, shall not a merchant, who by the same laborious means, has acquired a fortune and a high commercial reputation, be allowed a similar advantage?

We say, why should he not dispose of his credit, or in other words, pledge his property at such prices as it will naturally bear? But the truth is, that he cannot prevent this result, let him do what he will. He may sell his paper at one half per cent a month, but the moment it is out of his hands, it will rise to two or three per cent, if that be its real value. I say nothing now about obedience to the usury laws; I do not touch the point of conscience in that respect; but I believe that the laws themselves are both impolitic and unjust; unjust, because they conflict with the real value of things; and impolitic, because they never were, and never can be executed, and in fact, because they only increase the rates of interest by increasing the risk.

But is there, then, no limit it may be said, to the advantage which one man may take of the necessities of another? To ask this question in regard to the lender of money, is but the same thing as to ask it in regard to the man, in every other relationship of life. The duties of humanity, of philanthropy, of natural affection can never be abrogated by any circumstances, and the only question is, what line of conduct in the case before us, is conformable to those duties. That question cannot, I think, be brought within the compass of any assignable rules; and must be left for every man, seriously to consider for himself. He is put upon his conscience in this respect, as he is in every other case in life.

III. But the hardest case to determine, is that on which the question is raised, about the use of superior information. And perhaps this question cannot be better stated than in the celebrated case put by Cicero.* A corn merchant of Alexandria, he says, arrived at Rhodes in a time of great scarcity, with a cargo of grain, and with knowledge that a number of other vessels laden with corn, had already sailed from Alexandria for Rhodes, and which he had passed on the passage—was he bound in conscience to inform the buyers of that fact? Cicero decides that he was. Several modern writers on law dissent from his opinion—as Grotius, Puffendorf, and Pothier himself, though with very careful qualifications.†

It appears to me, that the answer to Cicero's question, must depend on the views which are taken of a contract. If a contract is a mere arbitrary convention, if business is a game, a mere contest of men's wits, if every man has a right to make the best bargain he can, if society really has power to ordain that such shall be the laws of trade, then the decision will be one way. But if a contract implies in its very nature the obligation of fair dealing and truth-telling, then the decision will be the other way. The supposition is, that the Alexandrine trader concealed a certain fact, for the sake of asking a price which he knew

* De Officiis, Lib. 3. Sec. 12–17.
† Traité du Contrat de vente, Part. II. ch. 2. Art. 3.

would not have been given, had that fact been public. Now what is implied in asking a price? What does a man say, when he sets a certain price on his merchandise? Does he, or does he not say, that the price he asks is, in his opinion, the fair value of the article? I think he does. If you did not so understand him, you would not trade with him. If you observed a lurking sneer on his lip, such as there must be in his heart, when he knows that he is taking you in, you would have nothing to do with him. The very transaction, called a contract, implies that degree of good faith. If this be true, if it is universally understood that he who asks a price, professes in that very act to ask a just and fair price, and if, moreover, he has a letter in his pocket assuring and satisfying him that it is not the just price; then he is guilty of falsehood. If the Alexandrine trader had asked a price, graduated exactly by his opinion of the probability that other vessels would soon arrive, and of the amount of the supply they would bring, his conduct would have been fair and honest. But if he had concealed facts within his knowledge, for the sake of asking an enormous price, or any price beyond what he knew to be the fair value, he would be guilty of falsehood and dishonesty. And the reason is, I repeat, that the very basis of a contract is mutual advantage; that its very essence lies in a supposed equivalency; that he who sets a price is understood to say as much as this, " I think the article is worth it." And if you allow a man to swerve from this truth and good faith at all, where will you stop? Suppose that the people of Rhodes had been suffering the horrors of famine, and the Alexandrine merchant had taken advantage of their situation to exact from them all their disposable property as the price of life, and had borne off that mass of treasure, all the while knowing that bountiful supplies were at hand—what should we have said? We should have said that his perfidy was equal to his cruelty—that he was both a pirate and a villain. But if a man may be guilty of falsehood in one degree, what principle is to prevent his being guilty of it in another? I know what may be said on the other hand. The master of the Alexandrine ship, it may be said, had outstripped the others, by superior sailing; and this superiority, in the management of his ship, may have been the fruit of a whole life of industry and ingenuity. He had also been on the alert, it may be supposed; had watched the course of the markets while others slept, and had been ready with his supply to meet the exigency which all others—even the Rhodians themselves, had been too dull to foresee. Is he not entitled to some premium for all this? Nay, but for the prospect held out of such a reward, the Rhodians might have starved. And yet if he gives the information in question, he loses the premium. No, the merchants of Rhodes say, "we will wait till to-morrow." But again; to-morrow comes; the vessels arrive; the market is glutted; and the Alexandrine trader loses money on his voyage. Will the merchants of Rhodes make it up to him, on account of his generosity in giving them the information? Not at all. "We buy at the market price," they say; "we cannot afford any more; if we give more we are losers;" and thus the Alexandrine by neglecting his own interests, and taking care of other people, loses not only his voyage, but his whole fortune perhaps, and becomes a bankrupt;

and by becoming a bankrupt, he injures those he is most bound to serve—his confiding friends, and beggared family. All this is a very good reason, to be sure, why the Alexandrine trader should be rewarded for his exertions, but it is not any good reason, nor *can* there *ever* be any good reason, why a man should tell a falsehood, why he should make a false impression, why he should deceive his neighbor.

Do we then propose to reduce the wise and the ignorant, the sagacious and the stupid, the attentive and the negligent, the active and the indolent, to the same level? Must the intelligent and the enterprising merchant raise up his dull and careless neighbor, to his own point of view, before he may deal with him? Certainly not. Let a wide field be opened, only provided that the boundaries be truth and honesty. Let the widest field for activity and freedom of action be spread, which these boundaries can enclose.

Indeed, a man *must* act in trade upon some opinion. That opinion must be founded on some knowledge. And that knowledge he may properly seek. Nay, and he may use it, to any extent, not implying deception or dishonesty. Nor are the cases frequent, in which commercial operations possess any such definite or extraordinary character, as admits of deception. It does not often happen that any great advantage is, or can be taken of complete and unsuspecting ignorance. Men are wary. They will not make questionable sales, when a packet ship from abroad is in the offing. They are set to guard their own interests, and they do guard them. They must assume some responsibilities in this way; they must take some risks. They are liable to err in opinion, and they must take such chance as human imperfection ordains for them. Business, like every other scene of human life, is a theatre for imperfection, for error, for effort, for opinion, and for their results. I do not see how it can possibly be otherwise, and therefore, I consider it as appointed to be so. Undue advantage may be taken of this state of things by the selfish, grasping, and unconscientious; right principles may be wrested to the accomplishment of wrong ends; a system of commercial morality may be good for the community, and yet may be abused by individuals: all this is true; and yet the doctrine which applies every where else must apply here, that abuse fairly argues nothing against use.

Let us see how the case would stand if it were otherwise: let us see what the assumption on the part of the trading community, that no man should ever act in any way on superior information, would amount to. "We may sleep," they would say, "we need not take any pains to inform ourselves of the state of the markets; we need not take a step from our own door. If our neighbor comes to trade with us, he must first inform us of every thing affecting the price of our goods. He makes himself very busy; and he shall have his labor for his pains; for the rule now is, that indolence is to fare as well as activity, and vigilance is to have no advantage over supineness and sloth." Suppose, then, that the vigilant and active man is up betimes, and goes down upon the wharf, or to the newsroom, and becomes apprized of facts that affect the price of his goods; he must not go about selling, till he has stepped into the shop of his indolent neighbor, and perhaps, of half a dozen such, to inform *them* of the state of things; for, although he does not directly trade with them, yet, by underselling or selling for more, in consequence of superior information, he injures them just as much as if he did : i. e., he takes profits out of the hands of the slothful, by acting on his superior knowledge. But now enlarge the sphere of the comparison. There is no real difference in the principle between a man's going down to the wharf, and his going to Europe, for information. And if, by superior activity, by building better ships and better manning them, he is accustomed to get earlier advices of the state of foreign markets, I see not, but as a general principle, a principle advantageous to commerce, and encouraging to human industry and ingenuity, he must be allowed to avail himself of those advices. The law of general expediency must be a law for the conscience. It is expedient that there should be commerce or barter; nay, it is inevitable. It is expedient that industry and attention should be rewarded, and that negligence and sloth should suffer loss. It is expedient, therefore, that all that sagacity, power and information, which are the result of superior talent, energy and ingenuity, should yield certain advantages to their possessor. These advantages he may push beyond the bounds of reason and justice; but we must not, on that account, be deterred from maintaining a principle which is right ; a principle which is expedient and necessary for the whole community.

And is not the same principle, in fact, adopted in every department of human pursuit? Two men engage in a certain branch of manufactures. The one, by his attention and ingenuity makes discoveries in his art, and thus gains advantages over his indolent or dull neighbor. Is he obliged to impart to him his superior information? Two young men in the profession of the law, are distinguished, the one for hard study, the other for idleness. They are engaged in the same cause; and the one perceives that the other is making a false point in the case. Is he obliged to go over to his brother's office, and explain to him his error; or is it not proper, rather, that both himself and his client should suffer for that error, when the cause comes to be argued in open court?

In fine, I hold that a distinction is to be made between general information and definite knowledge. If a man *knows* that an article is worth more than he buys it for, or less than he sells it for, he does not act with truth and integrity. It is just as if he knew the article were more or less in quantity than he alleges it to be. But if he acts on general information, open alike to all, if he acts on mere opinion, in which he may be mistaken, if he has no certain knowledge of the merchandise in question, but only a judgment, he is entitled to the full benefit of that judgment; while he is liable, at the same time, to the full injury of it, if it be mistaken.

But in regard to absolute certainty, how, I would ask, are we to distinguish between knowledge in regard to the real value of an article, from knowledge in regard to the real quality of an article? If I sell merchandise in which there is some secret defect, and do not expose that defect, I am held to be a dishonest man. But what matters it to my conscience, whether the secret defect lies in the article, or in the price? It comes to the same thing with my fellow-dealer. If I were to sell moth-eaten cloths at four dollars per yard more than they were worth—the defect known to me and not to my neighbor—all the world would pronounce me a knave. But there is another sort of moth, a secret in my own keeping, which may have as effectually eaten out four dollars from every yard of that cloth, as if it had literally cut the thread of the fabric. What difference now can it make to my neighbor, whether advantage is taken of his ignorance in one way or another, in regard to the quality or the price? The only material point is the value, and that is equally affected in either case. This is the only conclusion to which I find myself able, on much reflection, to arrive. Knowledge of prices is as material to the value of merchandise, as knowledge of its qualities. This knowledge, therefore, as it appears to me, should be common to all contracting parties. I cannot think that a trader is to be like a fisher, disguising his hook with bait; or like a slight-of-hand man, cheating men out of their senses and money with a face of gravity; or like an Indian, shooting from behind a bush, himself in no danger. Trade, traffic, contracts, bargains—all these words imply parity, equivalency, common risk, mutual advantage. And he who can arrange a commercial operation, by which he is *certain* to realize great profits and to inflict great losses, is a taker of merchandise, but can hardly be said to be a trader in it.

I am sensible that this is the nice and difficult point in the whole discussion. But, I put it to the calm reflection and to the consciences of my hearers, whether they would not feel easier in their business, if all use of superior and certain knowledge were entirely excluded from it. Long as this use has obtained, and warmly as it is sometimes defended, yet I ask, if the moral sentiments of the trading community itself, would not be relieved by giving it up? This, if it be true, is certainly a weighty consideration. I admit, indeed, as I have before done, that no vague sentiment is to settle the question. But when I find that there is even in vague sentiment, something like a hook that holds the mind in suspense, or will not let the mind be satisfied with departure from it, that circumstance deserves, I think, to arrest attention. I will frankly confess, that my own mind has been in this very situation. I did not see at one time, how the case of general information and opinion which it is lawful to use, could be separated from the case of particular knowledge. But I now entertain a different, and a more decided opinion. And the consideration, with me, which has changed uneasiness into doubt, and doubt into a new, and as I think, corrected judgment, is that which I have last stated—it is the consideration, that is to say, of the *very nature of a contract*. A contract does *not* imply equal powers, equal general information, equal shrewdness in the contracting parties; but it does imply, as it appears to me, equal actual knowledge. My neighbor may think himself superior to me in all other respects, and he may tell me so, and yet I will trade with him; we still stand upon ground that I am willing to consider equal. But let him tell me that he *knows* something touching the manufacture, quality, condition, or relations of the article to be sold, which I do not know, and which affects the value of the article; and I stop upon the threshold; we cannot traffic; there may be a game of hazard which he and I consent to play; but there is an end of all trading. If this be true, then the condition of a regular and lawful contract is, that there be no secrets in it; no secrets, either in the kind or quality of the merchandise, or in the breast, or in the pocket of the dealer. Let them all be swept away—let them be swept out, all secrets from all hiding-places, from all coverts of subterfuge and chicanery—and this, at least, I am certain of, that business would occasion fewer wounds of conscience, to all honorable and virtuous communities.

APPENDIX TO THE FOREGOING DISCOURSE.

Some remarks upon the foregoing discourse, which had reached the author's ear during the weekly interval, before the delivery of the next discourse, lead him before entering upon it, to offer the following observations.

It may be thought, that in my discourse of the last Sunday evening, I have leaned to a view of the principles of trade, which is too indulgent to its questionable practices. I am most anxious to guard against such an inference; and yet I must hesitate to yield exactly to the tone of objection which may possibly be adopted by some of my hearers. The pulpit is not to speak any peculiar language on this subject, because it is the pulpit. The language of truth is what we seek; the language which would be true any where. Neither is the pulpit to be looked upon as a post of duty, which is to serve only the purpose of assault, whose business it is to assail any particular class of persons, merchants or others; nor is the church a proper place for men to come to, in order to enjoy the gratification of seeing other men attacked. Nor is it the only business of the moral teacher, to denounce the sins of a violated conscience; it is sometimes quite as important to defend weak consciences. Nothing can be worse for a man than to act upon a principle of which he doubts the correctness. He is then doing wrong, even when the *thing* he does may be right. His conscience becomes weakened by wounds without cause; it is floating on a sea of doubt, and may be borne far beyond the bounds of rectitude. It is thus, that there arises in a community, a general and pernicious habit of paltering with conscience, of talking about certain principles as very good in theory, but as impracticable in fact, of slurring over the Christian rule with innuendoes, of commending it, indeed, and in a sort—but how? Why, of treacherously commending it, with those ironical praises, and ambiguous hints, and knowing glances of eye, which more effectually than any thing else, break down all principle.

On the contrary, let us come out fairly and establish the true doctrine, on independent grounds, with fair reasoning, without any bias against men of business or for them, and then shall we stand upon the stable basis of conscience and principle, and be able to define its boundaries. If it be expedient and inevitable, that men should, in business as in every thing else, act to a certain extent, upon their own superior sagacity, power and information, let us plainly say so; and then let us faithfully warn them against going too far. Now, nobody doubts, I presume, that they may go too far; that the man of sagacity may overreach an idiot; that the monopolist and the usurer may abuse his power; and that he who possesses superior information may dishonestly and cruelly use it. And, therefore, it was less necessary to insist upon these points, than it was to discuss the great question, and the only question; viz., whether these advantages may be used at all. If they may not be used at all, then all commerce, in its actual, and I think, inevitable procedures, is a system of knavery. If it is not a system of knavery, then it is important to defend it from that charge. And it is the more important, because, against merchants, from their acquiring greater wealth probably, there are peculiar prejudices in the community. The manufacturer may use his superior information—his particular invention that is—he may get a patent for it, i. e., a monopoly, and every other profession may do substantially the same thing, and not a word is said against it. But if the merchant does this, he is called into serious question. And influenced by this general distrust, he calls himself in question too. But unfortunately for him, instead of thinking deeply upon the matter, and settling himself upon some foundation of general principle, he is liable to give himself up to the suggestions of temporary expediency. He is not quite satisfied, perhaps, with what he is doing, and yet, he says, that he must do it or he cannot get along—a way of reasoning that I hold to be most injurious to his character. Let him then, I say, settle some just principle, and conscientiously act upon it.

They are general principles, I must desire you to observe, which I have attempted to establish. The questions that arise upon the application of these principles are, of course, numerous and complicated. I could not enter into them. My inexperience disqualified me. And besides, it was impossible to meet the the questions of every man's mind. But, by way of guarding against any false inferences from what I have said, let me offer two suggestions. In the first place, I have not intended to touch any questions about corporations, or about combinations and conspiracies to defraud. My discussion has been occupied with simple and single-handed dealings of man with man. In the next place, if my views have seemed to any one to lean to an unjust decision of any case, then, I say, that they are to be limited and restrained by that very case. The very principle I adopt, is that of restricting the fair action of trade within the boundaries of justice and philanthropy.

I must add, in fine, that in defending the right in trade, the impression upon the popular ear, may naturally enough have been, that I have not sufficiently considered the wrong. The wrong, let me observe here, will properly come under our consideration in another place. What I say now is, that if the principles I have laid down, have seemed to any one to verge towards an undue license, I must most earnestly protest against his inference. That very license, I say, is the point to which the principle shall not go. And I say more explicitly, that although the vender of any goods is not bound to assist the buyer with his judgment, yet that he is bound to point out any latent defect, and he is bound, by the general trust reposed in him on that point, to sell at the market price; and again, that monopoly, whether of money or other commodities, although it must inevitably raise the prices, although it must be governed in all ordinary cases, by the market value, yet when it can control the market price, is bound to use its power with moderation; and finally, that he who acts upon superior information, though he may lawfully do so, shall not press his advantage to the extent of any fraudulent use, or to the infliction of any gross and undeserved injury—that he shall not press it farther than is necessary, reasonably to reward vigilance and admonish indolence—that he shall not press it farther than the wholesome action of trade, and the true welfare of the whole community, requires.

DISCOURSE II.

ON THE MORAL END OF BUSINESS.

PROVERBS XX. 15. There is gold and a multitude of rubies, but the lips of knowledge, (i. e. of rectitude,) is a precious jewel.

My subject this evening is the moral end of business. Let me first attempt to define my meaning in the use of this phrase—the moral end of business.

It is not the end for which property should be sought. It is not the moral purpose to be answered by the acquisition, but by the process of acquisition. And again, it is not the end of industry in general—that is a more comprehensive subject—but it is the end of business in particular, of barter, of commerce. "The end of business?" some one may say, " why, the end of business is to obtain property; the end of the process of acquisition is acquisition." If I addressed any person whose mind had not gone behind that ready and obvious answer to ultimate and deeper reasons, I should venture to say, that a revelation is to be made to him, of a more exalted aim in business, of a higher, and at the same time, more perilous scene of action in its pursuits, than he has yet imagined. In other words, I hold that the ultimate end of all business is a moral end. I believe that business—I mean

THE MORAL END OF BUSINESS. 49

not labor but barter, traffic—would never have existed, if there had been no end but sustenance. The animal races obtain subsistence upon an easier and simpler plan; but for man there is a higher end, and that is moral.

The broad grounds of this position I find in the obvious designs of Providence, and in the evident adaptation to this moral end, of business itself.

There is, then, a design for which all things were made and ordained, going beyond the things themselves. To say that things were made, or that the arrangements and relations of things were ordained, for their own sake, is a proposition without meaning. The world, its structure, productions, laws and events, have no good nor evil in them—none, but as they produce these results, in the experience of living creatures. The end, then, of the inanimate creation, is the welfare of the living, and, therefore, especially of the intelligent creation. But the welfare of human beings lies essentially in their moral culture. All is wrong, every where, if all is not right there. All of design, that there is in this lower creation, presses upon that point. The universe is a moral chaos without that design, and it is a moral desolation to every mind in which that design is not accomplished. Life, then, has an ultimate purpose. We are not appointed to pass through this life, barely that we may live. We are not impelled, both by disposition and necessity, to buy and sell, barely that we may do it; nor to get gain, barely that we may get it. There is an end in business beyond supply. There is an object, in the acquisition of wealth, beyond success. There is a final cause of human traffic; and that is virtue.

With this view of the moral end of business, falls in the constant doctrine of all elevated philosophy and true religion. Life, say the expounders of every creed, is a probation. The circumstances in which we are placed—the events, the scenes of our mortal lot—the bright visions that cheer us, the dark clouds that overshadow us—all these are not an idle show, nor do they exist for themselves alone, nor because they must exist by the fiat of some blind chance; but they have a purpose; and that purpose is expressed in the word, probation. Now, if any thing deserves to be considered as a part of that probation, it is business. Life, say the wise, is a school. In this school there are lessons; toil is a lesson; trial is a lesson; and business, too, is a lesson. But the end of a lesson is, that something be learned. And the end of business is, that truth, rectitude, virtue, be learned. This is the ultimate design proposed by Heaven, and it is a design which every wise man, engaged in that calling, will propose to himself. It is no extravagance, therefore, but the simple assertion of a truth, to say to a man so engaged, and to say emphatically, " You have an end to gain beyond success; and that is the moral rectitude of your own mind."

That business is so exquisitely adapted to accomplish that purpose, is another argument with me to prove that such is the intention of its Ordainer, was its design. I can conceive that things might have been ordered otherwise; that human beings might have been formed for industry, and not for traffic. I can conceive man and nature to have been so constituted, that each individual should, by solitary labor, have drawn from the earth his sustenance; and that a vesture softer, richer, and more graceful than is ever wrought in the looms of our manufactories, might have been woven upon his body, by the same invisible hands that have thus clothed the beasts of the desert, and the birds of the air, and the lilies of the field, so that Solomon in all his glory was not arrayed like one of them. Then might man have held only the sweet counsel of society with his fellow, and never have been called to engage with him in the strife of business. Then, too, would he have been saved from all the dangers and vices of human traffic. But then, too, would the lofty virtues cultivated in this sphere of life, never have had an existence. For business, I repeat, is admirably adapted to form such virtues. It is apt, I know it is said, to corrupt men; but the truth is, it corrupts only those who are willing to be corrupted. An honest man, a man who sincerely desires to attain to a lofty and unbending uprightness, could scarcely seek a discipline more perfectly fitted to that end, than the discipline of trade. For what is trade? It is the constant adjustment of the claims of different parties, a man's self being one of the parties. This competition of rights and interests might not invade the solitary study, or the separate tasks of the work-shop, or the labors of the silent field, once a day; but it presses upon the merchant and trader continually. Do you say that it presses too hard? Then I reply, must the sense of rectitude be made the stronger to meet the trial. Every plea of this nature is an argument for strenuous moral effort. Shall I be told that the questions which often arise are very perplexing; that the case to be decided comes, oftentimes, not under a definite rule but under a general principle, whose very generality is perilous to the conscience? It is indeed. Here, perhaps, lies the great peril of business, in the generality of the rule. For conscience does not in most cases definitely say, "thou shalt do this thing, and thou shalt do that." It says always, "thou shalt do right," but what that is, is not always clear. And hence it is, that a man may take care to offend against no definite remonstrance of conscience, and that he may be, in the common acceptation, an honest man; and yet, that he may be a selfish, exacting and oppressive man; a man who can never recognize the rights and interests of others; who can never see any thing but on the side that is favorable to himself; who drowns the voice of his modest neighbor, with always and loudly saying, "Oh! this is right, and that can't be"—a man, in fine, who, although he seldom, perhaps, never offends against any assignable or definite precept of conscience, has swerved altogether from all uprightness and generosity. What then is to be done? A work, I answer, of the most ennobling character. A man must do more than to attain to punctilious honesty in his actions; he must train his whole soul, his judgment, his sentiments and affections, to uprightness, candour and good will.

In fine, I look upon business as one vast scene of moral action. "The thousand wheels of commerce," with all their swift and complicated revolutions, I regard as an immense moral machinery. Meanness and cunning may lurk amidst it, but it was not designed for that degradation. That must be a noble scene of action, where conscience is felt to be a law. And it is felt to be the law of business; its very violations prove it such. It is the enthroned sovereign of the plan; disobedience, disloyalty, give attestation to it. Nothing is too holy to connect with it. There is a temple in one of the cities of Europe, through which is the very passage to the market-place; and those who pass there, often rest their burthens, to turn aside and kneel at the altar of prayer. So were it meet that all men should enter upon their daily business. The temple of mammon, should be the temple of God. The gates of trade should be as the entrance to the sanctuary of conscience. There is an eye of witnessing and searching scrutiny fixed upon every one of its doings. The presence of that all-seeing One, not confined, as some imagine, to the silent church or the solitary grove—the presence of God, I think it not too solemn to say, is in every counting-room and warehouse of yonder mart, and ought to make it holy ground.

I have thus attempted to show that business has an ultimate, moral end—one going beyond the accumulation of property.

This may also be shown to be true, not only on the scale of our private affairs, but on the great theatre of history. Commerce has always been an instrument in the hands of Providence, for accomplishing nobler ends than promoting the wealth of nations. It has been the grand civilizer of nations. It has been the active principle in all civilization. Or, to speak more accurately, it has presented that condition of things, in which civilization has always rapidly advanced, and without which, it never has. The principles of civilization, properly speaking, are the principles of humanity—the natural desire of knowledge, liberty and refinement. But commerce seems to have been the germ, the original spring, that has put all other springs in action. Liberty has always followed its steps; and with liberty, science and religion have gradually advanced and improved; and never without it. All those kingdoms of central Asia, and of Europe too, which commerce has never penetrated, have been, and are, despotisms. With its earliest birth on the Mediterranean shore, freedom was born. Phœnicia, the merchants of whose cities, Tyre and Sidon, were accounted princes; the Hebrew commonwealth, which carried on a trade through those parts; the Grecian, Carthaginian and Roman States, were not only the freest, but they were the only free states of antiquity. In the middle ages, commerce broke down, in Europe, the feudal system, raising up in the Hanse Towns throughout Germany, Sweden and Norway, a body of men who were able to cope with barons and kings, and to wrest from them, their free charters and rightful privileges. In England, its influence is proverbial; the sheet-anchor it has long been considered, of her unequalled prosperity and intelligence. On our own happy shores, it has a still more unobstructed field, and is destined, I trust, to spread over the whole breadth of our interior domain, wealth, cultivation and refinement.

Its moral influences are the only ones of which we stand in any doubt, and these, it need not be said, are of unequalled importance. The philanthropist, the Christian, the Christian preacher, are all bound to watch these influences with the closest attention, and to do all in their power to guard and elevate them. To this work I am attempting to contribute my humble part; and I conceive, that I have now come to the grand principle of safety and improvement, viz., that trade is essentially a moral business, that it has a moral end more important than success, that the attainment of this end is better than the acquisition of wealth, and that the failure of it, is worse than any commercial failure; worse than bankruptcy, poverty, ruin.

It is upon this point that I wish especially to insist; but there are one or two topics, that may previously claim some attention.

If, then, business is a moral dispensation, and its highest end is moral, I shall venture to call in question the commonly supposed desirableness of escaping from it—the idea which prevails with so many of making a fortune in a few years, and afterwards of retiring to a state of leisure. If business really is a scene of worthy employment and of high moral action, I do not see why the moderate pursuit of it should not be laid down in the plan of entire active life; and why upon this plan, a man should not determine to give only so much time each day to his avocations, as would be compatible with such a plan; only so much time, in other words, as will be compatible with the daily enjoyment of life, with reading, society, domestic intercourse, and all the duties of philanthropy and devotion. If the merchant does not dislike or despise his employment—and it is when he makes himself the mere slave of business, that he creates the greatest real objections to it—if, I say, he looks upon his employment as lawful and laudable, an appointment of God to accomplish good purposes in this world and better for the next; why should he not, like the physician, the lawyer and clergyman, like the husbandman and artisan, continue in it, through the period of active life; and adjust his views, expectations and engagements to that reasonable plan? But now, instead of this, what do we see around us? Why, men are engaging in business—here, at home, in their own country, in the bosom of their families and amidst their friends—as if they were in a foreign and infectious clime; and must be in haste to make their fortunes, that they may escape with their lives to some place of safety, ease, and enjoyment!

And now, what sort of preparation for retirement is this life, absorbed in business? It is precisely that sort of preparation that unfits a man for retirement. Nothing will work well or agreeably in experience, which has not some foundation in previous habits and practice. But for all those things which are to be a man's resources in retirement, his previous life, perhaps, has given him not a moment of time. He has really no rural tastes; for he has scarcely seen the country for years, except on hurried journeys of business; the busy wheels of commerce now, alas! roll through the year, and he is chained to them every month. He has made no acquaintance with the fine arts; no music has there been for his ear but the clink of gold; no pictures for his eye, but fine colored drawings of houses and lots, or of fancy villages and towns. He has cultivated no habits of reading; and—what I hold to be just as fatal to the happiness of any life, retired or active—he has cultivated no habits of devotion. Add to all this, that he is thrown upon the dangerous state of luxurious leisure—that prepared, enriched, productive hot-bed of prurient imaginations and teeming passions—without any guards against its moral perils. And what is likely to be the consequence? He will become perhaps an indolent and bloate dsensualist, cumbering the beautiful grounds, on which he vegetates rather than lives; or, from the violent change of his habits, you will soon hear, perhaps, that, without any other cause than the change, he is dead; or he may live on, in weariness and ennui, wishing in his heart, that he were back again, though it were to take his place behind the counter of the humblest shop.

I do not pretend, of course, that I am pourtraying the case of every man, who is proposing to retire from business. There *are* those, doubtless, whose views of retiring are reasonable and praise-worthy; who do not propose to escape from all employment; who are living religiously and virtuously *in the midst* of their business, and not unwisely intending to make up for the deficiency of those qualities in retirement; who wish to improve and beautify some pleasant rural abode, and thus, and in many other ways, to be useful to the country around them. To such a retirement, I have nothing to object: and I only venture to suggest, as an obvious dictate of good sense, that he who proposes, some day, to retire from business, should, in the meantime, cultivate those qualities and habits, which will make him happy in retirement. But this I also say, that I do more than doubt, whether any man, who is completely engrossed in business, from morning till night, for twenty or thirty years, can be prepared to enjoy or improve a life of leisure.

Another topic, of which I wish to speak, is the rage for speculation. I wish to speak of it now in a particular view—as interfering, that is to say, with the moral end of business. And here, again, let me observe, that I can have nothing to do with instances, with exceptions. I can only speak of the general tendency of things. And it is not against *speculation simply*, that I have any thing to allege. All business possesses more or less of this character. Every thing is bought on the expectation of selling it for more. But this rage for speculation, this eagerness of many for sudden and stupendous accumulation, this spirit of gambling in trade, is a different thing. It proceeds on principles entirely different from the maxims of a regular and pains-taking business. It is not looking to diligence and fidelity for a fair reward, but to change and chance for a fortunate turn. It is drawing away men's minds from the healthful processes of sober industry and attention to business, and leading them to wait in feverish excitement, as at the wheel of a lottery. The proper basis of success—vigilant care and labor—is forsaken for a system of baseless credit. Upon this system, men proceed, straining their means and stretching their responsibilities, till, in calm times, they can scarcely hold on upon their position; and when a sudden jar shakes the commercial world, or a sudden blast sweeps over it, many fall, like untimely fruit, from the towering tree of fancied prosperity. Upon this system, many imagine that they are doing well, when they are not doing well. They rush into expenses, which they cannot afford, upon the strength, not of their actual, but of their imaginary or expected means. Young men, who, in former days, would have been advised to walk awhile longer, and patiently to tread the upward path, must buy horses and vehicles for their accommodation, and mounted upon the car of fancied independence, they are hurried only to swifter destruction. This system of rash and adventurous speculation, overlooks all the moral uses and ends of business. To do business and get gain, honestly and conscientiously, is a good thing. It is a useful discipline of the character. I look upon a man who has acquired wealth, in a laudable, conscientious and generous pursuit of business, not only with a respect far beyond what I can feel for his wealth—for which, indeed, abstractly, I can feel none at all—but with the distinct feeling that he has acquired something far more valuable than opulence. But for this discipline of the character, for the reasonableness and rectitude of mind which a regular business intercourse may form, speculation furnishes but a narrow field, if any at all; such speculation, I mean, as has lately created a popular phrenzy in this country about the sudden acquisition of property. The game which men were playing was too rapid, and the stake too large, to admit of the calm discriminations of conscience, and the reasonable contemplation of moral ends. Wealth came to be looked upon as the only end. And immediate wealth, was the agitating prize. Men could not wait for the slow and disciplinary methods, by which Providence designed that they should acquire it; but they felt, as if it were the order of Providence, that fortunes should fall direct from heaven into their open hands. Rather, should we not say, that multitudes did not look to heaven at all, but to speculation itself, instead, as if it were a god, or some wonder-working magician, at least, that was suddenly to endow them with opulence. Acquisition became the story of an Arabian tale; and men's minds were filled with romantic schemes, and visionary hopes, and vain longings, rather than with sobriety, and candor, and moderation, and gratitude, and trust in Heaven.

This insane and insatiable passion for accumulation, ever ready, when circumstances favor, to seize upon the public mind, is that "love of money which is the root of all evil," that "covetousness which is idolatry." It springs from an undue, an idolatrous estimate of the value of property. Many are feeling, that nothing—nothing will do for them or for their children, but wealth; not a good character, not well-trained and well exerted faculties, not virtue, not the hope of heaven—nothing but wealth. It is their god, and the god of their families. Their sons are growing up to the same worship of it, and to an equally baneful reliance upon it for the future; they are rushing into expenses which the divided property of their father's house will not enable them to sustain; and they are preparing to be in turn and from necessity, slaves to the same idol. How truly is it written, that "they that *will* be rich, fall into temptation, and a snare, and into many foolish and hurtful lusts, which drown men in destruction and perdition!" There is no need that they should be rich; but they *will* be rich. All the noblest functions of life may be discharged without wealth, all its highest honors obtained, all its purest pleasures enjoyed; yet I repeat it—nothing—nothing will do but wealth. Disappoint a man of this, and he mourns as if the highest end of life were defeated. Strip him of this: and this gone, all is gone. Strip him of this, and I shall point to no unheard of experience, when I say— he had rather die than live!

THE MORAL END OF BUSINESS. 61

The grievous mistake, the mournful evil implied in this oversight of the great spiritual end, which should be sought in all earthly pursuits, is the subject to which I wished to draw your attention in the last place. It is not merely in the haste to be rich, accompanied with the intention to retire from business to a state of luxurious and self-indulgent leisure ; it is not merely in the rage for speculation, that the evils of overlooking the moral aim of business are seen ; but they sink deep into the heart, in the ordinary walks of regular and daily occupation; dethroning the spiritual nature from its proper place, vitiating the affections, and losing some of the noblest opportunities for virtue, that can be lost on earth.

The spiritual nature, I say, is dethroned from its proper place, by this substitution of the immediate end, wealth, for the ultimate end, virtue. Who is this being, that labors for nothing but property; with no thought beyond it; with the feeling that nothing will do without it; with the feeling that there are no ends in life, that can satisfy him, if that end is not gained ? You will not tell me, that it is a being of my own fancy. You have probably known such ; perhaps, some of you are such. I have known men of this way of thinking, and men, too, of sense and of amiable temper. Who then, I ask again, is this being? He is an immortal being; and his views ought to stretch themselves to eternity—ought to seek an ever-expanding good. And this being, so immortal in his nature, so infinite in faculties—to what is he looking ? To the sublime mountain range, that spreads along the horizon of this world? To the glorious host of glittering stars, the majestic train of night, the infinite regions of heaven? No—his is no upward gaze, no wide vision of the world—to a speck of earthly dust he is looking. He might lift his eye, a philosophic eye, to the magnificence of the universe, for an object; and upon what is it fixed? Upon the mole-hill beneath his feet! That is his end. Every thing is naught, if that is gone. He is an immortal being, I repeat; he may be enrobed in that vesture of light, of virtue, which never shall decay; and he is to live through such ages, that the time shall come when to his eye all the splendors of fortune, of gilded palace and gorgeous equipage, shall be no more than the spangle that falls from a royal robe; and yet, in that glittering particle of earthly dust, is his soul absorbed and bound up. I am not saying, *now*, that he is willing to lose his soul for that. This he may do. But I only say now, that he sets his soul upon that, and feels it to be an end so dear, that the irretrievable loss of it, the doom of poverty, is death to him; nay, to his sober and deliberate judgment—for I have known such instances—is worse than death itself! And yet he is an immortal being, I repeat, and he is sent into this world on an errand? What errand? What is the great mission on which the Master of life hath sent him here? To get riches? To amass gold coins, and bank notes? To scrape together a little of the dust of this earth; and then to lie down upon it and embrace it, in the indolence of enjoyment, or in the rapture of possession? Is such worldliness possible? Worldliness! Why, it is not worldliness. That should be the quality of being attached to a world—to all that it can give, and not to one thing only that it can give—to fame, to power, to moral power, to influence, to the admiration of the world. Worldliness, methinks, should be something greater than men make it—should stretch itself out to the breadth of the great globe, and not wind itself up like a worm in the web of selfish possession. If I must be worldly, let me have the worldliness of Alexander, and not of Crœsus. And wealth too—I had thought it was a means and not an end—an instrument which a noble human being handles, and not a heap of shining dust in which he buries himself; something that a man could drop from his hand, and still be a man—be all that he ever was— and compass all the noble ends that pertain to a human being. What if you be poor? Are you not still a man—Oh! heaven, and mayest be a spirit, and have a universe of spiritual possessions for your treasure. What if you be poor? You may still walk through the world in freedom and in joy. You may still tread the glorious path of virtue. You may still win the bright prize of immortality. You may still achieve purposes on earth that constitute all the glory of earth, and ends in heaven, that constitute all the glory of heaven! Nay, if such must be the effect of wealth, I would say, let me be poor. I would pray God that I might be poor. Rather, and more wisely ought I, perhaps, to say with Agur, "give me neither poverty nor riches; lest I be full and deny thee, and say, who is the Lord? or lest I be poor, and steal, and take the name of my God in vain."

The many, corrupting and soul-destroying vices engendered in the mind by this lamentable oversight of the spiritual aim in business, deserve a separate and solemn consideration.

I believe that you will not accuse me of any disposition to press unreasonable charges against men of business. I cannot possibly let the pulpit throw burthens of responsibility, or warnings of danger on this sphere of life, as if others were not in their measure open to similar admonitions. I come not here to make war upon any particular class. I pray you not to regard this pulpit as holding any relation to you, but that of a faithful and Christian friend, or as having any interest in the world connected with business, but your own true interest. Above all things do I deprecate that worldly and most pernicious habit of hearing and approving very good things in the pulpit, and going away, and calmly doing very bad things in the world, as if the two had no real connection—that habit of listening to the admonitions and rebukes of the pulpit with a sort of demure respect, or with significant glances at your neighbors, and then of going away, commending the doctrine with your lips, to violate it in your lives— as if you said, " well, the pulpit has acted its part, and now we will go and act ours." I act no part here. God forbid! I endeavor to be reasonable and just, in what I say here. I take no liberty to be extravagant in this place, because I cannot be answered. I hold myself solemnly bound to say nothing recklessly and for effect. I occupy here no isolated position. I am continually thinking what my hearers will fairly have to say on their part, and striving fairly to meet it. I speak to you simply as one man may speak to another, as soul may speak to its brother soul; and I solemnly and affectionately say, what I would have you say to me in a change of place—I say that the pursuits of business are perilous to your virtue.

On this subject, I cannot, indeed, speak with the language of experience. But I cannot forget that the voice of all moral instruction, in all ages and in all countries, is a voice of warning. I cannot forget that the voice of Holy Scripture falls in solemn accents upon the perils attending the pursuit of wealth. How solemn, how strong, how pertinent those accents are, I may not know, but I must not, for that reason, withhold them. "Wo unto you who are rich," saith the holy word, "for ye have not received your consolation. Wo unto you that are full, for ye shall hunger." Hunger? What hath wealth to do with hunger? And yet there is a hunger. What is it? What can it be but the hungering of the soul; and that is the point which, in this discourse, I press upon your attention. And again it says, "your riches are corrupted; your gold and silver is cankered:" and is it not cankered in the very hearts of those whom wealth has made proud, vain, anxious and jealous, or self-indulgent, sensual, diseased and miserable?—" And the rust of them," so proceeds the holy text, "shall be a witness against you, and shall eat your flesh as it were fire." Ah! the rust of riches!— not that portion of them which is kept bright in good and holy uses—" and the consuming fire" of the passions which wealth engenders! No rich man—I lay it down as an axiom of all experience—no rich man is safe, who is not a benevolent man. No rich man is safe, but in the imitation of that benevolent God, who is the possessor and dispenser of all the riches of the universe. What else, mean the miseries of a selfishly luxurious and fashionable life every where? What mean the sighs that come up from the perlieus, and couches, and most secret haunts of all splendid and self-indulgent opulence? Do not tell me that other men are sufferers too. Say not that the poor, and destitute and forlorn, are miserable also. Ah! just heaven! thou hast in thy mysterious wisdom, appointed to them a lot hard, full hard, to bear. Poor houseless wretches! who "eat the bitter bread of penury, and drink the baleful cup of misery;" the winter's wind blows keenly through your "looped and windowed raggedness;" your children wander about unshod, unclothed and untended; I wonder not that ye sigh. But why should those who are surrounded with every thing that heart can wish, or imagination conceive—the very crumbs that fall from whose table of prosperity might feed hundreds—why should they sigh amidst their profusion and splendor? *They have broken the bond that should connect power with usefulness, and opulence with mercy.* That is the reason. They have taken up their treasures, and wandered away into a forbidden world of their own, far from the sympathies of suffering humanity; and the heavy night-dews are descending upon their splendid revels; and the all-gladdening light of heavenly beneficence is exchanged for the sickly glare of selfish enjoyment; and happiness, the blessed angel that hovers over generous deeds and heroic virtues, has fled away from that world of false gaiety and fashionable exclusion.

I have, perhaps, wandered a moment from the point before me—the peril of business—though as business is usually aiming at wealth, I may be considered rather as having only pressed that point to some of its ultimate bearings.

But the peril of business specifically considered; and I ask, if there is not good ground for the admonitions on this point, of every moral and holy teacher of every age? What means, if there is not, that eternal disingenuity of trade, that is ever putting on fair appearances and false pretences—of "the buyer that says, it is naught, it is naught, but when he is gone his way, then boasteth"—of the seller, who is always exhibiting the best samples, not fair but false samples, of what he has to sell; of the seller, I say, who, to use the language of another, "if he is tying up a bundle of quills, will place several in the centre, of not half the value of the rest, and thus sends forth a hundred liars, with a fair outside, to proclaim as many falsehoods to the world?" These practices, alas! have fallen into the regular course of the business of many. All men expect them; and therefore, you may say, that nobody is deceived. But deception is intended: else why are these things done? What if nobody is deceived? The seller himself is corrupted. He may stand acquitted of dishonesty in the moral code of worldly traffic; no man may charge him with dishonesty; and yet to himself he is a dishonest man. Did I say that nobody is deceived! Nay, but somebody is deceived. This man, the seller, is grossly, wofully deceived. He thinks to make a little profit by his contrivance; and he is selling, by penny-worths', the very integrity of his soul. Yes, the pettiest shop where these things are done, may be to the spiritual vision, a place of more than tragic interest. It is the stage on which the great action of life is performed. There stands a man, who in the sharp collisions of daily traffic, might have polished his mind to the bright and beautiful image of truth, who might have put on the noble brow of candor, and cherished the very soul of uprightness. I have known such a man. I have looked into his humble shop. I have seen the mean and soiled articles with which he is dealing. And yet the process of things going on there, was as beautiful, as if it had been done in heaven! But now, what is this man—the man who always turns up to you the better side of every thing he sells—the man of unceasing contrivances and expedients, his life long, to make things appear better than they are? Be he the greatest merchant or the poorest huckster, he is a mean, a knavish—and were I not awed by the thoughts of his immortality, I should say—a contemptible creature; whom nobody that knows him can love, whom nobody can trust, whom nobody can reverence. Not one thing in the dusty repository of things, great or small, which he deals with, is so vile as he. What *is* this *thing* then, which is done, or may be done in the house of traffic? I tell you, though you may have thought not so of it—I tell you that *there*, even *there*, a soul may be lost!—that that very structure, built for the gain of earth, may be the gate of hell! Say not that this fearful appellation should be applied to worse places than that. A man may as certainly corrupt all the integrity and virtue of his soul in a warehouse or a shop, as in a gambling-house or a brothel.

False to himself, then, may a man become, while he is walking through the perilous courses of traffic; false also to his *neighbor*. I cannot dwell much upon this topic; but I will put one question; not for reproach, but for your sober consideration. Must it not render a man extremely liable to be selfish, that he is engaged in pursuits whose immediate and palpable end, is his own interest? I wish to draw your attention to this peculiarity of trade. I do not say, that the motives which originally induce a man to enter into this sphere of life, may not be as benevolent as those of any other man; but this is the point which I wish to have considered—that while the learned professions have knowledge for their immediate object, and the artist and the artisan have the perfection of their work as the thing that directly engages their attention, the merchant and trader have for their immediate object, profit. Does not this circumstance greatly expose a man to be selfish? Full well I know that many are not so; that many resist and overcome this influence; but I think, that it *is* to be resisted. And a wise man, who more deeply dreads the taint of inward selfishness, than of outward dishonor, will take care to set up counter influences. And to this end, he should beware how he clenches his hand and closes his heart against the calls of suffering, the dictates of public spirit, and the claims of beneficence. To listen to them is, perhaps, his very salvation!

But the vitiating process of business may not stop with selfishness; it is to be contemplated in still another and higher light. For how possible is it, that a man while engaged in exchanging and diffusing the bounties of heaven, while all countries and climes are pouring their blessings at his feet, while he lawfully deals with not one instrument, in mind or matter, but it was formed and fitted to his use by a beneficent hand— how possible it is that he may forget and forsake the Being who has given him all things! How possible is it that under the very accumulation of his blessings may be buried all his gratitude and piety—that he may be too busy to pray, too full to be thankful, too much engrossed with the gifts to think of the Giver!

The humblest giver expects some thanks; he would think it a lack of ordinary human feeling in any one, to snatch at his bounties, without casting a look on the bestower; he would gaze in astonishment at such heedless ingratitude and rapacity, and almost doubt whether the creatures he helped, could be human. Are they any more human—do they any more deserve the name of men, when the object of such perverse and senseless ingratitude is the Infinite Benefactor? Would we know what aspect it bears before his eye? Once, and more than once, hath that Infinite Benefactor spoken. I listen, and tremble as I listen, to that lofty adjuration, with which the sublime prophet hath set forth *His* contemplation of the ingratitude of his creatures. " Hear, O heavens, and give ear, O earth! for the Lord hath spoken; I have nourished and brought up children, and they have rebelled against me. The ox knoweth his owner, and the ass his master's crib; but Israel doth not know; my people doth not consider." Sad and grievous error even in the eye of reason! Great default even to nature's religion! But art thou a Christian man—what law shall acquit thee, if that heavy charge lies at thy door—at the door of thy warehouse—at the door of thy dwelling. Beware, lest thou forget God in his mercies! the Giver in his gifts! lest the light be gone from thy prosperity, and prayer from thy heart, and the love of thy neighbor from the labors of thy calling, and the hope of heaven from the abundance of thine earthly estate!

But not with words of warning—ever painful to use, and not always profitable—would I now dismiss you from the house of God. I would not close this discourse, in which I may seem to have pressed heavily on the evils to which business exposes those who are engaged in it, without holding up distinctly to view the great moral aim on which it is my main purpose to insist, and attempting to show its excellence.

There is such a nobleness of character in the right course, that it is to that point I would last direct your attention. The aspirings of youth, the ambition of manhood, could receive no loftier moral direction than may be found in the sphere of business. The school of trade, with all its dangers, may be made one of the noblest schools of virtue in the world; and it is of some importance to say it:—because those who regard it as a sphere only of selfish interests and sordid calculations, are certain to win no lofty moral prizes in that school. There can be nothing more fatal to elevation of character in any sphere, whether it be of business or society, than to speak habitually of that sphere as given over to low aims and pursuits. If business is constantly spoken of as contracting the mind and corrupting the heart; if the pursuit of property is universally satirized as selfish and grasping; too many who engage in it will think of nothing but of adopting the character and the course so pointed out. Many causes have contributed, without doubt, to establish that disparaging estimate of business—the spirit of feudal aristocracies, the pride of learning, the tone of literature, and the faults of business itself.

I say, therefore, that there is no being in the world for whom I feel a higher moral respect and admiration, than for the upright man of business; no, not for the philanthropist, the missionary, or the martyr. I feel that I could more easily be a martyr, than a man of that lofty moral uprightness. And let me say yet more distinctly, that it is not for the generous man, that I feel this kind of respect—that seems to me a lower quality—a mere impulse, compared with the lofty virtue I speak of. It is not for the man who distributes extensive charities, who bestows magnificent donations. That may be all very well—I speak not to disparage it—I wish there were more of it; and yet it may all consist with a want of the true, lofty, unbending uprightness. That is not the man then, of whom I speak; but it is he who stands, amidst all the swaying interests and perilous exigencies of trade, firm, calm, disinterested and upright. It is the man, who can see another man's interests, just as clearly as his own. It is the man whose mind, his own advantage does not blind nor cloud for an instant; who could sit a judge, upon a question between himself and his neighbor, just as safely, as the purest magistrate upon the bench of justice. Ah! how much richer than ermine, how far nobler than the train of magisterial authority, how more awful than the guarded bench of majesty, is that simple, magnanimous and majestic truth. Yes, it is the man who is true—true to himself, to his neighbor and to his God—true to the right—true to his conscience—and who feels, that the slightest suggestion of that conscience, is more to him than the chance of acquiring an hundred estates.

Do I not speak to some such one now? Stands there not here, some man of such glorious virtue, of such fidelity to truth and to God. Good friend! I call upon you to hold fast to that integrity, as the dearest treasure of existence. Though storms of commercial distress sweep over you, and the wreck of all worldly hopes threaten you, hold on to that as the plank that shall bear your soul unhurt to its haven. Remember that which thy Saviour hath spoken—" what shall it profit a man, if he gain the whole world, and lose his own soul?" Remember that there is a worse bankruptcy than that which is recorded in an earthly court—the bankruptcy that is recorded in heaven—bankruptcy in thy soul—all poor, and broken down, and desolate there—all shame and sorrow and mourning, instead of that glorious integrity, which should have shone like an angel's presence, in the darkest prison that ever spread its shadow over human calamity. Heaven and earth may pass away, but the word of Christ—the word of thy truth, let it pass from thee never!

DISCOURSE III.

ON THE USES OF LABOR, AND THE PASSION FOR A FORTUNE.

II. THESSALONIANS III. 10. FOR EVEN WHEN WE WERE WITH YOU, THIS WE COMMANDED YOU, THAT IF ANY MAN WOULD NOT WORK, NEITHER SHOULD HE EAT.

I WISH to invite your attention this evening to the uses of labor, and the passion for a fortune. The topics, it is obvious, are closely connected. The latter, indeed, is my main subject; but as preliminary to it, I wish to set forth, as I regard it, the great law of human industry. It is worthy, I think, of being considered, and religiously considered, as the chief law of all human improvement and happiness. And if there be any attempt to escape from this law, or if there be any tendency of the public mind, at any time, to the same point, the eye of the moral observer should be instantly drawn to that point, as one most vital to the public welfare. That there has been such a tendency of the public mind in this country, that it has been most signally manifest within a few years past, and that although it has found in cities the principal field of its manifestation, it has spread itself over the country too; that multitudes have become suddenly possessed with a new idea, the idea of making a fortune in a brief time, and then of retiring to a state of ease and independence—this is the main fact on which I shall insist, and of which I shall endeavor to point out the dangerous consequences.

But let me first call your attention to the law which has thus, as I contend, in spirit at least, been broken. What then is the law? It is, that industry—working, either with the hand or with the mind—the application of the powers to some task, to the acheivement of some result, lies at the foundation of all human improvement.

Every step of our progress from infancy to manhood, is proof of this. The process of education, rightly considered, is nothing else but wakening the powers to activity. It is through their own activity alone, that they are cultivated. It is not by the mere imposition of tasks, or requisition of lessons. The very purpose of the tasks and lessons is to awaken, and direct that activity. Knowledge itself cannot be gained, but upon this condition, and if it could be gained, would be useless without it.

The state into which the human being is introduced, is from the first step of it to the last, designed to answer the purpose of such an education. Nature's education, in other words, answers in this respect, to the just idea of man's. Each sense, in succession, is elicited by surrounding objects, and it is only by repeated trials and efforts, that it is brought to perfection. In like manner, does the scene of life appeal to every intellectual and every moral power. Life is a severe discipline, and demands every energy of human nature to meet it. Nature is a rigorous taskmaster; and its language to the human race is, "if a man will not work, neither shall he eat." We are not sent into the world like animals, to crop the spontaneous herbage of the field, and then to lie down in indolent repose: but we are sent to dig the soil and plough the sea; to do the business of cities and the work of manufactories. The raw material only is given us; and by the processes of cookery and the fabrications of art, it is to be wrought to our purpose. The human frame itself is a most exquisite piece of mechanism, and it is designed in every part for work. The strength of the arm, the dexterity of the hand, and the delicacy of the finger, are all fitted for the accomplishment of this purpose.

All this is evidently, not a matter of chance, but the result of design. The world is the great and appointed school of industry. In an artificial state of society, I know, mankind are divided into the idle and the laboring classes; but such, I maintain, was not the design of providence. On the contrary, it was meant that all men, in one way or another, should work. If any human being could be completely released from this law of providence, if he should never be obliged so much as to stretch out his hand for any thing, if every thing came to him at a bare wish, if there were a slave appointed to minister to every sense, and the powers of nature were made, in like manner, to obey every thought, he would be a mere mass of inertness, uselessness and misery.

Yes, such is man's task, and such is the world he is placed in. The world of matter is shapeless and void to all man's purposes, till he lays upon it the creative hand of labor. And so also is the world of mind. It is as true in mind as it is in matter, that the materials only are given us. Absolute truth ready made, no more presents itself to us in one department, than finished models of mechanism ready made, do in the other. Original principles there doubtless are in both; but the result—philosophy, that is to say, in the one case is as far to seek, as art and mechanism are in the other.

Such, I repeat, is the world, and such is man. The earth he stands upon and the air he breathes are, so far as his improvement is concerned, but elements to be wrought by him to certain purposes. If he stood on earth passively and unconsciously imbibing the dew and sap, and spreading his arms to the light and air, he would be but a tree. If he grew up capable neither of purpose nor of improvement, with no guidance but instinct, and no powers but those of digestion and locomotion, he would be but an animal. But he is more than this; he is a man; he is made to improve; he is made, therefore, to think, to act, to *work*. Labor is his great function, his peculiar distinction, his privilege. *Can* he not think so? Can he not see, that from being an animal to eat and drink and sleep, to become a worker—to put forth the hand of ingenuity, and to pour his own thought into the worlds of nature, fashioning them into forms of grace and fabrics of convenience, and converting them to purposes of improvement and happiness—can he not see, I repeat, that this is the greatest possible step in privilege? Labor. I say, is man's great function. The earth and the atmosphere are his laboratory. With spade and plough, with mining-shafts and furnaces and forges, with fire and steam—amidst the noise and whirl of swift and bright machinery, and abroad in the silent fields beneath the roofing sky, man was made to be ever working, ever experimenting. And while he, and all his dwellings of care and toil, are borne onward with the circling skies, and the shows of heaven are around him, and their infinite depths image and invite his thought, still in all the worlds of philosophy, in the universe of intellect, man must be a worker. He is nothing, he can be nothing, he can achieve nothing, fulfil nothing, without working. Not only can he gain no lofty improvement without this; but without it, he can gain no tolerable happiness. So that he who gives himself up to utter indolence, finds it too hard for him; and is obliged in self-defence, unless he be an idiot, to *do* something. The miserable victims of idleness and ennui, driven at last from their chosen resort, are compelled to work, to do something; yes, to employ their wretched and worthless lives in—"*killing time.*" They must hunt down the hours as their prey. Yes, time—that mere abstraction—that sinks light as the air upon the eye-lids of the busy and the weary, to the idle is an enemy, clothed with gigantic armor; and they must kill it, or themselves die. They cannot *live* in mere idleness; and all the difference between them and others is, that they employ their activity to no useful end. They find, indeed, that the hardest work in the world is, to do nothing!

This reference to the class of mere idlers as it is called, leads me to offer one specification in laying down this law concerning industry. Suppose a man, then, to possess an immense, a boundless fortune, and that he holds himself discharged, in consequence, from all the ordinary cares and labors of life. Now, I maintain, that in order to be either an improving, worthy or happy man, he must do one of two things. He must either devote himself to the accomplishment of some public objects; or he must devote some hours of every day to his own intellectual cultivation. In any case, he must be, to a certain extent, a laborious man. The thought of his heart may be far different from this. He may think it his special privilege, as a man of fortune, to be exempt from all care and effort. To lounge on soft couches, to walk in pleasant gardens, to ride out for exercise, and to come home for feasting—this may be his plan. But it will never do. It never did yet answer for any human being, and it never will. God has made a law against it, which no human power ever could annul, nor human ingenuity evade. That law is, that upon labor, either of the body or of the mind, all essential well-being shall depend. And if this law be not complied with, I verily believe that wealth is only a curse, and luxury only a more slippery road to destruction. The poor idler, I verily believe, is safer than the rich idler: and I doubt, whether he is not happier. I doubt whether the most miserable vagrancy, that sleeps in barns and sheds, and feeds upon the fragments of other men's tables, and leaves its tattered garments upon every hedge, is *so* miserable, as surfeited opulence, sighing in palaces, sunk in the lethargy of indolence, loaded with plethory, groaning with weariness which no wholesome fatigue ever comes to relieve. The vagrant is, at least, obliged to *walk* from place to place, and thus far has the advantage over his fellow idler who can ride. Yes, he walks abroad in the fair morning— no soft couch detains him—he walks abroad among the fresh fields, by the sunny hedges and along the silent lanes, singing his idle song as he goes—a creature poor and wretched enough, no doubt—but I am tempted to say, if I must be idle, give me that lot, rather than to sit in the cheerless shadow of palace roofs. or to toss on downy beds of sluggish stupor or racking pain.

I have thus endeavored to state one of the cardinal and inflexible laws of all human improvement and happiness. I have already premised, that my purpose in doing so, was to speak of the spirit of gain, of the eagerness for fortune, as characteristics of modern business, which tend to the dishonor and violation of the law of labor.

In proceeding to do this, let me more generally observe, in the first place, that there has always been a public opinion in the world, derogatory to labor. The necessity of exertion, though it is the very law under which God has placed mankind for their improvement and virtue, has always been regarded as a kind of degradation—has always been felt as a kind of reproach. With the exception of a few great geniuses, none so great as those who do nothing. Freedom from the necessity of exertion is looked upon as a privileged condition; it is encircled with admiring eyes; it absolutely gathers dignity and honor about it. One might think that a man would make some apologies for it, to the toiling world. Not at all; he is proud of it. It is for the busy man to make apologies. He hopes you will excuse him; he *must* work, or he *must* attend to his business. You would think he was about to do some mean action. You would think he was about to do something of which he is ashamed. And he *is* ashamed of it !

The time has hardly gone by, when even literary labor—labor of the mind, the noblest of all labor, has suffered under this disparaging estimate. Authorship has always been held to be the proper subject for the patronage of condition. Some of the most distinguished authors, have lived in obscurity, compared with the rich and fashionable around them, and have only forced their way into posthumous celebrity. The rewards of intellectual toil have usually been stinted to the provision of a bare, humble subsistence. Not seldom has the reward been scarcely a remove from starvation. But when we descend to manual labor, the comparison is still more striking. The laboring classes, *operatives* as they are significantly called in these days, are generally regarded but as a useful machinery to produce and manufacture comforts and luxuries for those that can buy them. And the laboring classes are so regarded, mainly, not because they are less informed and cultivated, though that may be true, but *because* they are the laboring classes. Let any one of them be suddenly endowed with a fortune, let him be made independent of labor, and without any change of character, he immediately, in the general estimation, takes his place among what are called the upper classes. In those countries where the favoritism extended to the aristocracy, has made many of its members the vainest, most frivolous and useless of beings, it must be apparent, that many persons among the business classes are altogether their superiors in mind, in refinement, in all the noblest qualities; and yet does the bare circumstance of pecuniary independence carry it over every thing. They walk abroad in lordly pride, and the children of toil on every side, do homage to them

Let such an one enter any one of the villages of England or of this country, let him live there—with nothing to do and doing nothing, the year round—and those who labor in the field and the workshop, will look upon him, in bare virtue of his ability to be idle, as altogether their superior. Yes, those who have wrought well in the great school of providence, who have toiled faithfully at their tasks and learned them, will pay this mental deference to the truant, to the idler, to him who learns nothing and does nothing—aye, and because he does nothing. Nay, in that holy church, whose ministry is the strongest bond to philanthropic exertion, the clergy, the very ministry of him who went about doing good, and had not where to lay his head, sinks, in the estimation of the whole world to the lowest point of depression, the moment it is called "a working clergy." That very epithet, *working*, seems, in spite of every counteracting consideration, to be a stigma upon every thing to which it can be applied.

But besides this general opinion, there is a specific opinion or way of thinking, to which I have already referred, as opposed to our principle, and to which I wish now to invite your more particular attention. This opinion or way of thinking, I must endeavor to describe with some care, as it constitutes the basis of fact, from which the moral reflections of the remainder of this discourse will arise.

It will be admitted, then, in the general, I think, that modern business—*modern*, I mean, as compared with that of an hundred or even fifty years ago—has assumed a new character; that it has departed from the staidness, regularity and moderation of former days. The times when the business of the father descended to the son, and was expected to pass down as an heir-loom in the family; when the risks were small and the gains were moderate, or if ample, still comparatively sure, seem to have given way to the intense desire and the hazardous pursuit, of immediate and immense accumulation. It is not necessary to the statement I am making, that I should enter into the causes of this change. They are, doubtless, to be found in the unusual opportunities for gain, in the extraordinary extension of credits, and I think also, in the rapid expansion of the principle of liberty—that is to say, in the intellectual activity, personal ambition and unfettered enterprize, which that principle has introduced into society. But whatever be the causes of the change, it will not be denied, I presume, that there has sprung up in connection with it, a new view of acquisition; or rather, to state more exactly what I mean, that a view of acquisition, which, in former time, was confined to a few minds, has now taken possession of almost the entire business community, and constitutes therefore, beyond all former example, one of the great moral features of the times. I cannot, perhaps, briefly describe this view better than by denominating it, a *passion for making a fortune*, and for making it speedily. I do not, of course, mean to say that this *passion* has not existed before. The love of money has always been a desire so strong, that it has needed for its restraint, all the checks and admonitions of reason and religion. There have always been those who have set their affections and expectations on a fortune, as something indispensable to their happiness. There have also appeared, from time to time, seasons of rash and raging speculation, as in the case of the South Sea and Mississippi stocks in England; disturbing, however, but occasionally the regular progress of business. But the case with us, now, is different. We have, at length, become conversant with times, in which these seasons of excess and hazard in business are succeeding one another periodically, and with but brief intervals. The pursuit of property, and that in no moderate amount, has acquired at once, an unprecedented activity and universality. The views, with which multitudes now are entering into business, are not of gaining a subsistence—they disdain the thought—not barely of pursuing a proper and useful calling—that it is far beneath their ambition; but of acquiring a fortune—of acquiring ease and independence. In accordance with this view, is the common notion of retiring from business. It is true, that we do not see much of this retiring, but we hear much about it. The passion exists, though the course of business is so rash as constantly to disappoint, or so eager as finally to overcome it.

In saying that a great change is passing over the business character of the world, and that it is in some respects dangerous, I do not intend to say, that it is altogether bad, or even, that there is necessarily more evil than good in it. I hold it to be an advantage to the world, that restrictions, like those of the guilds of Germany and the Borough laws in England, are thrown off, and that a greater number of competitors can enter the lists, and run the race for the comforts and luxuries of life. The prizes, too, will be smaller as the competitors are more numerous; and *that*, I hold, will be an advantage. I believe, also, that the system of doing business on credit, in a young and enterprising country, is, within proper bounds, useful; and that our own, owes a part of its unexampled growth and prosperity to this cause. I only say, what I think all will admit, that from these causes, there are tendencies in the business of the country which are dangerous.

But to return to my statement; I undertake to say, not only in general, that there are wrong practical tendencies, but that there is a way of thinking about business which is wrong. Your practical advisers may tell you that there has been over-trading, that this is the great evil, and that it must be avoided in future. I do not say, for I do not know, whether this has been the great evil or not; but this I say, that it probably will not be avoided in future, if it has been the evil. And why not? Because there is an evil beneath the evil alleged, and that is an excessive desire for property, an eagerness for fortune. In other words, there is a wrong way of thinking, which lies like a canker at the root of all wholesome moderation. The very idea that property is to be acquired in the course of ten or twenty years, which shall suffice for the rest of life, that by some prosperous traffic or grand speculation, all the labor of life is to be accomplished in a brief portion of it, that by dexterous management, a large part of the term of human existence is to be exonerated from the laws of industry and self-denial—all this way of thinking, I contend, is founded in a mistake of the true nature and design of business, and of the conditions of human well-being.

I do not say—still to discriminate—that it is wrong to desire wealth, and even, with a favorable and safe opportunity, to seek the rapid accumulation of it. A man may have noble ends to accomplish by such accumulation. He may design to relieve his destitute friends or kindred. He may desire to foster good institutions, and to help good objects. Or, he may wish to retire to some other sphere of usefulness and exertion, which shall be more congenial to his taste and affections. But it is a different feeling, it is the desire of accumulation for the sake of securing a life of ease and gratification—for the sake of escaping from exertion and self-denial—this is the wrong way of thinking which I would point out, and which I maintain to be common. I do not say that it is universal among the seekers of wealth. I do not say that *all* who propose to retire from business, propose to retire to a life of complete indolence or indulgence; but I say that many do; and I am inclined to say, that all propose to themselves an independence, and an exemption from the necessity of exertion, which are not likely to be good for them; and, moreover, that they wed themselves to these ideas of independence and exemption, to a degree, that is altogether irrational, unchristian and inconsistent with the highest and noblest views of life. That a man should desire so to provide for himself, as in case of sickness or disability, not to be a burthen upon his friends or the public, or in case of his death, that his family should not be thus dependent, *is* most reasonable, proper and wise. But that a man should wear out half of his life in an almost slavish devotion to business, that he should neglect his health, comfort and mind, and waste his very heart, with anxiety, and all to build a castle of indolence in some fairy land—this, I hold, to be unwise and wrong. I am saying nothing now of particular emergencies into which a man may rightly or wrongly have brought himself; I speak only of the general principle.

And the principle, I say, in the first place, is unwise, wrong, injurious and dangerous, with reference to business itself. It is easy to see that the different views of business, implied in the foregoing remarks, will impart to the whole process a different character. If a man enters upon it as the occupation of his life, if he looks upon it as a useful and honorable course, if he is interested in its moral uses, and, what we demand of every high-minded profession, if he thinks more of its uses than of its fruits—more of a high and honorable character than of any amount of gains— and if, in fine, he is willing to conform to that ordinance of Heaven which has appointed industry, action, effort, to be the spring of improvement, then, of course, he will calmly and patiently address himself to his task, and fulfil it with wisdom and moderation. But if business is a mere expedient to gain a fortune, a race run for a prize, a game played for a great stake; then it as naturally follows that there will be eagerness and absorption, hurry and anxiety; it will be a race for the swift, and a game for the dexterous, and a battle for the strong; life will be turned into a scene of hazard and strife, and its fortunes will often hang upon the cast of a die.

I must add that the danger of all this is greatly increased by a circumstance already alluded to; I mean the rapid expansion of the principle of political freedom. Perhaps, the first natural development of that principle was to be looked for in the pursuit of property. Property is the most obvious form of individual power, the most immediate and palpable ministration to human ambition. It was natural, when the weights and burthens of old restrictions were taken off, that men should first rush into the career of accumulation. I say restrictions; but there have been restraints *upon the mind,* which are, perhaps, yet more worthy of notice. The mass of mankind, in former ages, have ever felt that the high and splendid prizes of life were not for them. They have consented to poverty, or to mediocrity at the utmost, as their inevitable lot. But a new arena is now spread for them, and they are looking to the high places of society as within their reach. The impulse imparted to private ambition by this possibility, has not, I think, been fully considered, and it cannot, perhaps, be fully calculated. And it should also be brought into the account, that our imperfect civilization has not yet gone beyond the point of awarding a leading, and, perhaps, paramount consideration in society, to mere wealth. Conceive, then, what must be the effect, upon a man in humble and straitened circumstances, of the idea that it is possible for him to rise to this distinction. The thoughts of his youth, perhaps, have been lowly and unaspiring: they have belonged to that place which has been assigned him in the old *regime* of society. But in the rapid progress of that equalizing system which is spreading itself over the world, and amidst the unprecedented facilities of modern business, a new idea is suddenly presented to him. As he travels along the dusty road of toil, visions of a palace—of splendor, and equipage and state, rise before him; his may be the most enviable and distinguished lot in the country; he who is now a slave of the counting-room or counter, of the work-bench or the carman's stand, may yet be one, to whom the highest in the land shall bow in homage. Conceive, I say, the effect of this new idea upon an individual, and upon a community. It must give an unprecedented and dangerous impulse to society. It must lead to extraordinary efforts and measures for acquisition. It will have the most natural effect upon the extension of traffic and the employment of credit. It may be expected, that in such circumstances, men will borrow and bargain as they have never done before; that the lessons of the old prudence will be laid aside; that the old plodding and pains-taking course will not do for the excited and stimulated spirit of such an age.

This eagerness for acquiring fortunes, tends equally to defeat the ultimate, the providential design of business. That design, I have said, is to train men by action, by labor and care, by the due exertion of their faculties, to mental and moral accomplishment. It is necessary to this end, that business should be conducted with regularity, patience and calmness; that the mind should not be diverted from a fair application of its powers, by any exaggerated or fanciful estimate of the results. Especially, if that contemplation of results involves the idea of *escaping* from all care and occupation, must it constantly hinder the fulfilment of the providential design. The very spirit of business *then*, is the spirit of resistance to that design. But even if it were not, yet it is evident, that neither the mental nor moral faculties of a human being have any fair chance, amidst agitations and anxieties, amidst dazzling hopes and disheartening fears. Certainly, it must be admitted, that a time of excessive absorption in business, is any thing but a period of improvement. How many in such seasons have sunk in character, and in all the aims of life—have lost their habits of reading and reflection, their habits of meditation and prayer!

Business, in its ultimate, its providential design, is a school. Neglected, forgotten, perhaps ridiculed, as this consideration may be, it is the great and solemn truth. Man is placed in this school, as a learner of lessons for eternity. What he shall learn, not what he shall get, is of chief, of eternal import to him. As to property, "it is certain," to use the language of an Apostle, "that as we brought nothing into this world, we can carry nothing out of it." But there is one thing which we shall carry out of it, and that is, the *character* which we have formed in the very pursuits, by which property has been acquired.

In the next place, this passion for rapid accumulation, thus pushed to eagerness and vehemence, and liable to be urged to rashness and recklessness, leads to another evil, which to any rational apprehension of things, cannot be accounted small; and that is the evil of sacrificing in business, the end to the means.

"Live while you live," is a maxim which has a good sense as well as a bad one. But the man who is sacrificing all the proper ends of life, for something to be enjoyed twenty years hence, can scarcely be said to live *while* he lives. He is *not* living *now* in any satisfactory way, he confesses; he is going to live by and by; that is, when and where he does not live, and never may live; nay, where, it is probable, he never will live. For not one man in thirty, of those who intend to retire from business, ever does retire. And yet, how many suffer this dream about retiring, to cheat them out of the substantial ends of acquisition—comfort, improvement, happiness, as they go on.

How then stands the account? In seeking property, a man has certain ends in view. Does he gain them? The lowest of them—comfort—does he gain that? No, he will tell you, he has little enough of comfort. That is to come. Having forsaken the path of regular and moderate and sure acquisition in which his fathers walked, he has plunged into an ocean of credit, spread the sails of adventurous speculation, is tossed upon the giddy and uncertain waves of a fluctuating currency, and liable, any day, to be wrecked by the storms that are sweeping over the world of business. The means, the *means*—of ease, of comfort, of luxury—he must have; and yet the things themselves—ease, comfort, and the true enjoyment of luxury, are the very things which he constantly fails to reach. He is ever saying, that he must *get out* of this turmoil of business, and yet he never does get out of it. The very eagerness of the pursuit, not only deprives him of all ease and comfort as he goes on, but it tends constantly to push the whole system of business to that excess, which brings about certain reaction and disappointment. Were it not better for him to live while he lives—to enjoy life as it passes? Were it not better for him to live richer and die poorer? Were it not best of all for him to banish from his mind, that erring dream of future indolence and indulgence; and to address himself to the business of life, as the school of his earthly education; to settle it with himself now, that independence if he gains it, is *not* to give him exemption from employment; that in order to be a happy man, he must always, with the mind or with the body, or with both, be a laborer; and, in fine, that the reasonable exertion of his powers, bodily and mental, is not to be regarded as mere drudgery, but as a good discipline, a wise ordination, a training in this primary school of our being, for nobler endeavors, and spheres of higher activity hereafter? For never surely is activity to cease; and he who proposes to resign half his life to indolent enjoyment, can scarcely be preparing for the boundless range and the intenser life that is to come.

But there are higher ends of acquisition than mere comfort. For I suppose, that few seekers of wealth can be found, who do not propose mental culture, and a beneficent use of property, as among their objects. And with a fulfilment of these purposes, a *moderate* pursuit is perfectly compatible. But how is it, when that pursuit becomes an eager and absorbing strife for fortune? What is the language of fact and experience? Amidst such engrossing pursuits, is there any time for reading? Are any literary habits, or any habits of mental culture, formed? I suppose these questions carry with them their own answer. But the over-busy man, though he is neglecting his mind now, means to repair that error by and by. That is the greatest mistake of all. He will not find the habits he wants, all prepared and ready for him, like that pleasant mansion of repose to which he is looking. He will find habits there, indeed; but they will be the habits he has been cultivating for twenty years; not those he has been neglecting. The truth he will then find to be, that he does not love to read or study, that he never did love it, and that he probably never will love it.

I do not say that reading is the only means of mental cultivation. Business itself *may* invigorate, enlarge and elevate the mind. But then it must be, because large views are taken of it; because the mind travels beyond the counter and the desk, and studies the geography, politics and social tendencies of the world; investigates the laws of trade, and the philosophy of mechanism, and speculates upon the morals and ends of all business. Nay, and the trader and the craftsman, if he would duly cultivate his mind, must, like the lawyer, physician and clergyman, travel beyond the province of his own profession, and bring the contributions of every region of thought, to build himself up in the strength and manhood of his intellectual nature.

And therefore, I say, with double force of asseveration, that he who has pursued business in such a way as to have neglected all just mental culture, has sacrificed the end to the means. He has gained money, and lost knowledge; he has gained splendor, and lost accomplishment; gained tinsel, and lost gold; gained an estate, and lost an empire—gained the world, and lost his soul.

And thus it is with all the ends of accumulation. The beneficent use, the moral elevation, which every high-minded man will propose to himself, are sacrificed in the eagerness of the pursuit. A man may give, and give liberally; but this may be a very different thing from *using* property beneficently and wisely. I confess, that on this account, I look with exceeding distrust upon all our city charities; because men have no time to look into the cases and questions that are presented to them; because they give recklessly, without system or concert. I believe that immense streams of charity are annually flowing around us, which tend only to deepen the channels of poverty and misery. He who gives money, to save time, cannot be acting wisely for others; and he who does good *only* by agents and almoners, cannot be acting wisely for himself. And yet, this is the course to which excessive devotion to gain must lead. The man has no time to think for himself; and, therefore, custom must be his law, or his clergyman, perhaps, is his conscience. He is an excellent disciple in the school of implicit submission. He attends a sound divine; he gives bountifully to the missions or to the alms-houses; he suffers himself to be assessed, perhaps, in the one tenth of his income; and there end with him all the uses and responsibilities of wealth. His mind is engrossed with acquisition to that extent, that he has no proper regard to the ends of acquisition. Nay more, he comes, perhaps, to that pass in fatuity, that he substitutes altogether the means for the end, and embraces his possessions with the insane grasp of the miser.

On the whole, and in fine, this passion for a fortune diverts man from his true dignity, his true function— which lies in exertion, in labor.

I can conceive of reasons, why I might lawfully, and even earnestly desire a fortune. If I could fill some fair palace, itself a work of art, with the productions of lofty genius; if I could be the friend and helper of humble worth—if I could mark it out, where failing health or adverse fortune pressed it hard, and soften or stay the bitter hours that are hastening it to madness or to the grave; if I could stand between the oppressor and his prey, and bid the fetter and the dungeon give up its victim; if I could build up great institutes of learning and academies of art; if I could open fountains of knowledge for the people, and conduct its streams in the right channels; if I could do better for the poor than to bestow alms upon them— even to think of them, and devise plans for their elevation in knowledge and virtue, instead of for ever opening the old reservoirs and resources for their improvidence ; if, in fine, wealth could be to me, the handmaid of exertion, facilitating effort and giving success to endeavor, then might I lawfully, and yet warily and modestly, desire it. But if wealth is to do nothing for me but to minister ease and indulgence, and to place my children in the same bad school, I fearlessly say, though it be in face of the world's dread laugh, that I do not see why I should desire it, and that I do not desire it!

Are my reasons asked for this strange decision? Another, in part, shall give them for me. " Two men," says a quaint writer, "two men I honor, and no third. First, the toil-worn craftsman, that with earth-made implement laboriously conquers the earth, and makes her man's. Venerable to me is the hard hand; crooked, coarse ; wherein, notwithstanding, lies a cunning virtue, indefeasibly royal, as of the sceptre of this planet. Venerable, too, is the rugged face, all weather-tanned, besoiled, with its rude intelligence ; for it is the face of a man, living man-like. Oh, but the more venerable for thy rudeness, and even because we must pity as well as love thee! Hardly-entreated brother! For us was thy back so bent, for us were thy straight limbs and fingers so deformed. Thou wert our conscript, on whom the lot fell, and fighting our battles, wert so marred. For in thee, too, lay a God-created form, but it was not to be unfolded; encrusted must it stand with the thick adhesions and defacement of labor; and thy body, like thy soul, was not to know freedom. Yet toil on, toil on; thou art in thy duty, be out of it who may; thou toilest for the altogether indispensable, for daily bread.

"A second man I honor, and still more highly; him who is seen toiling for the spiritually indispensable; not daily bread, but the bread of life. Is not he, too, in his duty; endeavoring towards inward harmony; revealing this, by act or by word, through all his outward endeavors, be they high or low? Highest of all, when his outward and his inward endeavor are one; when we can name him artist; not earthly craftsman only, but inspired thinker, that with heaven-made implement conquers heaven for us! If the poor and humble toil that we have food, must not the high and glorious toil for him, in return, that he have light and guidance, freedom, immortality?—These two, in all their degrees, I honor; all else is chaff and dust, which let the wind blow whither it listeth.

"Unspeakably touching is it, however, when I find both dignities united; and he, that must toil outwardly for the lowest of man's wants, is also toiling inwardly for the highest. Sublimer in this world know I nothing, than a peasant saint, could such now, any where be met with. Such a one will take thee back to Nazareth itself; thou wilt see the splendor of heaven spring forth from the humblest depths of earth, like a light shining in great darkness."[*]

And who, I ask, is that *third* man, that challenges

---

[*] Thomas Carlyle.

our respect? Say, that the world were made to be the couch of his repose, and the heavens to curtain it. Grant, that the revolving earth were his rolling chariot, and all earth's magnificence were the drapery that hung around his gorgeous rest; yet could not that august voluptuary—let alone the puny idler of our city streets—win from a wise man one sentiment of respect. What is there glorious in the world, that is not the product of labor, either of the body or of the mind? What is history but its record? What are the treasures of genius and art, but its work? What are cultivated fields but its toil? The busy marts, the rising cities, the enriched empires of the world—what are they, but the great treasure-houses of labor? The pyramids of Egypt, the castles and towers and temples of Europe, the buried cities of Mexico—what are they but tracks, all round the world, of the mighty footsteps of labor? Antiquity had not been without it. Without it, there were no memory of the past; without it, there were no hope for the future.

Let then labor, the world's great ordinance, take its proper place in the world. Let idleness too, have the meed that it deserves. Honor, I say be paid, wherever it is due. Honor, if you please, to unchallenged indolence—for that which all the world admires, hath, no doubt, some ground for it—honor, then, to undisturbed, unchallenged indolence—for it reposes on treasures that labor some time gained and gathered. It is the effigy of a man, upon a splendid mausoleum— somebody built that mausoleum—somebody put that dead image there. Honor to him that does nothing, and yet does not starve; he hath his significance still; he is a standing proof that *somebody* has worked.

Nay, rather let us say, honor to the worker—to the toiler—to him who produces, and not alone consumes—to him who puts forth his hand to add to the treasure-heap of human comforts, and not alone to take away! Honor to him who goes forth amidst the struggling elements to fight his battle, and shrinks not, with cowardly effeminacy, behind pillows of ease! Honor to the strong muscle and the manly nerve, and the resolute and brave heart! Honor to the sweaty brow and to the toiling brain! Honor to the great and beautiful offices of humanity—to manhood's toil and woman's task—to parental industry, to maternal watching and weariness—to teaching wisdom and patient learning—to the brow of care that presides over the state, and to many-handed labor that toils in the work-shops and fields, beneath its sacred and guardian sway!

DISCOURSE IV.

ON THE MORAL LIMITS OF ACCUMULATION.

PROVERBS XXX. 8, 9. GIVE ME NEITHER POVERTY NOR RICHES; LEST I BE FULL AND DENY THEE, AND SAY, WHO IS THE LORD? OR LEST I BE POOR, AND STEAL, AND TAKE THE NAME OF MY GOD IN VAIN.

IN my last discourse, I considered some of the evil consequences of the passion for accumulation; in the present, I propose to point out some of the moral limits to be set to that passion. In other words, the limits to accumulation, the wholsome restraints upon the passion for it, which are prescribed by feelings of general philanthropy and justice, by the laws of morality, and by a sober consideration of the natural effects of wealth upon ourselves, our children and the world— these are the topics of our present meditation.

I cannot help feeling here the difficulties under which the pulpit labors, in the discussion of the points now before us. Some, indeed, will think them unsuitable to the pulpit, as not being sufficiently religious. Others seem to be disposed to limit the pulpit to the utterance of general and unquestionable truths. To these views I cannot assent. The points which I am discussing are, in the highest degree, moral; they are practically religious; they belong to the morality and religion of daily life. And then again, as to what the preacher shall say, I do not think that he is to be confined to truisms, or to self-evident truths, or to truths in which all shall agree. We come here to deliberate on great questions of morality and duty; to consider what is true, what is right. In doing this, the preacher may bring forward views in which some of his hearers cannot agree with him; how, indeed, should it be otherwise. But he does not pretend to utter infallible sentences. He may be wrong. But he is none the less bound to utter what he does believe, and thinks to be worthy of attention. This office I attempt to discharge among you. And I ask you not to take ill, at my hands, that which you would not so take, if I utteredit by your fire-sides. And if I am wrong, on some such occasion, perhaps, you will set me right.

Let me proceed, then, frankly to lay before you some reflections that have impressed my own mind, in regard to the limitations which good feeling, justice and wisdom ought, perhaps, to set to the pursuit of wealth.

In the first place, then, I doubt whether this immense accumulation in a few hands, while the rest of the world is comparatively poor, does not imply an unequal, an unfair distribution of the rewards of industry. I may be wrong on this point, and if I were considered as speaking with any authority from the pulpit, I should not make the suggestion. Yet speaking as I do, with no assumption, but with the modesty of doubt, I shall venture to submit this point to your consideration.

It would seem to be an evident principle of humanity and justice, that property and the means of comfort should bear some proportion to men's industry. Now we know that they do not. I am not denying that, in general, the hard-working man labors less with the mind; and that he is often kept poor, either by improvidence and wastefulness, or because he has less energy and sagacity than others bring into the business of life. I do not advocate any absurd system of agrarian levelling. I believe that wealth was designed to accumulate in certain hands, to a certain extent; because, I perceive, that this naturally results from the superior talents and efforts of certain individuals. But I cannot help thinking, that the disproportion is greater than it ought to be.

In order to bring this question home to your apprehension, let me ask you to suppose that some years ago, any one of you had come to this city with a beloved brother, to prepare for a life of business. Let me suppose that you had been placed with a merchant, and he with a carman; both, lawful, useful and necessary callings in society; somebody must discharge each of these offices. Now you know that the results would probably be, that you would be rich, or at least possessed of an easy property, and that he would be poor; or at any rate, that you would have a fair chance of acquiring a fortune from your industry, and that he would have no such chance from his industry. Now let me further suppose, that you did not treat him as *some* men treat their poor relations; passing them by and striving to forget them—almost wishing they did not exist; but that you continued on terms of kind and intimate intercourse with him; that you constantly interchanged visits with him, and could compare the splendor of your dwelling with the poverty of his; I ask you if you would not feel, if you could help feeling, that society had dealt unjustly with you and with him in this matter? But I say that every man is your brother; and that what you would thus feel for your brother, you are bound to feel for every man!

I know that it is said in regard to accumulation in general, that capital has its claims; but I cannot help thinking that they are overrated, in comparison with the claims of human nerves and sinews. Suppose that of a thousand men engaged in a great manufacturing establishment, ten possess the capital and oversee the establishment, and the nine hundred and ninety do the work. Can it be right, that the ten should grow to immense wealth, and that the nine hundred and ninety should be for ever poor? I admit, that something is to be allowed for the risk taken by the capitalist. I have heard it pleaded, indeed, that he is extremely liable to fail, and often does so—while the poor, heaven help them! never fail. But it seems to me, that this consideration is not quite fairly pleaded. It is said, that there is a risk. But does not the capitalist, to a certain extent, make the risk? Is not his risk, often in proportion to the urgency with which he pushes the business of accumulation, and to that neglect and infidelity of his agents and workmen, which must spring from their having so slight a common interest with him in his undertakings? The risks will be smaller when the pursuit of property is more restrained and reasonable; and when the rewards of industry are more equal and just. But I hear it said again, that "the poor are wasteful; and that to increase their wages, is only to increase their vices."

Let me tell you, that poverty is the parent of improvidence and desperation. Those who have been brought up in that school may very probably, for a while, abuse their increased means. But in the long run, it cannot be so. Nay, by the very terms of your proposition, the abuse will cease with the desperation of poverty. Give the poor some hope; give them some means; give them something to lean upon; give them some interest in the order and welfare of society; and they will become less wasteful, less reckless and vicious.

Indeed, is it not obvious, can any one with his eyes open deny, that the extremes of condition in the world, the extremes of wealth and poverty, furnish us with the extremes of vice and dissipation? And does not this fact settle and prove, beyond all question, that it is desirable that accumulation should be restrained within some bounds, on the one hand, and on the other, that indigence should be lessened? What is the state of the operatives in the manufacturing districts of England? Only worse, than that of the idlers in that kingdom, who are living and rioting upon overgrown fortunes. Let the conditions of men approach the same inequality in this or any other country, and we shall witness the same results. The tendency of things among us, I rejoice to believe, is not to that result, but it is, no doubt, the constant tendency of private ambition.

I am sensible, my friends, that I have made a large demand on your candor, in laying this question before you. It is paying the highest compliment I could pay to your fairness of mind. I only ask that you will treat my argument with equal generosity.

But I proceed to another point. In order to the rapid accumulation of property, in all ordinary cases, a great expansion of credit is necessary. A man can not grow suddenly rich by the labor of his hands, and he must therefore use the property or the promises of others, in order to compass this end. Now, there is a question which I have never seen stated in the books of moral philosophy, which I have not heard discussed in the pulpit, and yet it is a point which deserves a place in the code of commercial morality; and that is, how far it is right for a man to use credit—that is, to extend his business, beyond his actual capital? I am sensible that it is extremely difficult, if it is not indeed impossible, to lay down any exact rule on this subject; and yet it seems to me none the less worthy of consideration. Certainly, it must be admitted, that there is a point somewhere, beyond which it is not prudent, and, therefore, not right, to go. Certainly, it can not be right, as it appears to me, for a man to use all the credit he can get. It could not be right, for instance, that upon a capital of ten thousand, a man should do a business of ten millions. No man ought to trust his powers to such an indefinable extent. No man's creditors, were he to fail, could be satisfied with his having accepted trusts from others in the shape of credits, which common prudence shall pronounce to be rash and hazardous. There is a common prudence, if there is no exact rule about this matter; and the borrower is most especially bound to observe it; and certainly, every honest man, being a borrower, would observe it, if he did but sufficiently think of it. The want of this thought is the very reason why I bring forward the subject.

With regard to the rule, I have it as the deliberate opinion of one of the greatest bankers in Europe, that a man should not extend his business to more than three times his capital, and if it be a large business, to not more than twice his capital. I do not say that this is the rule, though I have the greatest respect for the judgment that laid it down. I do not say that it is the rule, because I am advised on the other hand, by very competent judges, that the rule must vary exceedingly with the different kinds of business which a man may pursue.

I do not undertake, then, to lay down any particular rule, but I urge the claims of general prudence. I wish to call attention to this point. I am persuaded that it is for want of reflection and not from want of principle, that many have adventured out upon an ocean of credit, where they have not only suffered shipwreck themselves, but carried down many a goodly vessel with them. It is said, that the Government have spread temptation before the people, by adopting measures which lead to extraordinary issues of bank paper. It may be so; I believe that it is so; though this can scarcely be supposed by the most jealous, to have been a matter of design. But grant that it be so; what I maintain is, that the people ought not to have yielded to the temptation, to the extent that many have done. The borrower, I hold, is specially and solemnly bound to be prudent. He is bound to be more prudent in the use of other men's property, than of his own. A man should be more cautious in taking credit, than in using capital. But I fear that the very reverse of this is commonly the fact. I fear that most men are more reckless when they use the means which credit gives them, than they would be in using their own absolute and fixed property. In small matters, we know that immediate payment is a check to expenditure. Why is it, but for this, that every petty dealer is anxious to open a credit with your family? He knows that your expenditures will be freer, your purchases larger, and that a more considerable amount will be made up at the end of the year, because you buy on credit. But to look at the subject in a wider view; I know that some men do plunge more recklessly into the great game of business, because the game is played with credit; with counters, and not with coins. I have heard it observed, and I confess, that it was with a coolness and nonchalance that amazed me, that a man may as well take a good strong hold of business while he is about it, since he has nothing to lose by it. The sentiment is monstrous. It ought to shake the very foundations of every warehouse where it is uttered. There ought to be a sacred caution in the use of credit. And although I cannot pretend to define the precise law of its extension, yet this I will say, that never till I see a man adventuring his own property more freely than he adventures that which he borrows of his neighbor, can I think he is right. Let this great, and undeniably just moral principle be established; and I am persuaded that we shall at once see a wholesome restraint laid upon the use of credit.

There is one further point to which I wish to invite your attention; and that is the practice, in cases of bankruptcy, of giving preference to certain creditors, who have made loans on that condition. Now, I maintain, that no man ought to offer credit, and that no man ought to accept it, on that condition. The practice is abolished in England, and I know that *there* it is regarded as bringing a stain upon the commercial morality of this country.

I do not mean to charge with personal dereliction any person who has, in times past, taken advantage of this rule. It has been the rule of the country, and has passed unquestioned. And so long as it has been the rule, and money has been borrowed and lent on that principle, and it was considered right so to do, it was perhaps right, as between man and man, that cases of insolvency should be settled on that principle. But as a theoretical principle of general application, I hold, that it is utterly wrong. Our laws indeed disallow it, and public opinion ought not, for another hour, to sustain it.

The principle is dishonest. It is treachery to the body of a man's creditors. He appeared before them with a certain amount of means; and upon the strength of those means, they were willing to give him credit. Those means were the implied condition, the very basis of the loan; without them they would not have made it. They saw that he had a large stock of goods; that he was doing a large business, and they thought there was no danger. They depended, in fact, upon that visible property, in case of difficulties. But difficulty arises, failure comes; and then they find that much or all of that property is preoccupied and wrested from their hands, by certain confidential pledges. If they had known this, they would have stood aloof, and therefore, I say, that there is essential deception in the case.

Again, lending on such a principle loses all its generosity, and borrowing is liable to lose all the prudence and virtue that properly belong to it. If a man lends to his young friend or relative, on the sole strength of affection and confidence towards him, it is a transaction which bestows a grace upon mercantile life. But if he lends as a preference creditor, he takes no risk, and shows no confidence. For he knows, that the borrower upon the strength of *his* loan, can easily get property enough into his hands, to make *him* perfectly secure. And let it be observed, that in proportion as the acquisition of confidence is less necessary ; in proportion, that is to say, as virtue and ability are less necessary to set up a man in business, are they less likely to be cultivated: and so far as this principle goes, therefore, it tends to sap and undermine the whole business character of a country. Nay, it is easy to see, that under the cloak of these confidential transactions, the entire business between the borrower and lender may be the grossest and most iniquitous gambling. Of course, I do not say that this is common. But I say that the principle ought not to be tolerated, which is capable of such abuses.

This principle, I think, moreover, is the very keystone of the arch, that supports many an overgrown fabric of credit. And this observation has a two-fold bearing. Much of the credit that is obtained, could not exist without this principle. That is one thing ; but furthermore, I hold, that all the extension of credit which depends on this principle, ought not to exist at all. It ought not, because the principle is dishonest and treacherous. And it would not, because the first credit which often puts a man in the possession of visible means, is not given on the strength of confidence in him, but on the strength of the secret pledge; and then the after credits are based on those visible means. Let every man that borrows tell, as he ought to do, the amount of his confidential obligations, and many would find their credit seriously curtailed. And to that extent, most assuredly, it ought to be curtailed.

I have thus spoken of the spirit of gain as liable—not as *always being*, but as liable to be, in conflict with the great principles of social and commercial justice. I might add, that the manner in which the gains of business are sometimes clung to, amidst the wreck of fortunes, is a powerful and striking illustration of the same moral danger. He who regards no limits of justice in acquiring property, will break all bonds of justice to keep it.

And here I must carefully and widely distinguish. I give all honor to the spirit which many among us have shown in such circumstances; to the manly fortitude and disinterestedness of men, who have comparatively cared nothing for themselves, but who have been almost crushed to the earth by what they have suffered for their friends; to the heroic cheerfulness and soothing tenderness of woman in such an hour, ready to part with every luxury, and holding the very pearl of her life, in the unsullied integrity of her husband. I know full well, that that lofty integrity is the only rule ever thought of by many, in the painful adjustment of their broken fortunes. And I know and the public knows, that if they retain a portion of their splendor for a season, it is reluctantly, and because it cannot, in the present circumstances, be profitably disposed of—and in strict trust for their creditors. But, there are bankrupts of a different character, as you well know. I do not know that any such are in this presence; but if there were a congregation of such before me, I should speak no otherwise than I shall now speak. I say, that there are men of a different character; men who intend permanently to keep back a part of the price which they have sworn to pay; and I tell you, that God's altar, at which I minister, shall hear no word from me, concerning them, but a word of denunciation. It is dishonesty, and it ought to be infamy. It is robbery, though it live in splendor and ride in state; robbery, I say, as truly as if, instead of inhabiting a palace, it were consigned to the dungeons of Sing-Sing. And take care, my brethren, as ye shall stand at the judgment-bar of conscience and of God, that ye fall not at all beneath this temptation. The times are times of sore and dreadful peril to the virtue of the country. They are times in which it is necessary, even for honest men, to gird up the loins of their minds, and to be sober and watchful; ay, watchful over themselves. Remember, all such, I adjure you, that the dearest fortune you can carry into the world, will not compensate you for the least iota of your integrity surrendered and given up. Oh! sweeter in the lowliest dwelling to which you may descend, shall be the thought that you have kept your integrity immaculate, than all the concentrated essence of luxury to your taste, all its combined softness to your couch, all its gathered splendor to your state. Ay, prouder shall you be in the humblest seat, than if, with ill-kept gains, you sat upon the throne of a kingdom.

I come now to consider, in the last place, the limitations to be set to the desire of wealth, by a sober consideration of its too probable effects upon ourselves, upon our children, and upon the world at large. And here, let me ask two preliminary questions.

Can that be so necessary to human well-being, as many consider wealth to be, which necessarily falls to the lot but of a few? Can that be the very feast and wine of life, when but a few thousands of the human race, are allowed to partake of it? If it were so, surely God's providence were less kind and liberal, than we are bound to think it. God has not made a world of rich men, but rather a world of poor men; or of men, at least, who must toil for a subsistence. That then must be the good condition for man; nay, the best condition; and we see, indeed, that it is the grand sphere of human improvement.

In the next place, can that be so important to human welfare, which, if it were possessed by all, would be the most fatal injury possible? And here I must desire, that every person whose pursuit of property, this question may effect, will extend his thoughts beyond himself. He may say that it would be a good thing if *he* could acquire wealth, and perhaps it would. He may say that he does not see that riches would do *him* any harm, and, perhaps, they would not. He may have views that ennoble the pursuit of fortune. But the question is; would it be well and safe, for four-fifths of the business community around him to become opulent? He must remember that his neighbors have sought as well as he, and in a proportion, too, not far distant from what I have stated. They have sought, and had as good a right to succeed, as he had. Would it be well that so general an expectation of fortune, should be gratified? Would it be well for society; well for the world? Only carry the supposition a little farther; only suppose the whole world to acquire wealth; only suppose it were possible that the present generation could lay up a complete provision for the next, as some men desire to do for their children; and you destroy the world at a single blow. All industry would cease with the necessity for it; all improvement would stop with the demand for exertion; the dissipation of fortunes, whose mischiefs are now countervailed by the healthful tone of society, would then breed universal disease, and break out into universal license; and the world would sink into the grave of its own loathsome vices.

But let us look more closely, for a moment, at the general effect of wealth upon individuals and upon nations.

I am obliged, then, to regard with considerable distrust, the influence of wealth upon individuals. I know that it is a mere instrument, which may be converted to good or to bad ends. I know that it is often used for good ends. But I more than doubt whether the chances lean that way. Independence and luxury are not likely to be good for any man. Leisure and luxury are almost always bad for every man. I know that there are noble exceptions. But I have *seen* so much of the evil effect of wealth upon the mind—making it proud, haughty and impatient, robbing it of its simplicity, modesty and humility, bereaving it of its large and gentle and considerate humanity; and I have *heard* such testimonies, such astonishing testimonies to the same effect, from those whose professional business it is to settle and adjust the affairs of large estates, that I more and more distrust its boasted advantages. I deny the validity of that boast. In truth, I am sick of the world's admiration of wealth. Almost all the noblest things that have been achieved in the world, have been achieved by poor men; poor scholars and professional men; poor artisans and artists; poor philosophers, and poets, and men of genius. It does appear to me, that there is a certain staidness and sobriety, a certain moderation and restraint, a certain pressure of circumstances, that is good for man. His body was not made for luxuries; it sickens, sinks and dies under them. His mind was not made for indulgence. It grows weak, effeminate and dwarfish, under that condition. It is good for us to bear the yoke; and it is especially good to bear the yoke in our youth. I am persuaded that many children are injured by too much attention, too much care; by too many servants at home; too many lessons at school; too many indulgences in society. They are not left sufficiently to exert their own powers, to invent their own amusements, to make their own way. They are often inefficient and unhappy, they lack ingenuity and energy, because they are taken out of the school of providence; and placed in one which our own foolish fondness and pride have built for them. Wealth, without a law of entail to help it, has always lacked the energy even to *keep* its own treasures. They drop from its imbecile hand. What an extraordinary revolution in domestic life is that, which, in this respect, is presented to us all over the world! A man, trained in the school of industry and frugality, acquires a large estate. His children possibly keep it. But the third generation almost inevitably goes down the rolling wheel of fortune, and *there* learns the energy necessary to rise again. And yet we are, almost *all* of us, anxious to put our children, or to ensure that our grand-children shall be put, on this road to indulgence, luxury, vice, degradation and ruin!

This excessive desire and admiration for wealth, is one of the worst traits in our modern civilization. We are, if I may say so, in an unfortunate dilemma in this matter. Our political civilization has opened the way for multitudes to wealth, and created an insatiable desire for it; but our mental civilization has not gone far enough, to make a right use of it. If wealth were employed in promoting mental culture at home, and works of philanthropy abroad; if it were multiplying studios of art, and building up institutions of learning around us; if it were every way raising the intellectual and moral character of the world, there could scarcely be too much of it. But if the utmost aim, effort and ambition of wealth, be to procure rich furniture, and provide costly entertainments, I am inclined to say, that there could scarcely be too little of it. " It employs the poor," do I hear it said? Better that it were *divided* with the poor. Willing enough am I, that it should be in few hands, if they will use it nobly—with temperate self-restraint and wise philanthropy. But on no other condition, will I admit that it is a good, either for its possessors or for any body else. I do not deny that it may lawfully be, to a certain extent, the minister of elegancies and luxuries, and the handmaid of hospitality and physical enjoyment; but this I say, that just in such proportion as its tendencies, divested of all higher aims and tastes, are running that way, are they running to evil and to peril.

That peril, moreover, does not attach to individuals and families alone; but it stands, a fearful beacon, in the experience of cities and empires. The lessons of past times, on this subject, are emphatic and solemn. I undertake to say that the history of wealth, has always been a history of corruption and downfall. The people never existed that could stand the trial.

Boundless profusion—alas! for humanity—is too little likely to spread for any people, the theatre of manly energy, rigid self-denial, and lofty virtue. Where is the bone and sinew and strength of a country? Where do you expect to find its loftiest talents and virtues? Where its martyrs to patriotism or religion? Where are the men to meet the days of peril and disaster? Do you look for them among the children of ease and indulgence and luxury?

All history answers. In the great march of the races of men over the earth, we have always seen opulence and luxury sinking before poverty and toil and hardy nurture. It is the very law that has presided over the great processions of empire. Sidon and Tyre, whose merchants possessed the wealth of princes; Babylon and Palmyra, the seats of Asiatic luxury; Rome, laden with the spoils of a world, overwhelmed by her own vices more than by the hosts of her enemies—all these, and many more, are examples of the destructive tendencies of immense and unnatural accumulation. No lesson in history is so clear, so impressive, as this.

I trust, indeed, that our modern, our *Christian* cities and kingdoms are to be saved from such disastrous issues. I trust that, by the appropriation of wealth, less to purposes of private gratification, and more to purposes of Christian philanthropy and public spirit, we are to be saved. But this is the very point on which I insist. Men must become more generous and benevolent, not more selfish and effeminate, as they become more rich, or the history of modern wealth will follow in the sad train of all past examples; and the story of American prosperity and of English opulence, will be told as a moral, in empires beyond the Rocky Mountains, or in the newly-discovered continents of the Asiatic Seas!

DISCOURSE V.

ON THE NATURAL AND ARTIFICIAL RELATIONS OF SOCIETY.

LUKE X, 29. AND WHO IS MY NEIGHBOR?

WHAT is society? And what are the ties that give to society its strength, dignity and beauty?

Let us make the attempt, though it will be difficult, to lay aside all conventional ideas of this subject; and endeavor to contemplate it in the spirit of generous philosophy, and more beneficent Christianity. What is society, not as man has made it, but in its original elements and just relations?—what is it, in the constitution of God? What did he design that man should be to man, and what the bond between them?

The answer is given in words of authority. "Thou shalt love thy neighbor as thyself." It is the bond of kind neighborhood, of gentle affinity, of gracious sympathy. And "who is my neighbor?" Again, the sacred text answers. It is the Samaritan, the sinner, the sufferer. It is he who is cast down and trodden under foot. It is he who lies by the way-side, neglected and despised. Every man is your neighbor. No matter what is his condition, his clime, his nation. No matter from what country, trodden down with oppression, he hath come. No matter in what prison-house he hath toiled ; or in what mournful garb, poverty or neglect hath clothed him. If he can say, "I am a man," he puts forward a sacred and venerable claim. If he who could say, "I am a Roman citizen," could rouse in his behalf the sympathies of a whole mighty people ; he who can say, "I am a man," should touch the heart of all mankind.

It is the claim of a common nature which God has laid upon us. As strong as the bond of humanity itself, he has made the common tie. Nay, more ; and dear as are the interests which he has committed to the sacred depository of each human bosom, and powerful as are the influences which one human being can exert upon another, has he made the obligation of love, pity and humanity to the common welfare. Humanity! the universal counterpart of each man's self! the multiplication of one's self into millions of suffering or happy beings !—well might the Latin poet say, "I am a man, and nothing is foreign, nothing far from me, that is human." And when a crowded Roman theatre once rose up in admiration of that noble sentiment, it was a homage as fit as it was beautiful. And fitly, from that day to this, has been borne, in the literature and on the bosom of nations, the record of that touching and noble saying.

But when I look more deeply into that humanity, and consider what it is, I feel that such a sentiment rises above generosity, and takes the character of sanctity and even of sublimity. I see a circle drawn around each human being, which it is not only sin, but sacrilege, to invade. For *what* is within that sacred pale that girds about every human heart ? Joy, sorrow ;

fear, hope; *need*; the need of happiness, and—more sacred and awful still—the need of virtue! There, God hath made a being, whom nothing but virtue can suffice; whom nothing but infinity and eternity will content. I speak not the language of theology, but of fact. So God hath made us. That mighty burthen of a spiritual and divine *need* rests upon every human heart; and nothing but the Almighty power that placed it there, can ever relieve it. It is your soul, my friend, that bears this dread charge; but it is the soul of him, whosoever he be, that standeth next you in the worldly crowd; it is every soul in this assembly; it is every man in the world. Human society is the society of beings so charged and entrusted. And if a congress of kings and potentates shall be thought an imposing spectacle, and to demand the most heedful consideration and treatment from one to the other, what shall be the higher law for beings who act for virtue, for heaven and for eternity!

Were it only happiness that is concerned, yet in the mysterious and inexplicable feeling of individuality which we all possess, the veriest outcast by the wayside, has as much at stake, as the monarch on his guarded throne. Poor men and rich men have, indeed, their distinct resorts and reliances; but there are no such things as a rich man's joy, and a poor man's joy. Happiness hath no respect of persons. It is as dear to one man as to another; and the feeling that makes it so, is not of man's, but of God's creating. And the sharp visitation of pain, whether it finds its way through the beggar's rags or the prince's cloth of gold, is alike sore and bitter to abide. Suffering is not an accident of our condition, but an ingredient of our being. Disease, whether it knocks at the cottage-wicket or the castle-gate, sends its thrilling summons, in equal disregard of haughty grandeur and shrinking penury. The inmates of the one, when revolving, beneath their humble roof, the fortunes of their lives, feel that they have, in their happiness, as much at stake, as the lofty possessors of the other; and in that essential respect, they have as much at stake.

To what conclusion, then, do we arrive? Is it a strange or an unexpected conclusion?—for this it is—that without any respect to external condition, one man has just as much right to have his virtue and happiness regarded, as another man! Is there a man here, who can look upon joy or sorrow with indifference, because they are found in a meaner garb than his own? I will not compromise, for one moment, the principle I maintain. I abhor that man, and I will say it. I abhor him, as worse than a traitor to his country, as a traitor to humanity. And I appeal, for my justification, to the most ordinary sentiments of every generous mind. Would you make that man your friend, who could take pleasure in wantonly crushing an insect? What will you think, then, of the man, who could coldly disregard, or carelessly wound, the feelings of a fellow-creature?

I have not wished to linger upon these preliminary steps; and, therefore, I hasten to observe that we have thus come, by a direct path, to the consideration of social relationships. They are of two kinds, natural and artificial; and my purpose is, of course, not to go over the whole ground—which would require volumes for the survey of it—but only to touch upon such points as are particularly pressed upon our noice, by the present condition of society. The natural relations of society are such as spring from necessity, and may be considered as ordained by our Creator; the artificial are those which are devised and regulated by man.

Of those which are natural, or necessary to society itself—though there are many, such as those of husband and wife, parent and child, guardian and ward, brothers and sisters, I shall consider only the single but comprehensive relation of employers and employed; or, in other words, that of master and apprentice, householder and domestic, rich and poor. These are certainly among the inevitable relations of human beings; and no progress of the world, in civilization or Christianity, may ever be expected to abolish them.

Our business with them, then, is not to extirpate but to improve them; and the questions that arise on this point, are of some delicacy, and need to be touched with a careful hand. I frankly confess myself to be among the number of those, who think that the feudal distinctions of former days, the old relations of master and servant, have transmitted to us some errors, which need to be done away; and which, in this country, must be done away. But, on the contrary, I do not hold at all, with those visionary persons, who expect that all distinctions in society will cease, and that men will stand on the level of perfect equality. Nay more, I maintain, that both necessity and propriety demand that the *manners* of different classes of society towards each other, shall differ. The manner of him who directs, must differ from the manner of him who is directed. On the one hand, there must be authority, or direction, if you please so to call it; and, on the other, acquiescence. The relation, indeed, is voluntary; no man among us is obliged to be the agent, workman, or domestic of another. But if he is such, then the relation requires that he should yield the acquiescence in question. And to that acquiescence, I repeat, a certain manner is appropriate: not slavish or obsequious, but cheerful and courteous. And I especially insist, that neither party is ever to forget the respect and kindness which are due from one human being to another.

But this great bond of humanity is, doubtless, often disregarded by both parties. Men strive and wrangle with each other, and are guilty of scorn or spite in their behavior, forgetting what they are—forgetting that they are creatures of the same God, children of one common Father. On which side the fault chiefly lies, at the present era of American society, I confess, that I am in doubt. Up to this time, or nearly to this time, I should have confidently said, that it was, where it always has been—with the class of employers. Power is ever liable to beget pride, injustice, and a haughty demeanor. But in a community where the class of the employed has become so independent, as it is in ours; where the sense of past injuries is rankling in the mind; where many false maxims tend to make all apparent inferiority peculiarly galling, and where the old conventional manners, once considered appropriate to that condition, are breaking up, the consequence is but too likely to be in many, revolt, recklessness, discourtesy and despite.

On which side the greatest courtesy and kindness are to be found, I will not decide; nor is it necessary in order to urging the duties that belong to both.

ON SOCIETY. 123

Let me offer it as a leading observation, that these duties, in this country, have assumed a new character, and a new importance. The relation of employers and employed among us is new. The workman here does not come to his employer, bowing and cringing for service, as the only thing that can keep him from starving. He stands before the great and powerful contractor or merchant, on a footing of comparative independence—of such independence, at least, as was never before known in any country. His labor is in request; if one man does not want it, another does. He is not obliged to sell it on such terms, as often grind to the dust, the artisan of Birmingham and Manchester, or the lazzaroni of Naples, or the palankin-bearer of Calcutta. This state of things, indeed, suggests some admonitions to the laboring classes, which I shall not fail to address to them. But at the same time, it imposes on employers some things, which I shall ask them to do more than submit to, as a matter of necessity. It calls them to consider and respect, more than employers have ever before done, the great claims of a common humanity.

I protest, then, against all overbearing haughtiness, and every thing that indicates a want of respect and kindness, on the part of the employer. I do not say how common this treatment of the poor man is. I do not say, that there are ten men in this assembly who are guilty of it. But if there is one, then, I say, that upon that case, I lay the heaviest weight of moral reprobation. I plead the great cause of humanity. I tell you that he who stands before you with a coarse garb and sweaty brow, is yet a man; and that he is to be regarded and felt for as a man. Must I resort to the very alphabet of Christianity, to teach you what is due to him? Must I remind you, that "God hath made of one blood all nations of men to dwell on the face of the earth?" Must I tell you, that "God hath made the poor of this world rich in faith, and heirs of a kingdom," amidst whose splendors all the appendages of your condition are but perishing bawbles? Must I tell you, that the man, whom you are liable in your power to treat with injustice or indignity, may be a nobler man than you; dearer to God, and more worthy of all true respect than you are? Must I say in so many words, that he has feelings, as keen and sensitive, it may be, as your own? Must I say, that all the touching and venerable claims of humanity are stamped upon him as well as upon you—that wife and children and home, happiness and hope and heaven, are as dear to him as to you? What right have you, and where did you find it, to treat him any otherwise than as a brother man! You are, indeed, to give directions, and he is to follow them. But that is a simple compact between you, and does not compromise the respectability of either. And beyond that, I say, that there is no law of substantial courtesy and kindness which is not to be observed between you. It is true, that men whose hands and eyes are occupied with strenuous toil or business, cannot be engaged with making bows to each other; and this is not what I insist upon. But I would make the laborer understand, that I respect him according to his merits, as truly as I respect the gentleman; and I would make the gentleman, who had no merits, understand, that I respect the honest and worthy laborer a thousand times more. What! shall I bring down the principles of eternal truth and justice, so low, that they may be buried in the plaited folds of a rich man's garment? Truth and justice forbid! Worth is worth; and no garb, before my eyes, shall ever clothe meanness with honor, or sink virtue to contempt.

We are all possessed, it is probable, with conventional notions on this subject, which expose us to do considerable injustice. Man looketh on the outward appearance. But, I hold, that he who does not strive in favor of principle and humanity, to correct the mistakes of worldly sense and fashion, is no noble or Christian man. And I say, too, that he who would assume all the airs of unfeeling superiority, which the spirit of society will tolerate, is either inexcusably thoughtless, or detestably unprincipled, and is just fit to be an oppressor in Russia, a tyrant in Constantinople, if not a man-stealer in Africa. And, I maintain, moreover, that Christianity itself has made but little progress, where this care and consideration for our kind are not cherished. Vainly will you try to reconcile any man's claims to Christian virtue, with harshness and insolence to his dependants. He may go from the very worship of God to this scorn and despite of man—it avails not. The spirit of Christ is the spirit of philanthropy. "He who loveth not his brother whom he hath seen; how doth he love God whom he hath not seen!"

Nor is it enough to refrain from oppression and insolence. There are *duties* belonging to the relation of the employer. He is bound to feel an interest in his dependants, beyond that of obtaining their services. This interest he takes in his horse or his ox. This is not enough, to be felt for a human being. The man who labors in your garden, or in your warehouse, or your manufactory, is not to be looked upon as a mere machine that is accomplishing so much work, and after it is done, to be dismissed without a further thought. You ought to think kindly of that man, and to consider how you can, as a fellow-being, act towards him a brotherly part. You may find ways enough of doing this, without going out of your sphere, and without being officious, or ostentatious, or offensively patronising in your kindness. Your very manners, inspiring in those who labor for you, good will, cheerfulness and self-respect, may do much. Yes, your very manners may do more for their happiness and virtue, than if you doubled their wages, or gave them the most liberal presents. You may also speak kindly to them, of their welfare and of their families. You may become their adviser and friend. You may induce them to deposit a portion of their earnings in a savings' bank; and that money, so laid up and gradually accumulating, will be one of the best securities for their growing virtue and courage and self-respect. You may sometimes give them an interesting book to read—at least, during the leisure of Sunday, if they have no other time—and it will be a means both of safety and improvement on that holy day. You may make them feel that they have, in you and in your family, those who know them and take a friendly interest in their respectability and good conduct; and they might be made to know, that if you should some day go home to your splendid dwelling, and say, that such or such an one had been, that day, intoxicated, or a brawler in the streets, it would spread a sadness over the face of that bright and happy circle. Your children might sometimes go to their children in sickness or in trouble, and kindly take them by the hand. No fear, that the hand, nurtured and softened in the bosom of luxury, would be soiled by that contact. There is a work of our greatest sculptor,* which represents a child-angel as conducting another child to heaven. Were it not a beautiful vision, realized into life? Oh! when I think what rich families might do for poor families, what ministering angels they might be, to raise up the low and the fallen, to comfort, to virtue and to heaven, my heart swells at the contemplation; and I say, when, *shall* the vision be realized into life?

Yet, let us not despair. There are things already done in our noble city, which forbid despair. I say, our noble city; and when I say this, I am not thinking of our splendid dwellings, of our wealth pouring in through a thousand channels, of our commerce spreading the sounding banners of its prosperous march over every sea, nor of that mighty repairing of our desolations, which the last year has witnessed; but I am thinking of the works of mercy that are done in this city. It is a fact, and I must state it with some formality, because to most persons it will be new and astonishing, that there is scarcely a poor family in our city, which is not regularly visited, by some Sunday-school teacher, or tract distributor, or minister at large, with a view to its moral enlightening and renovation. God bless and prosper the noble band, who have thus gone forth into our waste places!—they are young men, many of them, rising into life, with their own cares and affairs to attend to; they are young women,

---

* Greenough.

some of them of our wealthiest families, and others, who depend upon the labors of their needle for their subsistence; noble missionaries of mercy! fair sisters of charity!—again, I bid them God speed! I bless them for my own sake, and for your sake—and in the name of Christ. When I came to this city, a little more than two years ago, I confess, that the mighty mass of what seemed to me its desperate wickedness and misery, weighed upon my mind as a heavy burthen. It was a professional feeling, if you please so to consider it; my office called me to look upon the moral interests of men; and I almost shrunk from a residence in the presence of evils so stupendous, and, as I thought, so incapable of any but the most distant relief. But within two years, I have learned that the dread wastes which stretched out before me, in darkness and silence, are filled with benevolent action; that their long-neglected thresholds are tracked thickly over with footsteps of mercy, and their desolate walls are echoing the voices of Christian truth and love. Let the good work be *deepened* in any proportion to its *extent*; and this city will present the long-desired example, of a great commercial emporium, purified by the beneficent instrumentality of its own prosperous inhabitants.

But to return; there is another sphere for female talent and virtue which I wish to point out; and that is beneath the domestic roof. I say talent; for to regulate a family of domestics in this country, is really an acheivement of intellect as well as of virtue. The difficulties springing from the state of domestic service among us, I need not dwell upon. They are well known. They are, in fact, the great palpable difficulties of domestic life throughout the country. The real difficulties, indeed, are not those which are palpable; they lie deeper; they lie in the mind; and it is to the removal of these, that I would solicit your attention. And let it be considered that the difficulties of the case, so far as they lie in the situation of the parties, cannot be removed; and that if any relief is to be found, it must be found in the mind. The relation of householders and domestics, in this country, is new. The latter are not dependant on the former, as they are in other countries. They have not the same interest to satisfy you. They have not the same anxiety to keep their place, as if the alternative were penury or starvation: and I trust they never will have. Whether you are satisfied, is not the only question. If they are not satisfied too, they may retire from your service, and readily find employment elsewhere. What then, amidst all the difficulties of this situation is to be done? Perpetual changes in a domestic establishment; no security against its being half broken up almost any day; no necessity, on the part of those who temporarily compose it, of holding their place longer than the caprice or the whim of the moment may dictate; no bond of necessity for their good behavior, like that which presses upon every other occupation, since they do not look upon their station as a permanent one, nor feel that they are taking a character to live and die by —they are looking to better their condition, to establish themselves in life, to pursue an independent course —all these things, I say, occasion immense inconvenience, and the severest trials of temper. What then, is to give us relief? I say plainly and firmly, that I do not regret this independence of the class of domestics. I am glad that they can look to separate and permanent establishments. It is a fortunate condition for them. But even if it were not, it is *theirs* beyond recovery; and, therefore, the only relief must come through a consideration towards them, hitherto unknown in the world—a consideration respectful, wise, Christian-like and kind. And here is the field for female talent and virtue, to which I have already referred. She who has the immediate charge of a family, should make her assistants feel from the first, that she does not wish to regard them as hirelings, but as faithful friends. If, hardened by custom, or puffed up with pride, or absorbed in fashion, she never thinks of them but to exact from them their tasks, she must not wonder, if they never think of her but to earn the price of those tasks. Committed to her care, subjected in a measure to her influence, as fellow-beings, she is bound to respect, cherish and love them. She ought to study their character, to consider their situation, wants and feelings, to promote the improvement of their minds and hearts, to provide for their gratification and entertainment, to make them cheerful and happy if possible, to make them feel that her interest is common with theirs, and, in fine, to treat them, as she might reasonably wish to be treated in change of circumstances. Will you tell me that when all this is done, many of them will prove extremely ungrateful? I must be allowed to doubt, when such is the result, whether all this *is* done. That is the very point to be reached; the removal of that ingratitude; the removal of that soured and irritated feeling, that often settles at the bottom of the heart, even when there is the effervescence of many kind emotions on the surface. And it is not to be forgotten, that there are grievances too, in the condition of the employed, which furnish some ground for this irritated feeling. Those who listen to me, may imagine that all the complaint, since they hear no other, is on one side. What incessant trials, you say, there are with servants! But I can tell you of places where all the complaint is on the other side—of departments in the domestic establishment, where all the confidential communings together, are filled with complaints of the master or mistress, or of their children.

This is a case, in short, where there are faults on both sides. And this is the impression, in fine, which I wish to make on the heads of families. I know that there are families where all is going on kindly and quietly, and I think that the number of such is increasing. But where it is not, I would admonish you against the injustice of supposing that all is right on your part. It was Pestalozzi, I think, who had the generosity to say, when his pupils did not learn, that the fault was his own; and this, doubtless, as a general maxim, is partly true. And this, without doubt, if not equally, is, in a measure, true of the masters of families, who fail in their office. If they would generously admit this, instead of constantly complaining of their difficulties, they would be prepared resolutely to address themselves to the task of working out that great reform in domestic manners and morals, which the very constitution of society among us demands. The general, who cannot command men; the contractor or overseer, who is always vexed by the insubordination and insolence of his workmen, is usually reputed to be guilty of some fault or deficiency on his part. And this, I think, must be accounted equally true of the heads of a family who fail in like manner. I will only add, that the mighty power which controls all human beings, whether in the camp, the manufactory, or the workshop, is judicious kindness; and that this must be the controlling power in all well-ordered and happy families.

Let me now say one word to the class of the employed; and especially, of domestics. Why should it be thought a hardship or a degradation, to minister to the comfort and happiness of our fellow-beings? It is the high office, the noble bond of humanity to assist, to serve one another. It appears to me, that I could take a sincere pleasure in ministering to the daily and hourly satisfactions of any one, with whom circumstances had for a time connected me; in smoothing his path for him; in relieving him from annoyances and vexations; in facilitating his business, his studies, or his enjoyments. What an affection, in this domestic relation, what a true friendship might one win from another, never to end but with life? And what a happiness would this be to carry away from a family, rather than to retire in anger, and to have one's retirement felt as a relief!

I say, that it is no disgrace to give this domestic assistance. It is not slavery; it is a respectable compact, which one finds it expedient to make with another. And the only real disgrace is in being unfaithful to the terms of that compact. We are made to serve one another. We are all servants. The man who stands in his warehouse or behind his counter, and sells goods to another, is his servant for the time. The lawyer is the servant of his clients, the physician of his patients, and the clergyman of his people. The highest in the land is only so much more, the servant of all.

The domestic but stands in one of the many relations of service ; one that is alike ordained of Heaven, and which, therefore, cannot be intrinsically dishonorable. He is apt, I know, to imagine that the distinctions which are made between him and his employers, the different situations and apartments which he occupies, his separation from them in the offices of life, in conversation, amusements, meals, &c., imply some discredit. But all this, let him observe, is necessary to the general comfort, and to his own comfort. If any ten persons were to unite to form a domestic establishment, they would find the very distinctions now complained of, to be inevitable. Some must give directions, and others must follow them. Some must provide entertainments, and others must give them. Some must prepare and serve dinner, and others must partake of it. These conditions cannot be blended, without absolute confusion and discomfort. All that could be demanded in the case supposed, would be a rotation of these offices. But can this be fairly demanded in actual life? Can it be expected, that he who has built a house, and furnished it, and who pays all its expenses, should not occupy the highest situation in it? I might as well demand that my neighbor, who lives at the next door, should not occupy a grander house than mine, should not have a more splendid equipage, or keep a more luxurious table. Nay, many domestics live in more style, dress better, and feed more daintily, than multitudes of the poor, who live in their own dwellings. And those poor might as well demand, that those above them, should not be better off than they are. In short, the feeling that would resist the conditions of domestic service, could not stop till it levelled all human conditions to literal equality. The rich man must part with his riches, the industrious with his gains, the advanced in life with the acquisitions of many years, that he may share his advantages with the young, the negligent, or the poor.

It appears to me, that any sensible young man or woman entering into life, may easily comprehend this argument. And if he does, let him patiently and cheerfully address himself to his task, as appointed to him by Providence. Let him endeavor so to discharge it, that the result in him shall be, not an irritated temper, a soured mind, an unfaithful practice, but that gentleness, kindness and fidelity, that shall raise him above all human distinctions.

I must turn now to a consideration, more brief indeed, of the artificial relations of society; and here, too, I shall confine myself to a single point—to the relations created in society by fashion. They are artificial, inasmuch as they are not founded on merit or mental culture, or even on wealth; nor are they required by the necessities of society. They are the ordinances not of nature, but of caprice, pride and ambition. They do not depend on different modes of living; because in this country, at least, the same conveniences, comforts and elegances, substantially, are found in different circles; and we *have* no idle class. They seem to depend more than upon any thing else, upon the determination of those who consider themselves as above, to keep down, and to keep out, those who are below. That refinement should shrink from vulgarity, and intelligence from ignorance, and sense from folly, I can understand, and understand to be reasonable; but whether these are the terms on which the fashionable classes, of this or any other country, stand towards the rest of the world, I leave you to judge. I confess, that to me, fashion seems to stand upon a much coarser and more worldly estimate of things than this.

It is difficult, I allow, to assign any law to its caprice. But that which appears to me to go farther than any thing else, to explain its movements, changes and vagaries, is the desire to escape from the (so called) vulgar multitude. The silly multitude strives hard to keep up with fashion, in dress, equipage, etiquette and modes of living; but the moment it comes in sight, that Proteus thing changes its form. The multitude comes up, and finds nothing but a tawdry and forsaken image. The spirit of fashion has taken another form. Wealth is the most favorite handmaid of fashion, as enabling it to make the most frequent and splendid changes, and as being itself, indeed, the distinction but of a few. If wealth could purchase the exclusive privilege of wearing coarse apparel, it would, doubtless, avail itself of the distinction. We see opulent fashion, indeed, in its fantasies as it would seem, but really on principle, sometimes putting on coarse garments, for the sake of a day's singularity.

This passion has lead its votaries, in the great cities of Europe, to resort to a device, which there seems to be some disposition among ourselves, absurdly enough, to copy; and that is the notable device of turning night into day. There the multitude cannot follow. Business must be done in the day-time. The idle and luxurious classes of Europe, have, therefore, found at last, a world for themselves. They have surrounded themselves with a wall of darkness; and they strive within it, to make a day of their own, which God has not made. But this violation of the laws of nature, exacts of them sharp penalties. Disease lurks in the splendid purlieus of fashionable indulgence; and the dews of night penetrate their frames with aches and pains, that pay dear for hours of unnatural dissipation and excess. But that in a country which has no idle class, where all must do business, and where, too, the earlier hours of eating, leave the body exhausted at late evening, and so demanding stimulants to support it—that in such a country and under such circumstances, this absurd practice should be gaining ground, is a striking proof to what lengths the folly of fashionable imitation will go.

It is on this account that I protest against the spirit of fashion. The spirit of fashion I say; for I am less concerned with its particular arrangements. And when I speak of its spirit, let me not be understood to ascribe it to all the members of this class. I have lived too long to judge men by classes. I am far enough from saying, that all who belong to this class in particular, are heartless and insincere, or exclusive and proud. I am happy to know that the contrary is the fact.

But there is a spirit that is properly denominated the spirit of fashion. It is a spirit of exclusion. It is a spirit that wars against the great claims of humanity. It is a spirit that is haughty, cold and unkind, to those who are deemed inferior. It does not regard their rights, interests and feelings. It forgets that they are men.

It is on this account, on account of its essential inhumanity, that I regard that exclusiveness, which fashion has introduced, not into one circle only, but into the entire mass of society, as worthy of the severest reprehension. And when I say this exclusiveness, I do not speak of any particular rules of exclusion. Distinctions there must be, certainly; different circles, doubtless. Intimacies are to be forced upon no man. Every man has a right to accept such associates as he chooses. It is not of the particular arrangements of society that I now speak, but of its general spirit, of the unchristian exclusion and scorn that prevail in it. And it is not purse-proud ignorance, or vulgar assumption alone, that is liable to this charge. It is not those only, who treat those, reputed to be beneath them, with contempt, or speak to them in the tones of harsh authority. There are many, who have too much good breeding and good sense, to assume these rude manners, yet in whom the feeling of exclusion and superiority, is just as strong. The veil of courtesy, that is thrown over the feeling, does not at all diminish its power.

The claim to notice, from such persons, is some distinction. It may be talent, it may be wealth, but it is, above all, the opinion of others; it is eclat in the eyes of the world—it is, especially, *belonging to a certain class in society.* There is an instinctive shrinking, as if from contagion, from all but this. There is a certain distinction, then; there is a charmed circle, within which the social exclusionist entrenches himself, and that circle is surrounded as with an electric chain, which sends quick and thrilling sensibility through every part. But touch an individual in that circle—but mention his name, and the man or the woman we are speaking of, feels it instantly; attention is on the alert; the ear is opened to every word; there is the utmost desire to know, or to seem to know, the individual in question;—there is an eagerness to talk about him, a lively interest in all that concerns him. Is he sick, or is he well?—is he in this place, or in that place?—the most ordinary circumstances rise to great importance, the moment they are connected with him. But, now, do you speak of a person *out* of that circle—be it of fashion, or birth, or wealth, or talent, or be it a circle composed of some or all of these; and suddenly the social exclusionist has passed through a total metamorphosis. He *says* not a *word*, perhaps: he settles the matter more briefly, and at less expense. His manner speaks. There is an absolute, an *un*speakable indifference. He knows nothing about persons of that class, who, alas! have nothing in this world to make them interesting, but their mind and heart. And if you speak of such one, he opens his eyes upon you, as if he scarcely comprehended what part of the creation you are talking about. And when he is made, at length, to recognize a thing so unimportant, as the concerns of a fellow-being, held to be inferior, you find that he is included with a multitude of others, under the summary phrase of "those people," or, "that sort of people;" and with such, you would find that he scarcely more acknowledges the tie of a common nature, than with the actually inferior beings of the animal creation.

This feeling of selfish and proud exclusion is confined to no one class. I wish we could say, that it is limited to any one grade of character. I wish we could say, that it did not infect the minds of many persons,

ON SOCIETY. 139

otherwise, of great merit and worth. I wish we could say, that any one is exempt from it. Living, growing up, as we all have been, in a selfish world, educated, more or less, by worldly maxims, we have none of us, perhaps, felt as we ought, the sacred claim of human nature—felt our minds thrill to its touch, as to an electric chain—felt ourselves bound with the bands of holy human sympathy—felt that all human thought, desire, want, weakness, hope, joy and grief, were our own—ours to commune with and to partake of. Few have felt this; for it is always the attribute of the holiest philanthropy, or of the loftiest genius. Of the loftiest genius, I repeat ; for I venture to say, that all such genius has ever been distinguished by its earnest sympathy and sacred interest in all human feeling. And why should we not feel it? The very dog, that goes and lies down and dies upon the grave of his master, will almost draw a tear from us, so near does he approach to human affection. And when the war-horse, that has carried his rider through many battles, bows his neck, and thrills through his whole frame, at the approach and touch of that master's hand, we feel something more than respect, towards the noble animal. Oh! sacred humanity! how art thou dishonored by thy children, when the merest appendage of thy condition, the mere brute companion of thy fortunes, is more regarded than thou !

What a picture does human society present to us ! If I were to represent the world in vision, I should say that I see it, not as that interchange of hill and dale which now spreads around me, but as one vast mountain; and all the multitudes that cover it, are struggling to rise ; and those who, in my vision, seem to be above, instead of holding friendly intercourse with those who are below, are endeavoring, all the while to look over them, or building barriers and fences to keep them down; and every lower grade is using the same treatment towards those who are beneath *them*, that they bitterly and scornfully complain of, in those who are above; all but the topmost circle, imitators as well as competitors, injuring as well as injured; and the topmost circle—with no more to gain, revelling or sleeping upon its perilous heights, or dizzy with its elevation—soon falls from its pinnacle of pride, giving place to others, who share in constant succession the same fate. Such is the miserable struggle of social ambition all the world over. And every thing, I had almost said, is helping it on: every thing, but the loftiest—I say not common—every thing but the loftiest intellect, like that of Milton, or of Shakspeare; every thing but simple and holy religion, like that of the Gospel—but that religion which came to bless the poor, and the broken in fortune, and the bruised in heart. These holier influences, alas! have as yet been comparatively but little felt. All else, I repeat, has helped on the evil strife—institutions, maxims, passions, the tone of education, the spirit of society; nay, even history, poetry, romance; the entire body of our literature has been prostituted to the unholy work. The image of human pride has been set up, like the abomination of desolation spoken of by the prophet, in the holy place; it has stood where it ought not—in the holy places of human nature; it has removed the altar where men ought to worship; it has overshadowed the paths of society; it has blighted the fruits of honest and ingenuous virtue; it has crushed many of the noblest and most generous affections of the human heart. It is time that wise and good men, men who can afford to rest on their intrinsic dignity and worth, who, in imitation of the holy Master, are above the fear of being confounded with the mean and base, but not above the blessed labor of doing good to all, as they have opportunity—it is time that Christians, especially, the followers of the meek and lowly Jesus, should see this subject in a new light. We talk about "ordinary people;" and this phrase, you will often hear pronounced in a tone the most self-sufficient and disdainful. Now, I shall venture to say, that in a most material, in *the* most material respect, *nobody is ordinary*. *Human nature is not an ordinary thing.* That nature which is capable of knowledge, which can rise to heavenly virtue, which is destined to immortality, is not an ordinary thing, to be trampled down with a hasty footstep, or to be passed by with a tone or phrase of compendious scorn. There is many a work of *human* hands, that we should not treat in this manner. There are names of ancient genius, which bring a glow into the cheek, as we mention them. And if the work of such an one was before us—if we saw the most common statue or monument that had come from the chisel of Phidias, or a faded cartoon from the pencil of Raphael, we should not contemptuously pronounce it an "ordinary thing." If we used this phrase at all, we should do it with a care and consideration, conveying the highest compliment. And are less care and consideration to be used, when we are speaking of the "offspring," the work, "the very image" of our Creator? I would not fastidiously restrict the freedom of colloquial language. But I do think it a serious question, whether any language, implying scorn of our fellow-beings, should be used without extreme caution and discrimination, and without a feeling of evident pity and regret, that a being so nobly gifted, should so degrade himself. The meanest knave, the basest profligate, the reeling drunkard— what a picture does he present of a glorious nature in ruins! Let a tear fall, as he passes. Let us blame and abhor, if we must, but let us reverence and pity still. What hopes are cast down! what powers are wasted! what means, what indefinite possibilities of improvement are turned into gloomy disappointment! what *is* the man, and what might he be! The very body, with its fine organization, with its wonderful workmanship, groans and sickens when it is made the instrument of base indulgence! The spirit sighs, in its secret places, over its meanness, its treachery and dishonor! There is a nobler mind, in the degraded body, that retires within itself, and will not *look* through the dimmed eye, and will not *shine* in the bloated and stolid countenance: there is a holier conscience, that will not strengthen the arm that is stretched out to defraud—but sometimes makes that arm tremble with its paralyzing touch, and sometimes shakes, as with thunder, the whole soul of the guilty transgressor!

But it is not so extreme a case, that comes within the range of ordinary and practical consideration. You are surrounded with a mass of fellow-beings, most of whom have not lost the common and natural claims to respect. You have a wrong and unworthy pride—(let him that heareth, understand—let him that to whom this belongs, receive it—I say not to whom—but I say without much fear of misapplication)—you have a wrong and unworthy pride, which leads you to pass by your inferiors, as you consider them, with cold neglect or slight, or to bestow upon them those patronizing airs, that are more difficult to bear. And I say that you degrade not others, so much as you degrade yourself, by these manners. You show a mind bound up in worse than spiritual pride; that says, " stand by thyself, for I am—not holier; that were indeed a claim to respect, could it be sustained—but I am more fashionable than thou." You show that your mind has not been in the noblest school.

The celebrated Walter Scott has somewhere observed, in his popular works, that, in an ordinary ride in a stage-coach, he never found a man so dull, as not to communicate to him—if a free conversation were opened—something, which he would have been very sorry not to have heard. It was a noble observation; and the practice which it implied, no doubt, contributed much to that deep knowledge of human nature, for which this great author is so much distinguished.

But it is not as a fine sentiment, or as a useful maxim, that I urge this mutual respect. I say it is a duty. I will listen to no language of haughty pretension, or fastidious taste, or over-refined doubt; I say it is a duty. I say it is a duty, most especially binding on all Christians; yes, *binding* upon all who make any pretensions to a belief in the religion of Jesus Christ. And remember, too, my brethren, that it is a duty which will one day be felt, which will enforce conviction through sanctions more commanding, through a judgment more awful, than that of the sages, or the preachers of this world. There is an hour coming, when all worldly distinctions shall vanish away; when splendid sin, with all its pride, shall sink prostrate and cowering before the eye of the eternal Judge; when the modest merit that it could not look upon here, nay, when the virtuous poverty that was spurned from its gate, shall wear a crown of honor; when Dives shall lift up his eyes being in torment, and Lazarus shall be borne in Abraham's bosom to the presence of the angels of God; when the great gulf which shall separate men from one another, shall separate not between outward splendor and meanness, but between inward, spiritual, essential purity and pollution. Let the judgment of that hour be our judgment now. That which will be true there, is true here—is true now. Let that severe and solemn discrimination find its way into *this* world. For it is written, "He that exalteth himself shall be humbled, and he that humbleth himself, shall be exalted."

DISCOURSE VI.

ON THE MORAL EVILS TO WHICH AMERICAN SOCIETY IS EXPOSED.

ACTS XVII. 27. AND HATH MADE OF ONE BLOOD ALL NATIONS OF MEN, TO DWELL ON ALL THE FACE OF THE EARTH.

THE principle of equality here stated, lies at the foundation of our political institutions. It is the first and main principle in our celebrated declaration of Independence. I have heard some flippant disputers maintain, that that declaration is false; because (they say) men are, in fact, *not* " born equal." As if it could have been intended to assert, that all men are born with equal wit or wealth, or of equal strength or stature. The equality which we contend for in this country is an equality, not of powers, but of rights. It is an equality before the law.

But this qualification being made, our assertion of the doctrine of equality, is strong and emphatic. That which I have said in a former discourse is, in fact, a part of our political creed—" that, without any respect to external condition, one man has as much right to have his virtue and happiness regarded as another." The feeling which every human being entertains, that he has, in his welfare, as dear an interest at stake, as any other man, is here perfectly respected. No man among us is allowed to say to any one of his fellow-citizens, "you are of a meaner class, and it matters little what becomes of you; you may be trodden under foot with impunity." The law spreads its protecting shield over the weakest and humblest man in the community, and it says to the highest and the haughtiest, " thou shalt not touch a hair of his head, but by the judgment of his peers."

But the leading feature of our political condition is, that this law is ordained by the majority of the people. The law allows a certain freedom, and it imposes certain restrictions; but it is the majority that determines the extent of the one, and the limit of the other. This, I say, is the peculiar feature of our political condition. While, in most other countries, these points are determined by prescriptive usages, or by irresponsible orders of men, it is here left to the whole body of the people.

This state of things, of course, raises every individual in society to power and importance. Meanwhile, the collective body has already swept from its path, all permanent, hereditary distinctions. It has opened to merit a free course, by which it may rise to the highest places in society and government.

This principle of equality, thus obviously fitted to produce a direct and powerful effect on society, lends extraordinary force to another power of equal importance, in its bearing on our social character; and that is the power of public opinion. Public opinion, in this country, is the aggregate of universal opinion. It is not the opinion of the rich and fashionable, nor of princes and nobles; it is the opinion of every body.

It is the opinion of every body, and it affects every body. It is like suffrage, universal, and awarding all distinction. It is like the atmosphere; it presses every man, and on every side. And—what is especially worthy of consideration—like the atmosphere, it leaves men unconscious of its power. You move your hand easily and freely in the air, though philosophers tell you, that the weight of the air is equal to fifteen pounds upon every square inch of it. Let a vacuum be made on one side of you, and that invisible force, of which you are so insensible, would hurl you to the earth as with a thunderbolt. It seldoms happens, indeed, that a man is so circumstanced with regard to public opinion; and there is, too, a moral power which, against all opinion, can stand firm ;—" faithful found amidst the faithless." There is such a power; but few men are conscious on how many lesser occasions it is necessary to exert it; how liable they are to be, not crushed indeed, but swayed from their integrity and independence, by those potent influences, assent and dissent, praise and dispraise, flattery and ridicule; and above all, by the breath of the boundless multitude—the mighty atmosphere of opinion that surrounds us. The effect of every thing that is universal, is, in like manner, apt to be unperceived ; and I think it the more important, therefore, to point out some of those dangers to our social character, which arise both from our equality, and from that public opinion to which it gives an almost despotic power.

I. And the first danger which I shall notice, and this arises particularly from our equality, is that of coldness and reserve in our manners.

I may observe here, in entering upon these details,

that our exposures in the respects which I shall mention, are only such as appertain to *human nature* in such circumstances. Thus, with regard to this trait of reserve, I shall venture to lay it down as an unquestionable fact, that the progress of nations towards equality, has always been marked by it. England has long been the freest country in Europe. Its manners are proverbial for their reserve. I do not deny that there are other causes for this, but I have no doubt that the rise of the lower classes in the scale of society, is one. Nay, and it is observable that with the more rapid steps of reform, this reserve has been more rapidly gaining upon the English character. It is remarked, that the higher classes are more and more withdrawing themselves from the amusements and sports of the common people.

A writer[*] on the manners and customs of Spain, fifteen years ago, has, unintentionally, given a very striking illustration of the general position, on which I am insisting. "The line of distinction," he says, "between the *noblesse* and the unprivileged class, being here drawn with the greatest precision, there cannot be a more disagreeable place for such as are, by education, above the lower ranks, yet have the misfortune of a plebeian birth." We shall immediately see the reason of this. "An honest respectable laborer," he says, "without ambition, yet with a conscious dignity of mind not uncommon among the Spanish peasantry, may, in this respect, well be an object of envy to many of his betters. Gentlemen treat them with a less haughty and distant air, than is used in England to-

---

[*] Doblado's Letters.

wards inferiors and dependants. A *rabadan*, (chief shepherd,) or an *aperador*, (steward,) is always indulged with a seat, when speaking on business with his master; and men of the first distinction will have a kind word for every peasant, when riding about the country. Yet they will exclude from their club and billiard table, a well-educated man, because, forsooth, he has no legal title to a Don before his name."

The author here states important facts, but he does not give the reasons for them. Why, then, is it, that the Spanish gentry treat their dependants with a less haughty and distant air, than the English? It is, precisely, because the line of distinction between them is drawn with the greatest exactness. And why is it, that those plebeians, who have the misfortune to be well-educated, are an exception to this liberal treatment? It is simply because, in cultivation and manners, they approach nearer to their superiors. It is because they have claims, which it is found necessary to resist by some means; and the natural barrier is reserve.

But in this country there is no other barrier. All the defences of birth and rank are broken down. Here, every man not only has claims, but claims which he is allowed freely to put forward. Hence, the guards against intrusion among us; the cautions and contrivances used to avoid intercourse with persons held to be inferior; the engagements pleaded, ay, and planned, to escape such fatal contact and contamination. Hence, the sensitive dread of being thought vulgar; and hence, for one reason, the decline of almost all the homely old domestic and village sports, lest they should bring with them that terrible opprobium. An aristocratic state of society naturally produces courtesy, contentment, order; a republican, ambition, energy, improvement. I have seen a tree on the smooth and verdant lawn, which spread far its branches in unchallenged majesty to the sky, and whose outermost boughs nodded to the violets that grew by its side, and kissed the greensward beneath it; and in its shadow were the games and sports of a contented and cheerful peasantry. And I have seen a forest, whose intrusive underwood choked up the passages, and forced the loftier trees to stretch away from their companions, and tower up towards heaven; and there was neither space nor time there for games or sports.

This, no doubt, in the mouth of an adversary, would be thought a most invidious comparison. But I am prepared to accept the very ground on which it places us, and to defend it. If the agriculturist may hold it to be an advantage, that ten trees should grow where one grew before; surely, the humane political economist may value that condition which is favorable to the growth of men—to the growth of the many. So well am I satisfied with our institutions on this account, that I can afford to look fairly at the inconveniences and dangers that attend them. I trust, indeed, that much of the inconvenient under-*brush* will be cleared away from our paths, and that we shall see a fairer growth; in other words, that more perfect relations in society will spring up from the general and equal claims of all. In the meantime, we have less fawning and sycophancy among us, than prevail in other countries. We have fewer parasitical plants in our forest state, than are found clinging around the oaks and elms of Europe. But it must not be denied, that we are sometimes chilled by the shadow of this thick growth of society; that we are too liable, each one to stand stiffly up for his rights; that we are liable to want gracefulness and amenity in our manners; that we are exposed to have our hearts locked up in rigid and frozen reserve. A prince or a nobleman, in a state of unbroken aristocracy, does not fear that his dignity or reputation will be compromised, by the presence of an inferior, in his house or in his society. He is at ease on this point, because his claims stand on an independent basis. But with us, he who would hold a higher place, must obtain it from the general voice. He is dependant on suffrage as truly as the political aspirant. Hence, every circumstance affecting his position, is important to him. And the circumstance that most immediately and obviously affects it, is the company he keeps. On this point, therefore, he is likely to be extremely jealous. And this, I conceive, to be one reason, for the proverbial reserve of our national manners.

I have thus far endeavored to unfold the danger on this point, to which I think that our situation exposes us. Let me now observe, that it is one of the most serious moral importance. There is an intimate connection between the manners and feelings of a people. A cold demeanor, though it may not prove coldness of heart, tends to produce it. The feelings that are locked up in reserve, are liable to wither and shrink, from simple disuse. He who stands in the attitude of perpetual resistance to the claims of others, is very apt to acquire a hardness and inhumanity towards them. He is liable to be cold, harsh and ungracious, both in feeling and deportment. He is in the very school, not of generosity and love, but of selfishness and scorn and pride. And vainly might any Christian people boast of its intelligence, refinement or freedom, if it fail thus, of the essential virtues of the Christian religion.

The domestic affections are peculiarly liable to suffer under the same influence. "A poor relation"— says an English writer, satirizing the manners of his countrymen—"is the most irrelevant thing in nature; a piece of impertinent correspondency; an odious approximation; a haunting conscience; a preposterous shadow, lengthening in the noontide of your prosperity; an unwelcome remembrancer; a perpetually recurring mortification; a drawback upon success; a rebuke to your rising; a mote in your eye; a triumph to your enemy; an apology to your friends."* Where, I was ready to say, but in England—but I will generalize the observation—where, but in countries that give birth and insecurity at once to individual aspirings, could such a satire have been framed? Not among the wild Highlanders of Scotland; not among the barbarous chieftains of our own native forests; not, I think, with the same force at least, in Germany, in France, in Spain, or in Italy. I will not undertake to say how far the satire applies to our own people. But this I say, that we are very liable to deserve it. And I would warn my countrymen, could I speak to them, against this odious and barbarous treatment of their poor and depressed or uncourtly relatives, as against a sin worse than sacrilege and blasphemy!

Religion, too, is liable to lose much of its expansion, generosity and beauty, under the pressure of this na-

* Elia.

tional reserve. I have sometimes doubted, whether a religion so cold, inaccessible and repulsive, ever could have existed in any other country, as that which has prevailed in this. The manners of the country foster a peculiar reserve among us, an austerity, a sanctimoniousness, nowhere else to be found. The enthusiasm of the country, checked in every other direction, is checked in this, no less. The same fervor, the same freedom of action, will not be borne in our pulpit, that is welcomed in most other countries. Ridicule—" the world's dread laugh"—is scarcely any where in the world so much feared as here; and the reason is, that here, the world—every body is judge. The preacher is begirt with a thousand critical eyes. He does not step forth from his lofty stall to his loftier pulpit, to address an ignorant multitude, as he might in Italy or Spain; but he stands up to address those who are to judge him; and not only to judge, but to award him life or death in his profession.

But not to wander from the point I have in view; I declare my conviction, that religion in this country, has a peculiar hardness and repulsiveness; that it is not genial and gentle, gracious and tender, in the common administration of it; that it speaks, I do not say to heretics, but to the mass of the people, from the sealed up bosom of a more pitiless exclusion, than it does any where else in the world. The Church of Rome is, indeed, severe and exclusive towards heretics; but to its own people, it is all graciousness and love, compared with the Puritan and Presbyterian forms of administration. Individual exceptions, of course, are always to be allowed in representations of this general character; but I hold that, in the main, the Protestantism of other countries—the Church of England, for instance, and the Lutheranism of Germany—are more genial ; that they speak with a kinder tone to the people, than the Protestantism of America. And the consequence is, that multitudes among us, and especially of the young, are more repelled from religion, than the people of any other Christian nation. We are a very religious people, it is said, and it is true ; so it would appear to the eye of a stranger ; and the best foreign writer* who has visited us, has said, that he never saw a people so religious ; and yet I fear, that many among us are *very religious,* who do not heartily *love* religion. But especially with regard to the young in this country, I am inclined to think that their state is, in this respect, very singular. It is not the want of religious affections and habits only ; this, though it is to be regretted in all countries, is not peculiar to the young any where. But it is a state of the sentiments here, of which I speak. It is a feeling of strange and almost preternatural superstition about religion ; a feeling, in the young, as if religion were shut up from them in seclusion and reserve ; a feeling as if they had nothing to do with it. Why is this ? Why, but because the clergy, in the first place, constitute a peculiar and reserved class—because they are guarded and sequestered from all the amusements of society, from almost all the scenes of cheerful, social enjoyment ; and because, in the next place, professors of religion mostly are shut up in the iron mask of peculiarity, and communicate with the world, in their religious capacity, as it were

---

* De Tocqueville.

only through the bars of an ugly and distorting visor. And these two classes are considered as the representatives of all the religion of the country. How, then, can the young and unreflecting be expected to feel attracted to such a religion? Suppose that all the churches of a country were built in lonely places, like the shrine of Dodona; were set far apart from all human habitation, and were to be approached only by taking a painful pilgrimage, away from all the cheerful haunts of life. This would be only a visible, though, as I admit, a strong representation of the isolated and reserved character which religion has assumed among us. Suppose that all the clergy should put on sackcloth, and wear long, sad weeds, hanging from the head, the hands, the arms, and every part of their person, and should walk forth among the people with slow and melancholy steps, and an abstracted air; this, I say again, would be only a visible representation of the ideas with which a people may clothe the ministers of religion. And how far does the fact differ from the representation, when the sight of a clergyman at places of amusement, where every body else may go with perfect propriety, would be accounted a kind of sacrilege, a desecration of his office! You may clothe a man with an intellectual costume, as repulsive as any visible costume. You may thus as truly make him a spectre and a bugbear to the young, as if you made him wear weeds and sackcloth. And if this man, the official representative of religion, is thus invested with a peculiarity, and forced into a solemn reserve, unknown in other countries—a reserve, especially, from most of the cheerful resorts and recreations of society; if he is seldom seen where men are gay and happy ; and if, when he is seen, his presence lays an irksome restraint upon the company he visits, how is it surprising, that our youth should feel that peculiar strangeness and alienation towards religion, of which I am speaking. Suppose that a father were to treat his children in this way; could they love him ? I allow that in all these things a gradual improvement is showing itself. But he cannot have looked deeply into the spirit of society around him, who does not yet see much to lament. And how saddening is the reflection, that at the very time when religion is wanted to mould, to soften, to control and satisfy the bursting affections of the heart, when youth is beginning to feel its nature's great want, when it is swayed by alternate enthusiasm and disappointment, and has not yet stepped deep into vice and worldliness; how lamentable that it should stand before the altar of religion, listening as to a cold, stern oracle from a heathen shrine, instead of hearing the words, Abba, Father ; instead of feeling that God is its Father, and the Saviour its friend, and every Christian minister its brother!

II. But I must proceed to speak briefly of another trait of the social character, to which the state of political equality exposes us ; and that is discontent. To this I may add, the danger of imprudent and extravagant expenditures.

But to speak distinctly of the feeling of discontent, in the first place; it may be observed, that there is scarcely a limit among us, to any man's aspirings. And yet, it is no more possible that all should be first, in this country, than in any other. And the very circumstance that these aspirings are universal and importunate, creates among us, as I have said, a peculiar reaction. This demand, on the one hand, and this resistance on the other, are likely, it is obvious, to give birth to an unusual and prevalent feeling of discontent.

Doubtless, the feeling prevails sufficiently in other countries: and it may be thought, since one class only, and that a small one, is elevated by birth and rank above the rest, that the feeling may have as full scope among their inferior circles, as it has among ourselves. But the truth is, that the existence of this class in those countries, gives a tone to the whole body of society. The distinction of classes is not an offence with them, as it would be with us. People there more willingly consent to permanent inferiority. Men expect to live and die, in the condition of life in which they were born, and in the calling to which they have been brought up. The case with us, is widely different; and the exposure to discontent is proportionably increased.

To exhibit the various forms which this trait assumes, would require the liberty of dramatic or fictitious writing. In the necessarily sober and didactic discussions of the pulpit, I can scarcely do more than refer you, for its existence, to your own consciousness or observation. I say, your observation; and yet, this is a feeling that so sedulously shrinks from notice, that you can hardly gain from that source, any just idea of its prevalence and depth. Could I get an honest confession written out from the hearts of many around us, I have no doubt, that it would reveal an extent and poignancy of suffering from this cause, of which you may be little aware. For this conviction, I need only to be acquainted with the principles of human nature,

I only need to know, that all men are made to desire the approbation and attention of one another; and then to know, that here are circumstances unusually fitted to afford expansion at once, and dissappointment to this desire, in order to feel myself justified in making a very strong representation. Indeed, the indirect proofs of it, under the circumstances, are, perhaps, the clearest. As an author, by showing an apparent indifference to the success of his writings, commonly betrays, by that very manner, the keenest interest about it; so do I think that the coldness and hauteur of many persons towards their neighbors, leads to the same inference. They never speak of them, perhaps, for the very reason that they are always thinking about them; or they speak with guarded indifference, because they have something within them to guard. But not to rest on indirect disclosures; you must know that many of the dissensions, shall I say quarrels, of families, and many of the manifest jealousies and heart-burnings of society, arise from mortified pride. A man feels that he is not known to society as he ought to be, that he has not the acquaintances to which he is entitled; the fashionable reject him; or if he has gained that first-rate object, as it is usually considered, then there is a literary circle to which he does not belong; some exclusive circle there is, of some kind, to which he is not admitted; and he broods over it; he feels it; he thinks of it with ill-suppressed anger and vexation. He has got property or talent, perhaps, but he cannot get that for which, as one inducement, he sought property or distinction. In some minds, this is an honorable feeling, a just and reasonable desire for the acquaintance of congenial minds. But it is too apt to sink into the baser feeling of chagrin and spite.

It is not to be forgotten, in this connection, that society does great wrong to many, and great injury to itself, by the neglect of merit. By a superficial estimate of the claims to notice, by bestowing its chief attention upon wealth, beauty, and the eclat of talent, rather than upon talent itself, and by setting up a standard of expense in its entertainments, which makes a considerable property a necessary passport to its advantages, society cuts off a great deal of worth, intelligence and refinement, with which it can very ill afford to part. The simple entertainments, the intellectual *soirees* of the cultivated cities of Europe, open a door to merit, that is nearly closed among us. It is the true policy of society to collect and concentrate, as much as possible, the scattered rays of mental illumination. But if, instead of this, it goes about, virtually putting an extinguisher upon all the lights that are burning in silence and obscurity, instead of bringing them into notice, the loss is its own; and it is an irreparable loss. Mind is the only thing which it cannot afford to lose. Let the fashion of the country look to it, that it does not become degraded before the eyes of all the world, by this illiberal exclusion. Show me a society where wealth, dress and equipage, are the chief titles to advancement; from which the great body of the educated, reading and thinking men of the country are excluded, or choose to exclude themselves; and I shall not hesitate to say, that you show me a frivolous and vulgar society. Depend upon it, the conversation will become mean and insipid; and the manners will want the last graces of manner, ease and simplicity. Intellect, cultivated and spiritualized intellect, is the only true refiner.

But I spoke, also, as connected with the worldly pride and discontent of society, of the temptations to imprudent and extravagant expense. In a state of society like ours, does not every one see, that these temptations are carried to the utmost length; that no condition of things on earth can, in this respect, more endanger the prudence and virtue of men? In regard to their expenses, men are apt to govern themselves, by the consideration of what is proper to their condition, rank or class in society. It is often a decisive argument for the purchase of a certain article of furniture or apparel, or for offering entertainments in a certain style, that others are doing the same thing. But what others? This question unfolds the peculiar temptation that besets us. Families, in this country, scarcely *have* any fixed and ascertained condition or rank. They are separated from each other, not by visible lines, but by imperceptible shades of distinction. In following others, they do not readily see where to stop. All, at the same time, are aspiring to a higher condition. And in the absence of hereditary distinctions, *the style of living* is too apt to be considered as the grand, visible index of that condition. The coat of arms is nothing; and it is the coat that a man wears, that must mark him out. The hatchment has passed away from our house-fronts; those houses themselves, then, must set forth our respectability. In houses, therefore, in apparel, and in every species of expense, we are liable to go too far; to cross, one after another, the shadowy intervals that separate us from those who are above us in their means, and to be urged on to inconvenient and ruinous expenditures.

I think I have properly connected this topic, extravagance, with what I have said of the discontent of society. An irritated sense of inferiority, a diseased ambition, at once blinds and goads a man into the snares of rash expense and ruinous debt. It is often a word of discontent pronounced in a domestic consultation, that decides the question; and carries a man to do what he feels to be unnecessary, and knows to be imprudent. He knows that it is rather beyond his means; but he hopes that his business will be prosperous, that his speculations will be fortunate; and he has, at least, the satisfaction of gratifying those who are dearest to him. His daughter *shall* have such and such decorations, his wife, a certain equipage; others have them, and "they *must*." If those others were any body in particular; and if any body had a limit, the case would be better. But those others are every body in their sphere, that is a little beyond them. Thus a man enters upon the hazardous "experiment of living beyond the means"—of living upon resources that are not yet realized. For a while, the business of the country may be so prosperous as to bear him through all. But the times are likely to change; and the speculations that were to relieve, may become obligations that bind and fetter him. Or, if not, yet the domestic ambition which, restrained by no definite rule, is for ever saying, "give, give," is likely to bring about the same result. The man is in debt. He is obliged to look in the face, people, and perhaps poor people, whom he cannot pay. It is a situation, infinitely irritating and mortifying. We are a people, I know, to a proverb, reckless of debt; reckless, at least, about plunging into it; but no man can be in it, and find the situation an easy one. No man can, without passing, I had almost said, through worse than purgatorial torments, become callous to the demand for payment. It turns the whole of life into a scene of misery and mortification—makes its whole business and action a series of sacrifices and shifts and subterfuges. Home itself, the last refuge of virtue and peace—the very home, that has lost its independence in its splendor—that is not protected from the intrusive step and contemptuous tone of the unsatisfied creditor, has lost its charm. It is no longer a sanctuary; and it is but too likely to be forsaken for other resorts. Many a man, not only in the city but in the country, has gone down in character and self-respect, in virtue and hope, under the accumulated weight of these overwhelming embarrassments.

Now I maintain, that in such a country as this, special guards are to be set up against discontent and extravagance. With regard to the last, let every man be resolute; let him firmly set his limit, and resolve to live far within the means. It is the only way to be happy in his condition, and, in fact, it is the only way to be honest. With regard to the first of these exposures, it is less easy to lay down any definite rule. We all desire the esteem of society; and its notice is the only visible mark of its esteem. Yet, let a man beware how he barters away for it the peace of his mind. Let him live *at home,* in his own bosom; and not abroad, in the thoughts of others. His mind must thus travel abroad sometimes, no doubt; but let it *live* at home. Let it find content in self-culture, in the few fast and strong friendships, and, above all, in the resources of religion. Never, and nowhere, perhaps, has the strong sentiment of religion been so necessary, in any age and in any country, as it is in this age, and in this country.

III. But I must hasten to notice, in the last place, another exposure of the national character, and that is, to pusillanimity.

You will think, perhaps, as I offer this further consideration, and in such undisguised language, that I am the accuser of my country, rather than its defender. My answer is, as before, that I have such a calm and strong conviction of its merits and advantages, that I can afford to speak plainly of its dangers and faults. The irritable sensitiveness to blame among us, I hold, is not the true self-respect. And more than this; the errors to which we are exposed, *must* be fairly canvassed, frankly admitted, and fully corrected, that we may be justly entitled to our own respect, or that of other nations.

And now, I desire you to look at the exposure in question, and see if it is not peculiar ; and so powerful, too, that a complete and immediate escape from it, would, in fact, have proved us more than human. Every man in this country is dependant for his position upon public opinion. There is no exception. But in most other countries, there are many exceptions. In the first place, there is the class of nobles who hold their place by birth. In the next place, the clergy generally are presented to their livings, and are not dependant on the popular voice. Then there are a multitude of minor situations and offices, for which their incumbents are indebted, not to election, but to appointment. Even wealth, I think, holds a more independent position abroad, than it does with us. This may be thought a surprising opinion; because it is constantly said, that where hereditary distinctions do not exist, wealth is apt to take their place, and to be more eagerly sought. It may be more eagerly sought; and yet, it may have a less independent power when it is gained. Abroad, wealth shines by the reflected light of an opulent aristocracy. The possession of it is thus associated with the highest titles to respect and deference. And it is able, as an undoubted matter of fact, to command a deference and observance, which it never receives with us. It can speak to its dependants and agents there, as it does not here; and as, I trust, it never will. One of the most painful aspects of society abroad, is the cringing and fawning of so many worthy and intelligent men, at the feet of rank and opulence.

But we, in this country, have our own dangers. And the greatest of all dangers here, as I conceive, is that of general pusillanimity, of moral cowardice, of losing a proper and manly independence of character. I think that I see something of this in our very manners, in the hesitation, the indirectness, the cautious and circuitous modes of speech, the eye asking assent before the tongue can finish its sentence. I think that in other countries, you oftener meet with men, who stand manfully and boldly up, and deliver their opinion without asking or caring what you or others think about it. It may, sometimes, be rough and harsh; but, at any rate, it is independent. Observe, too, in how many relations, political, religious and social, a man is liable to find bondage instead of freedom. If he wants office, he must attach himself to a party, and then his eyes must be sealed in blindness, and his lips in silence, towards all the faults of his party. He *may* have his eyes open, and he may see much to condemn, but he must *say* nothing. If he edits a newspaper, his choice is often between bondage and beggary. That may actually be the choice, though he does not know it. He may be so complete a slave, that he does not feel the chain. His passions may be so enlisted in the cause of his party, as to blind his discrimination, and destroy all comprehension and capability of independence. So it may be with the religious partisan. He knows, perhaps, that there are errors in his adopted creed, faults in his sect, fanaticism and extravagance in some of its measures. See if you get him to speak of them. See if you can get him to breathe a whisper of doubt. No, he is always believing. He has a convenient phrase that covers up all difficulties in his creed. He believes it "for *substance* of doctrine." Or if he is a layman, perhaps he does not believe it at all. What, then, is his conclusion? Why, he has friends who do believe it; and he does not wish to offend them. And so he goes on, listening to what he does not believe; outwardly acquiescing, inwardly remonstrating; the slave of fear or fashion, never daring, not once in his life daring, to speak out and openly the thought that is in him. Nay, he sees men suffering under the weight of public reprobation, for the open espousal of the very opinions *he* holds, and he has never the generosity or manliness to say, "*I* think so too." Nay, more; by the course he pursues, he is made to cast his stone, or he holds it in his hand, at least, and lets another arm apply the force necessary to cast it, at the very men, who are suffering a sort of martyrdom *for his own faith!*

I am not now advocating any particular opinions. I am only advocating a manly freedom in the expression of those opinions, which a man does entertain. And if those opinions are unpopular, I hold that, in this country, there is so much the more need of an open and independent expression of them. Look at the case most seriously, I beseech you. What is ever to correct the faults of society, if nobody lifts his voice against them; if every body goes on openly doing what every body privately complains of; if all shrink behind the faint-hearted apology, that it would be over-bold in them to attempt any reform? What is to rebuke political time-serving, religious fanaticism, or social folly, if no one has the independence to protest against them? Look at it in a larger view. What barrier is there against the universal despotism of public opinion in this country, but individual freedom? Who is to stand up against it here, but the possessor of that lofty independence? There is no king, no sultan, no noble, no privileged class; nobody else, to stand against it. If you yield this point, if you are for ever making compromises, if all men do this, if the entire policy of private life here, is to escape opposition and reproach, every thing will be swept beneath the popular wave. There will be no individuality, no hardihood, no high and stern resolve, no self-subsistence, no fearless dignity, no glorious manhood of mind, left among us. The holy heritage of our fathers' virtues will be trodden under foot, by their unworthy children. *They* feared not to stand up against kings and nobles, and parliament and people. Better did they account it, that their lonely bark should sweep the wide sea in freedom—happier were they, when their sail swelled to the storm of winter, than to be slaves in palaces of ease. Sweeter to their ear was the music of the gale, that shrieked in their broken cordage, than the voice at home that said, " submit, and you shall have rest." And when they reached this wild shore, and built their altar, and knelt upon the frozen snow and the flinty rock to worship, they built that altar to freedom, to individual freedom, to freedom of conscience and opinion; and their noble prayer was, that their children might be thus free. Let their sons remember the prayer of their extremity, and the great bequest which their magnanimity has left us. Let them beware how they become entangled again in the yoke of bondage. Let the ministers at God's altar, let the guardians of the press, let all sober and thinking men, speak the thought that is in them. It is better to speak honest *error*, than to suppress conscious truth. Smothered error is more dangerous than that which flames and burns out. But do I speak of danger? I know of but one thing safe in the universe, and that is truth. And I know of but one way to truth for an individual mind, and that is, unfettered thought. And I know but one path for the multitude to truth, and that is, thought, freely expressed. Make of truth itself an altar of slavery, and guard it about with a mysterious shrine; bind thought as a victim upon it; and let the passions of the prejudiced multitude minister fuel; and you sacrifice upon that accursed altar, the hopes of the world!

Why is it, in fact, that the tone of morality in the

high places of society, is so lax and complaisant, but for want of the independent and indignant rebuke of society? There is reproach enough poured upon the drunkenness, debauchery and dishonesty of the poor man. The good people who go to him can speak plainly—ay, very plainly, of his evil ways. Why is it, then, that fashionable vice is able to hold up its head, and sometimes to occupy the front ranks of society? It is because respectable persons, of hesitating and compromising virtue, keep it in countenance. It is because timid woman stretches out her hand to the man whom she knows to be the deadliest enemy of morality and of her sex, while she turns a cold eye upon the victims he has ruined. It is because there is nobody to speak plainly in cases like these. And do you think that society is ever to be regenerated or purified under the influence of these unjust and pusillanimous compromises? I tell you never. So long as vice is suffered to be fashionable and respectable—so long as men are bold to condemn it only when it is clothed in rags, there will never be any radical improvement. You may multiply Temperance Societies, and Moral Reform Societies; you may pile up statute books of laws against gambling and dishonesty; but so long as the timid homages of the fair and honored are paid to splendid iniquity, it will be all in vain. So long will it be felt, that the voice of the world is not against the sinner, but against the sinner's garb. And so long, every weapon of association, and every baton of office, will be but a missile feather against the Leviathan, that is wallowing in the low marshes and stagnant pools of society.

Would that the world were changed, we say; but

how is it to be changed? Would that the evils and vices of society were done away; but how are they to be done away? Whence is the power to come? I answer. One fearless voice—that of Luther—broke up the spiritual despotism of centuries. One fearless voice in England—that of Hampden—shook the throne of corruption to its base. Any one human arm, lifted up in indignant rebuke, is clothed by the power of God, with all-conquering might. The popular mind ever wants leaders. The people want that some one should interpret the voice that is in them—should speak the commanding word that marshals the hosts of society to the work of reform. If there shall be no such voices in this country, no lofty seers, no stern prophets—if all shall basely seek to lose themselves in the multitude; then shall the sluggish wave of mean mediocrity and slavish acquiescence roll over the land, giving birth to broods of serpents and reptiles, and it shall only fatten the soil for some other and future empire, of more generous freedom and more magnanimous virtue. So sunk the glorious land of Grecian liberty, when nothing but cowering flattery would suit the people; temples and statues and thrones went down, bemired and trodden under the feet of its "fierce" and flattered "democracies;" and the vision of Plato's republic lingers only as a bright dream upon its beautiful shores. If that vision or any part of it is ever to be realized here, there must be a genial confidence and warmth breathed into the soul of the people; there must be a noble simplicity and self-respect free from all base discontents; and there must be a lofty magnanimity free from all time-serving and slavish fear.

DISCOURSE VII.

ON ASSOCIATIONS.

GALATIANS V. 1. AND BE NOT ENTANGLED AGAIN WITH THE YOKE OF BONDAGE.

In the close of my last discourse, I considered the tendency of a controlling public opinion to abridge private and personal independence. The subject appears to me of such importance, that I am induced to resume the discussion of it. The general effect of public opinion, otherwise sufficiently great, is increased, I believe, to an unsuspected extent, by the principle of association: and it is this, which I wish particularly to consider in the present discourse.

I have lately ventured to say that the great danger to our national character is, that of wanting personal, individual independence—independence of mind; and I have once, in another form of communication to the public, expressed the opinion, that "there is less private and social freedom in America, than there is in Europe."

A striking confirmation of these views I have lately met with, in the intelligent French traveller, de Tocqueville; a man remarkably qualified by previous study, by singular candor, and by a thorough investigation of the subject, to write on this country. "I am not acquainted," he says, "with any country, in which there is so little true independence of mind, and so little freedom of discussion, as in America. The authority of a king," he continues, "is purely physical; it controls the actions of the subject without subduing his private will; but the majority in America is invested with a power, which is physical and moral at the same time; it acts upon the will, as well as upon the actions of men, and represses not only all contest, but all controversy."

Though the result is too strongly expressed, especially in the last clause of this passage, yet the tendency is unquestionable; and it being so, I hold that public opinion is more than sufficiently strong, without any artificial aids or arrangements to give it greater power. That the majority shall rule, is the chosen and comprehensive principle that lies at the foundation of our political institutions. Under such an administration of things, there is no reason to fear that public opinion will be too weak; that majorities will be too timid and scrupulous. On the contrary, the danger is, that individuals will lose all courage and independence; that all individual opinion will be merged in prevailing opinion; that intellect and virtue together will sink to an all-levelling tameness and mediocrity. The danger, I repeat, however little it may have been anticipated or suspected, is, that the very principle of our freedom—the rule of majorities —will " entangle us again with the yoke of bondage." In such circumstances I insist, that all artificial aids and arrangements which give force to public opinion, are to be looked upon with jealousy, and that their efforts are to be guarded against, on the part of individuals, with strenuous resistance. And by artificial arrangements, I mean all those parties, sects and associations, whose tendency it is to invade or abridge personal freedom.

But it is necessary, before I proceed farther, to say something definitely of the principle of association; to say, in other words, how far and for what reasons it is to be resisted or restrained.

That principle has had, in this country, a most extraordinary development. It is the very country of parties, sects and societies. But to consider the latter particularly, as being most remarkable; it would seem as if nothing could be done in this country but by societies; and wo to the man, claiming any place among the *good* men of the country, who thinks to escape them! Wo to him who thought to stand apart and aloof, and to go to his grave, quietly and alone! Some society will be certain to find and ferret him out, and bring him into the great trained bands of benevolence, that are spreading themselves over the country.

It would be curious, if not useful, to inquire into the causes of this singular social movement of the country. It arises in part, doubtless, from the popular character of our institutions. It has been the fashion abroad, for governments to do every thing for the people. It is the tendency of our political forms to make the people do every thing for themselves. Besides, the pervading intellectual activity of this country, leads the people to take an interest in every thing that is going forward, which is not found to an equal extent, in any other. This interest, perhaps, naturally expresses itself in associations; since associated action is obviously more powerful than any other mode of operation. But I am inclined to think, that the very trait of national character, on which I have lately commented, has had something to do with the multiplicity of our associations. They enable the individual to shrink from responsibility, and to lose himself in the crowd. They are convenient intrenchments to shelter the timid and faint-hearted. If a man wishes to advocate or advance an unpopular measure, and has not moral strength enough to stand alone, a society offers to him the very resource he wants; then there is a body of associates to lean upon, and to divide with him the risk and opprobrium.

And yet I do not deny that societies have their use; and I am inclined to say, that it is in this very emergency that they have their use and scope. An unpopular opinion or doctrine may well gather its friends about it, if it has any. An aggrieved minority may well associate for its own defence. It is the very policy of our social condition to give to remonstrance, strength. But the same policy requires that the principle of association should be limited by that consideration. If this were a proper subject for legislation, and the power of enacting such a rule were given me, I would cause every association, whose object it is to operate upon public opinion, to die the moment it reached the point of predominant influence; success should dissolve it. Public opinion wants no such aid to make it strong. It is too strong already.

But we must further distinguish. There are societies whose main purpose is to produce an effect upon public opinion. Such were the anti-masonic, and are now, the temperance and abolition societies; and such are all political associations and parties. Upon all such combinations, I should look with jealousy. In this remark, I do not intend to pronounce any judgment upon their particular objects. I might approve of them, but I should be on that account none the less jealous of their tendency, when successful, to narrow and enslave the minds of individuals. Then, again, there are other associations, whose object is charity, or to do some good work ; such as bible, tract, missionary and relief societies of various sorts. With regard to these, it appears to me, that a different judgment is to be entertained. Their object being simply charitable, is so far unexceptionable, let it be carried as far as it will. But this I should say, that while their success is no ground for apprehension, while their success, to almost any assignable extent is to be desired, their coercive influence upon individual minds is no less to be guarded against.

In fine, I do not say that societies, *as* societies, are to be opposed. Were it even desirable, it is certainly impossible in this country at least, by any such weak means or arguments, to check or discourage the spirit of association. It is in the very air about us, ready to come at every call, and to take some new form every day ; and no power, at our command, can exorcise it. This is all, then, that I say, and this is the ground I take ; that all societies ought to beware how they unduly press their influence upon individual minds, and that every individual is to be exhorted to guard his freedom against them: to be exhorted, not, indeed, to withhold his countenance and aid, but to limit them **exactly** to his independent convictions. He is to be warned, I say, not against liberality, but against bondage, and societies are to be warned against imposing it. Some of the cases in which this injury is both done and suffered, it shall now be my business to point out; and then I shall proceed to consider their general influence upon the intellect and virtue of society. Thus with regard to the cases—when a political party says to its members, "You shall support every thing, and oppose nothing, that is done among us, or else, expect no favor or office at our hands," what is this but an enactment in a code of slavery? And what can its legitimate effect be, but to make slaves? Doubtless, a man may honestly and honorably attach himself to some particular doctrine in politics ; and on that basis, a party may be formed; and if the party confined itself to the support of that or similar, or associated doctrines, or of any *doctrines* in fact, all might be well. There would not necessarily be any bondage in such an adherence to party. But the evil is, that the little circle of individual and independent opinions, which at first was calmly gathering and slowly revolving about its proper centre, soon increases to a whirlwind, and raises a cloud of dust, and takes up straws and rubbish in its course, and sweeps every thing in its train. A man finds himself, ere long, mixed up with the agitated and irregular action of many things altogether irrelevant to the original questions. If it were only a certain measure or set of measures, that he was pledged to support, he might be free, Therein he might act upon his own independent opinion. But he soon finds that other questions and interests are thrust into the case ; that he must help to compass party ends ; and hardest of all, that he must support party leaders. Folly must become wisdom to him, if it is found in the party idol; every political vice, a virtue; incapacity, honest, homely sense, unpractised in the tricks of office; intrigue, prudence; sycophancy to the multitude, the love of the people; the most tortuous policy, straight-forward integrity. Let it not be thought that I overdraw the picture. If any man will think to be independent of these considerations, let him try it. Let him dare to say, what, if he has any sense or candor, it is probable that he honestly thinks; let him say, that although he approves the general object of his party, there are some of its measures that he cannot approve, and some of its men, that he will not support. Let him do this; and he will find that the batteries of an hundred presses are immediately opened upon him. He is denounced as a false friend, a spy in the camp; he could hardly be a worse man, if he meditated treason to his party, or to his country; and the end of this experiment on party toleration is, that he is flung off, and left to struggle alone, in the wake of the great ship, that has borne his friends to their haven.

With regard to those great associations, denominated religious sects, I fear that the case involves no less peril to the mental independence of our people. I allow, that the multiplicity of sects in this country, is some bond for their mutual forbearance and freedom. But the strength and repose of a great establishment are, in some respects, more favorable to private liberty. If less favor is shown to those without, there is usually more liberality to those within it. It is in the protected soil of great establishments, that the germs of every great reform in the church have quietly taken root. For myself, if I were ever to permit my liberty to be compromised by such considerations, I would rather take my chance in the bosom of a great national religion, than amidst the jealous eyes of small and contending sects. And I think it will be found, that a more liberal and catholic theology has always pervaded establishments, than the bodies of dissenters from them. Nay, I much doubt, whether intolerance itself, in such countries—in England and Germany, for instance—has ever gone to that length of Jewish and Samaritan exclusion, that has sometimes been witnessed among us.

In saying this, I am not the enemy of dissent. Nor do I deny that it is often the offspring of freedom. It certainly is the usual condition of progress. But this I say; that dissent sometimes binds stronger chains than it broke. And this is especially apt to be the case, for a time, when several, rival and contending sects spring from the general freedom. Then the parent-principle is often devoured by its own children.

But there are other associations to be noticed in this connection. The great benevolent societies of the day, however much good they may propose, and may actually do, are liable to do this evil—to give, that is to say, a form to public opinion, which shall make it press too hard upon individual freedom.

This may be less felt in cities. Individuals there, are lost in the crowd, and possess a certain freedom in their comparative insignificance. The many and conflicting claims to public attention in cities, also, make each particular claim to be less distinct and imposing. And the heterogeneous mass of mind collected in them, enables every dissentient or opposing opinion, to draw forth strength and courage for its support. Hence, I believe it will be found, that all great reforms, political, religious or social, have commenced in cities. Hence it is, that cities have ever been the strongholds of freedom; and if I should add, its corrupters also, I should only point out an extension of the same principle; that is, freedom becomes licentiousness. And thus it is, at this moment, in our American cities, that we have at once, more freedom of mind and more licentiousness of opinion, than there is in the country. Still, amidst all this, there is, no doubt, enough and too much of bondage among us.

But if you would know how great associations may invade the freedom of individuals, go with one of their agents to some retired village or township in the country. His object is to form a Missionary, Tract, or Temperance Society. He first approaches the clergyman, and finds him, perhaps, a convert already to the project. But if not, he is but too likely to find in him an instance of timid and pitiable vacillation; a person unwilling to express that decided opinion, or that decided doubt about the plan, that becomes his place. Next, the agent, with or without the support of the pastor, applies himself to the church and the people. And here, of course, there will be a certain amount of objection. There will be those who think that they cannot afford the money required, or who prefer some other plan, or who dislike pledges. How are these feelings of objection treated? Does the applicant for aid respect them? Is he anxious that every man should act freely, upon his own individual and unbiassed conviction? Does he remember, that "God loveth a cheerful giver," and no other? How much more likely is he to bring the whole weight of public opinion to bear upon the case; to content himself, if he can wring forth reluctant assent! His own reputation is, in a measure, involved. A society of ten or twenty will not satisfy him. It is very likely that these are the only numbers, which, on any new proposition, would justly express the state of the public mind; but these will not content him. He wants an hundred members. He would fain *press* men into the cause. Even if this were not the case, if he were ever so scrupulous about the motives he employed, yet the bare fact, that he comes backed by the example of a thousand villages, of almost the entire country in fact, will be likely to leave little enough freedom among the people he addresses. Shall they stand up against the whole world? Shall all be darkness and death among them, while all is life and brightness around them? What a sad report to go forth among the churches, that no Missionary Society, no Tract Society, no Temperance Society, could be formed there? What will people think of that congregation, or of its pastor? What can they think, but that they are all sunk in spiritual death, or else are opposed to all truth and righteousness? This will not do. There must be a society. They cannot go on without one. I am not denying, of course, that better feelings have their share in the result; but I wish to show you, how liable these bad, unworthy and slavish feelings are to have place in it.

But I need not confine myself, in this survey, to any locality. Every one must be aware that, with regard to several of the great moral enterprises of the day, there is, in this country, a considerable mass of dissent. Take, for instance, the Temperance Reform. I have no doubt, that I might express the opinion of a multitude of sober and reflecting men in the country, in terms like these; "that there was, indeed, great and crying need of this reform; that the evil was one of tremendous magnitude; that it was meet, the whole country should be aroused to its danger; that a pledge of abstinence might have been advisable as a temporary expedient, to give form and force to that strong protest, which was rising in the public mind; but that the pledge, as it has actually been framed, is based upon a false principle; that what the temperance reformers say, when they assert, that it is a sin *per se* to take any substance or liquid in which alcohol is mingled, is not true; that it is altogether an unwarrantable and mischievous refining upon the case, so to state the doctrine of temperance; that there is alcohol in every thing, as there is an exciting quality in every thing, even in the simplest food; that gluttony is as bad as intemperance, though not so common, but that it does not follow that men should not eat; that the proscription of wine, and the sacrilegious and most gratuitous disputes about the use of that element in the Lord's supper, are really as legitimate as they are hurtful inferences from a false principle—because, if alcohol may not be drank, then wine may not be drank, and if it is a sin to drink wine, then it ought not to be used in the Communion; and, finally, that no good is ultimately to be expected, but only a sad reaction from the propagation of any error. Warn the public mind," they would say, "alarm it as much as possible; but do this by legitimate considerations;

none other are needed, and none other can do any eventual good." There are many, I say, who entertain these views; but where, I had almost said, is the speech, sermon or newspaper, that has ever given one single solitary expression to them? And the consequence has been, that the Temperance Reform has gone on without that open and frank opposition to keep it judicious and right, which is necessary to all human action, to every government, to every mind in fact, and therefore, especially, to every heterogeneous and irresponsible association.

Every great association, if it were wise, would welcome an honest, intellectual, argumentative opposition. This is precisely what it wants to preserve it from that extavagance, to which the fervor and confidence of united action are ever apt to lead. But the evil is, that every such association, in proportion as it grows strong, silences remonstrance. It is not here as in politics, where interest insures an opposition. Men feel no immediate interest in resisting any enterprise of a moral nature; and therefore, they are apt to content themselves with expressing their objections in private, and they leave the multitude to rush on without control. But I predict that the day will come, when reflecting men will find, if they would preserve any personal influence or independence, that they have a duty to perform, widely at variance with their present supine indifference or shrinking timidity. Nay, to some, has not the time already come? Have you never known a man in the country, of somewhat conspicuous standing, of unexceptionable morals and many virtues, but who gave nothing to missionary societies, nothing to tract societies, nothing to education societies, and who would sign no pledges to temperance associations, or to associations for promoting the observance of the Sabbath? What is the position of that man in his neighborhood? Why, he is "a great opposer:"—brief, but significant and comprehensive phrase, which none but they who have observed its effect, can understand. It draws a mysterious circle around its object; the very children of the neighborhood come to regard him as a strange and bad man— they know not why; he is cut off from the sympathies of the world around him; kept aloof, (and well if he is not made a misanthrope)—mentioned to strangers with disparagement; prayed for in meetings; and sent to his grave, unblessed, lonely, and perhaps, sad at heart. His very family, it may be, and especially, the female members of it, who are more susceptible to the influence of public opinion, are brought over to the side of distrust and suspicion. Stand up for him, fair ministers at the altar of domestic love, and sacrifice him not on *that* altar! I am not now saying, that the principles he has adopted with regard to societies is right; but this I do say, that for public sentiment to visit upon him such calamities for his dissent, is an insufferable presumption, and ought to bring the power of associations under the most jealous watch of a free people.

But there are other dangers, besides that of producing individual suffering and bondage, which should lead us carefully to guard against the uncontrolled influence and tendency of associations.

And here I must desire you to observe, that it is not against associations as such, that I am directing these observations, nor against them altogether. It is with no hostility to societies, that I am pointing out some of their incidental effects upon the public mind. The best things are liable, by abuse, or by an oversight of their injurious tendencies, to become the worst; and this *because* they are the best; because they win unbounded confidence. Moral associations are such good things—they are so humane and benevolent, they engage such pious and excellent people in their measures, that it is scarcely possible to think any evil of them. So, also, is public opinion a good thing. An enlightened public opinion is to do more, perhaps, than any other agent, except truth itself, to reform the world. But still it is obvious, that this same power may, in certain circumstances, become an instrument of bondage. That it is liable to be such in this country, I think, will scarcely be denied. I say, then, that it is not against associations as such, but against associations, as auxiliaries of a public opinion already too strong, that I would put you on your guard. I have said, that public opinion is like the atmosphere, surrounding and pressing upon every man in the country. Associations may be compared to the atmosphere put in motion. They sweep across a country like the trade-winds or monsoons. Nay, and it may be the sun of truth, pouring its rays upon a certain portion of the firmament, that sets in motion those trade-winds of society, associations. It is the sun of truth, I think, that has set in motion the moral elements of the abolition societies; and yet they may rise and swell, till they bring wreck and ruin upon the dearest interests of the country. I say it was the sun of truth, and I will explain my meaning. The abolition societies began, I believe, in a just and generous impulse. *It is true*, that human beings ought not to be bought or sold, or held in bondage. The only question is, about a practicable and wise measure of relief, from the evil and wrong that is done. But not only have abolitionists failed, in my opinion, to offer any such measure; but, what it particularly falls in with my design to observe is, that the excitement, if it increases, threatens to be one of the most alarming character. You perceive, already, how fearfully it is mixing itself up with the politics of the country.

Indeed, this is one of the general dangers which I was about to notice. Every association among us, and especially, every one that is designed to operate upon public opinion, is liable to take on a political character. It may begin in a very simple intention; it may be conducted for a while with great singleness of purpose; but ere long, it is likely to feel the impulse, which, in this country, is hurrying every thing to the ballot-box. That is the real source of power; and honest men, who find themselves unable speedily enough to accomplish their purposes by any other means, may be so far wrested from their simplicity, as to be willing to bring their cause to that dangerous ordeal. Or even if they retain their simplicity, elements may mingle with their enterprise, which they did not seek; and they may discover at last, that, in the array of their numbers, they have only raised up an army, convenient and ready to the hand of some artful demagogue. The party leader will smile in himself at their zeal, and use their services; and they will find, like the Independents and Round-heads in the time of the second Charles, that they have been deceived and betrayed.

Another danger from the sway of public opinion, and especially, of associations is that of narrowing and prostrating the intellect of the country. It has been maintained by a modern French historian,* that the free action and rapid progress of the body of the people, is unfavorable to the production of great men ; that the nurturing of great minds needs leisure, repose, a fixed order of things, freeing them from the distraction of surrounding events. This opinion, though it obviously requires many qualifications, has a certain plausibility ; and it suggests the inquiry, whether the ratio of individual greatness among us, has not decreased with the general advancement of society. One thing, at any rate, is certain, that mind cannot grow but in freedom. It must be bold, fearless, independent, or it cannot rise. But the tendency of an overwhelming public opinion, is to make it timid and time-serving. The multiplicity of associations increases this effect. It multiplies the questions on which it is dangerous or disagreeable to speak plainly. One can scarcely speak on any subject now, but there is some adherent of some society or some party present, to be wounded or offended by his freedom. Really, we are tempted to say, that something must be done, some compact formed, some new freedom obtained in society ; or all liberty of general conversation will sink into whispers and innuendoes. Besides, associations naturally tend, not only to restrain general freedom of mind, but to narrow and contract the views of their votaries. Opinion naturally loses expansion and freedom amidst the action and pressure of an association. A pledge, or a test,

* Guizot.

must be brief and general; and is likely to sacrifice truth as well as freedom, in the cautious and politic terms with which it must be announced. Associations are scarce likely to be the school of philosophy; still less of a philosophical spirit. A votary is apt to think that there is no plan like his plan. Every plan must yield to it; all means flow to it, all voices be secured for it. He would gladly forestall all that ministers to the decoration of life, and turn it into his treasury. He will not look with a wide and comprehensive survey upon life, and see how many and varied are the means that contribute to its welfare. With him there is but one thing in the world, and that is the Missions, or the Education Society, or the Poor's Fund, or the Ministry for the Poor.

Finally, there are moral dangers of a general nature, arising from that concentrated action of public opinion which is witnessed in associations. There is danger that virtue will lose something, and not a little, of its manliness, simplicity, and spontaneity; that men will be more attentive to outward appearances than to inward qualities; more religious than good, more correct than virtuous, more charitable than generous, and more strict than pure.

It is said that intemperance has decreased in this country. Is it an honest, and not an enforced reform? Has no evasion, concealment, or hypocrisy resulted from the mode in which this enterprise has been carried forward? The very history of the temperance pledges shows that there is such a danger. At first, they contained a promise of abstinence from spirituous drinks, except when they were used as medicine. But it soon appeared, that it was not safe to leave this qualification in the hands of the people ; and the prescription of a physician was required. But as a single prescription of this kind might spread license over a man's whole life, it was found necessary to restrict his use to the single instance prescribed for. Then, again, abuses crept in, under the disguises, the new and false appellations, which spirituous drinks received ; till, at length, no barrier against hypocrisy could be framed but an unqualified pledge of total abstinence from every thing that can intoxicate. This is throughout, a history of evasions ; and it should admonish the temperance societies to beware how they press assent beyond conviction ; to beware lest they make men the slaves of opinion, rather than willing subjects of the law of conscience.

Again, the charities of our people, their contributions to the various benevolent enterprises of the day, are immense and unexampled. I rejoice to see it. I wish they were doubled. They ought to be doubled, at least, on the part of the rich. But while I yield my sympathy and admiration to the spectacle of a great people rising up with associated power, to fulfil its duties to the poor and neglected, and to the heathen, I cannot help charging it upon this people, to see that its charities be really pure and generous. I must confess that I look with some doubt and pain, upon the moral administration of this business of soliciting charities. I fear that there is no delicate or proper regard paid to the freedom and conscience of the giver ; that all sorts of influences are, too often, unscrupulously brought to bear on him, and to wrest from him a reluctant donation. A great association, when it presents itself before an individual, may very properly urge upon him his duties; but let it not urge its own authority, or the universal example to induce him to do that, which he is not in his own mind and conscience prepared and ready to do. I once knew the agent of a religious charity to receive this answer from the person applied to. "I shall give, because you have asked me, but not because I wish to give, or because I take any interest in your object." "Then, sir," was the reply, "I cannot receive your donation." The answer was right. Any other ground is degrading both to the giver and receiver. But I fear that this is not the ground usually taken by the solicitors of charity. I must confess that I have never heard of another instance, yet, I would hope, for the honor of our national liberality, that it is not rare. Charity loses all its sublimity and beauty the moment it ceases to be voluntary and free. There are miseries enough, God knoweth, and man may see, to touch our hearts with unforced pity. There are wastes of ignorance spreading far and wide; there are vices whelming thousands in wo and shame; there are victims of penury and guilt sighing in ten thousand dwellings all around us. Let then charity stand forward to relieve —with pitying heart, and open hand—and not with an iron palm, half closed by a feeling baser than avarice, and doling out just so much as will maintain its reputation. Odious gifts, that profane the name of mercy! not, if so I could fill a thousand treasuries, would I touch one of them. Dishonored would be the very glory of a nation's benevolence, if its gifts are cankered, if its fountains are poisoned, by that taint of slavish homage to public opinion.

Do you ask, in fine, why I lay such stress on this

point—freedom? This is my answer; and my apology, if any be needed, for occupying so much attention with this point. I know of no intellect worth possessing, without freedom. I know of no virtue worth the name, without freedom. A mind chained, a virtue enforced, lose entirely their proper character. They are no longer mind and virtue. But mind and virtue are the only enduring treasures of individuals or of nations. You may present to me the picture of boundless physical prosperity, but if these are gone, all is gone. An iron materialism will press, like incumbent fate, upon the heart of the nation; and quench for ever, the hope and heroism, the light and glory, of the country! You may tell me of free institutions, and they may be your boast; you may tell me of suffrage and the ballot, of the constitution and the laws; unreal mockery is it all, if there is not a free mind and a free heart in the people! A temple of freedom, fair and majestic as the dreams of philosophy or poetry ever fancied, may be built on these shores; but if slaves walk beneath it, if the very ministers at its altars are held in abject bondage to those tyrants of the spirit, fear and opinion; what will it be but a temple deserted of its Divinity?—what will it be, but the great Tomb of Liberty?

DISCOURSE VIII.

ON SOCIAL AMBITION.

MARK IX. 34. By the way, they had disputed among themselves, who should be the greatest.

This dispute is not yet ended. And as Jesus reasoned with it in the case referred to in our text, and in many others, so do I conceive that this questioning of the mind about worldly distinctions, still needs to be reasoned with. Nay, the progress of modern society, is daily furnishing additional occasion for the argument.

There are, indeed, many and high reasonings required, to meet the exigences of modern civilization. Questions concerning governments, concerning the balance of political powers, concerning the rights that are to be acknowledged and the restraints that are to be enforced, are spreading themselves among all reading and reflecting persons, throughout the civilized world. Thinking men, in an age like this, must think about questions such as these. Nor is it an easy, nor would it be a thankless task to solve them. But I confess that I should be yet more grateful to him, who would answer satisfactorily all the questions that arise concerning the social relationship of man to man; and who could effectually teach men to dwell together, not

ON SOCIAL AMBITION. 191

merely as brethren in equality, but as brethren in spite of inequality. This is, indeed, a larger theme than I propose now to discuss. It would involve an inquiry into the manners of society, into the manners of different classes towards each other, not only transcending my present limits, but requiring, perhaps, greater freedom of treatment than public discourse allows, for its proper illustration.

I shall invite your attention, at present, to a single point—social ambition; and the spirit with which its trials are to be met.

Why, let us ask, in the first place, is such a field opened in life, for the display of this passion? Between creatures of the same birth, of the same soul and faculty, and especially, of the same passion for the notice and admiration of their fellows, why, in general, are such immense distinctions permitted? Why is one clothed with purple and fine linen, and why fareth he sumptuously every day, while his brother-man sitteth by his gate in rags and beggary? Why does one stand in the cold shadow of neglect, while another passes by, amidst throng and shout and festal splendor? Why do such extremes of power and weakness present themselves, in the form of our common humanity? Why is it so ordained that a man, ay, and many a man, is obliged to say this—" I am as industrious and honest, I am as rich and wise as my neighbor, and perchance, no worse; and yet it availeth me not; I have striven hard for a place in the world and in society, and yet, mere birth or connections, or fortuitous fashion, or clanship social or political, gives that to another which I cannot obtain?" In short, for natures, craving approbation and regard, and the visible expression of those sentiments, why is a condition of things ordained, which constantly disappoints this passion, and often unjustly?

To such questioning, I know it is common to reply, that difference of situation gives occasion for the exercise of various social virtues; that for man, if there were none above him, there would be no call for reverence; if none below, there would be no opportunity for condescension and forbearance; that without power, there could not be protection, nor submission without dependance; that riches and poverty are appointed spheres, the one for generosity, the other for gratitude. Now, with this answer, I confess I am not satisfied. To those who stand in higher situations, it may, no doubt, be very acceptable doctrine; but I scarcely think it can be, or ought to be, very satisfactory to the poor or neglected, to be told that they are placed in that state, in order that they may learn to reverence their superiors; especially, when those very superiors frequently owe their elevation to the caprice of fashion, the worldliness of society, or the injustice of political institutions. Nor does this inequality of the social condition seem necessary for the end stated. Suppose that all men stood upon a *perfect level;* there would still be occasion for reverence and pity, for generosity and forbearance, for mutual help and kindness. Besides, it would be but a gross view of society, and a still grosser view of our great and spiritual humanity, to see the virtues of either, as chiefly dependant on a mere transient, perishable condition—as if nothing but inferiority could inspire a man with emotions of gratitude and admiration, and nothing but lofty state could fill him with benignity and kindness—as if a rich man were never to be pitied, and a poor man never to be envied—as if all the great and trying experiences of a sensitive and suffering nature, were to be merged in the mere conditions of being well or ill clothed, well or ill fed.

It may seem quite unnecessary and useless, to advert to reasonings such as I have now noticed. It may be thought enough to say, that the inequalities of the human condition result from the very attributes of human nature. It is true that they do. Yet one may seek, perhaps, if not a final cause, yet the proper use to be made, even of that which belongs to the inevitable constitution of things. And so doing, I should say that inequality of condition is to be regarded as a grand *trial* and *test* of our fidelity to high principle—to the loftiest rectitude. If I stood by one who towered far above me; if he were conspicuous before the world, and the shadow of his greatness flung me into obscurity; if, moreover, we had been companions and competitors, and I had labored as hard as he, and yet had failed to rise to the same elevation in talent, or in social claims, or if I had risen to it, and yet the world would not see it; if, I say, I stood thus contrasted with another, thus neglected in comparison with him, and then should ask myself, whereto served this difference, I should say—not to work in me necessarily any reverence or gratitude towards my fellow, but to prove and test and work out in me, a reverence for the greatness of virtue—to put me upon those deep, unfathomed principles of my nature, that absorb all considerations of self—to fill me with a divine disinterestedness towards another's virtue, with a divine calmness in the consciousness of my own; to raise me above, and carry me beyond, all worldly complainings, to the recognition of the supreme privilege, blessing, happiness of loving the infinite beauty of truth, the infinite glory of God. It is in this sharp contrast, in this sore conflict, that virtue gains, perhaps, its highest triumph on earth. Nor will it ever, either in this or a future world, escape this trial, this great challenge to the noblest elevation; for *there* it is written, that "one star differeth from another in glory." But there, as the eternal ages roll, as everlasting difference makes everlasting harmony—there will the happy soul be for ever " satisfied with the likeness" of the Divinity—be for ever "filled with all the fulness of God."

I have alluded to certain reasonings with regard to the inequalities of the social condition; but the controversy which the human heart has with this state of things is full practical. How this controversy has been carried on, and how it has failed of true success; how it ought to be carried on, and how it may attain to the most exalted triumph—these are the points which I propose now to consider.

It has been carried on, first, with strife. A man has seen his fellow rising above him; succeeding beyond him in business and the acquisition of property, or gaining the praise of talent, distinguishing himself by professional ability, or literary success; and either way, and, indeed, every way, winning the regard of society—and in fine, taking that place in public estimation, or in social life, which was the object of *his* ambition. Stung with jealousy and envy, he strives to equal or to surpass his prosperous competitor. Day and night he thinks of this; it is the secret, the unacknowledged, perhaps, but powerful impulse, which urges him on, to study, to business, to speculation, and to all sorts of plans and schemings, by which he may rise. For this, the ambitious man builds his house; adorns it with costly furniture; clothes his family with splendor; buys horses and carriages; gives rich entertainments; seeks acquaintances that are above him, neglects those that are below him; puts on the best appearances; talks much of his rich or distinguished relations, keeps out of sight things that make against him; is silent about his origin, his lowly, perhaps, but virtuous parentage; lives, a hypocrite—labors, a drudge—wears out his life with toil and anxiety; and all—to rise. Does he succeed? Can he, in fact, succeed in any manner, that ought to satisfy a rational being? I say, no. First, because his course is always agitating, irritating, full of trouble and discomfort; and secondly, because the end of a selfish and worldly ambition, when it is reached, is scarcely more satisfactory than its beginning. Why? Because, there are always things beyond it, just as much desired as those which it has already gained. Ask any of the thousands who have succeeded, from among the millions who have sought, and they will tell you, that they are not yet satisfied; that the circle of their ambition is only widened; that the passion for distinction is only stimulated: and as for those few of them, who are approaching the goal of supreme power, they need not tell you, for you will see, that they are only straining every nerve harder to the course on which they are running. Can it be wisdom to live in this manner? Can that be wisdom, whose progress is continual vexation, and whose end is inevitable disappointment?

But, in the next place, there is another, a rarer, and, indeed, it is seldom more than an *occasioual*, mood of mind, in which the trial of social inequality is met. With this mood, the strife of ambition is over for the time, and it sinks in low murmuring complaint, or wraps itself in the cheerless garment of misanthropy, or takes refuge behind the hard and hidebound shield of scorn. The man looks out and around upon the splendor of earthly distinctions, and says, " let it pass; I will not see it ; I will not know it. The proud and unjust world—I will not seek its favor, nor love its praise. Sink, thou gorgeous phantom of this world's magnificence! into the depths of eternity—where thou shalt soon go. Ha! thou art gone! Thou *wert* but a breath, a dream, a cloud-castle ; and thou art *gone;* and now I am as wise and good, as if I were rich and great, and as if all the world rang with my name alone. Empty breath of praise! why should I desire ye! Let me alone ; leave me to obscurity ; leave me to toil— and tears—I can bear them!" But I say to that erring complainer—Is *this*, then, to bear them? Is all this scorn—not *caring* for the world? No ; the poor man's despite, the neglected man's disdain, the humble man's misanthropy, so far from being lofty wisdom, is not even simple sincerity, nor ordinary good sense. No; it is not *so* that we are to battle with the gauds and honors, and the pride of this world.

Nor, in the third place, is it any more justly, to do this battle, to fly, as some do, to the heights of a mystic pietism. The one sinks beneath the conflict ; the other strives to rise above it ; both endeavor to escape from it. I look upon a man whom disappointed ambition, whom earthly mortification and chagrin only, have driven to religion, as upon a coward who has run to a high tower from a post of danger and of duty. True piety is not to lift a man above all comparison with his fellows, but to sustain him *in* that comparison; to enable him, though feeling that he is inferior, yet to be happy; to enable him to say, as John said of Jesus, "he must increase, but I must decrease," and yet to be happy—even as when that noble-minded forerunner said, "the friend of the bridegroom, who standeth and heareth him, rejoiceth greatly, because of the bridegroom's voice; this my joy, therefore, is fulfilled." It is only a false and erring piety, which leads a man to say, " I am one of the elect of God; I am a favorite of Heaven; and I compare not myself with the sons of earth; I am altogether above and beyond all their questions about precedence and honor and respectability." He who stands above all other men, only in his conventicle or his conference-room, may very well doubt whether his elevation be real, or his religion sound and true. And it is only a false and erring piety, I repeat, which receives earthly discontent and disdain into its bosom, but to lap them in celestial visions, and to buoy them up to dreamy heights of contemplation, above all the rough and stanch conflicts of social life. Many such refuges of modern pietism have there been, answering, in this respect, the same purpose as the monasteries and hermitages of old.

Extremes, indeed, there have always been, one way or the other, to which men have ever been retreating from the close and pressing trials of social ambition. On the one hand, worldliness, wealth, rank, insignia, costumes, have defended them against the searching and honest comparison of themselves with one another. On the other hand, they have escaped into conventual seclusion and wild forest retreats—and farther yet, into spiritual pride, mysticism, asceticism, and every strange vagary of fanciful virtue and imaginary devotion.

This will not do. These artificial defences must be removed; these refuges of lies must be swept away. So are not the trials of society to be met. No victory is to be gained through such means, but only a kind of safety. No courage is to be nurtured in this way; no fearless truth, no gentle humility, nothing half so beautiful even as the virtue of the old chivalry; but only haughtiness, pride, either worldly or spiritual, a dreamy self-importance, an imbecile reliance on circumstances. The man whom wealth, office or a title —whom parentage, cast, or a mystic pietism, lifts above the fair comparison of himself with others, is so far safe, indeed; and he may bless his condition, his defences, his armour, if he pleases—may bless the friendly cloud that wraps him from the glittering weapons of his adversary; but he stands not up in the manly, brave and beautiful conflict of social competition.

For that conflict, I say, may be beautiful. I know that it commonly elicits the worst passions, and unfolds the worst aspects of human nature. That is precisely because it is the severest trial of human nature. But the severest trial is always designed to develope the noblest virtue, and may develope it. The result *need* not be what it is often seen to be—anger, envy, bitterness—the quarrels of authors, the strifes of rivals, the poor contentions of families, the miserable jealousies and heart-burnings of society. The result may be as beautiful as the trial is severe.

How this effect is to be wrought out, it is now my purpose to show.

You stand then among those, who in common with yourselves, are desirous of the attention, the esteem, the praise of society. You are naturally led to compare your success, in this respect, with theirs. You do not escape this comparison by fleeing to a hermitage, far from the converse of man. You do not escape it by taking refuge behind the escutcheon of rank, the honors of a noble birth. You do not escape it, let us suppose, by mounting up into the heights of a false and mystic devotion. You are a man; you stand among men; and are one of them. Especially, in *this* country, do you thus stand. There are no nurselings of church or state *here;* no baby-favorites of society here, to be fondled in the lap of primogeniture; no froward children, to be pacified with bright toys, with coronets and titles. The swaddling-clothes of old feudal institutions are here flung aside. You stand among men only as a man, and—be it for good or for evil—altogether as a man. You may be a child of wealth, but the son of the poorest man from the most barren mountain-side in the country, has a fair chance to outstrip you in the race of honor, and to take a higher place in the world than you; and he probably will do so. But not to insist on this—here you stand, I say, among a thousand competitors; and of almost every man to whom I could speak in society, I might safely say, somebody is above you—somebody has surpassed you—some other, in your own walk. Another preacher has more hearers; another lawyer, more clients; another physician, more patients; another author, more readers; another candidate for the attention of society, educated and trained up with yourself perhaps, has more notice, more invitations, more caressings, from the great world than you have. Now, how is this to be met?

There are three conditions under which this superior success may be gained, to which different considerations are applicable. Let us dwell upon them for a moment.

In the first place, you may say, that it has been unfairly gained; that management and chicanery in a profession, dishonesty in business, or insincerity and sycophancy in society, have carried it over you. Then, I ask, would you take that success on condition of adopting the same expedients, the same character? Would you exchange your happiness, for such happiness? Is such advancement any real success? If you think so, you are not true to yourself. If you cannot stand calmly, and see such air-bubbles as quackery, falsehood and vanity, rising around and above you, you have yet to learn what is the true dignity and self-respect of a man. "But it is rather hard, after all," you may say; and besides, the questions, you may remind me, are not such unmixed questions as I state; your rivals have certain merits; it is by mixing up certain other and lighter things with them, that they rise above you. Then, I say, you must make your election. If you will avail yourself of those other things, you may also have the envied success, such as it is—unsatisfactory while it lasts, and likely enough to be short-lived—but such as it is, you may have it. But if you will not make that compromise, if you will keep your integrity, then be your integrity your reward. It is reward enough. It is, indeed, the true success. I do not deny that it will cost you an effort, a trial. I look upon society as designed, through its very injustice, to put our truth, simplicity and independence to severe proof. But let them stand the proof, and they shall come forth as gold purified from the furnace.

But, in the next place, it may be true, that others have surpassed you, by superior industry, by harder study, by greater efforts to accomplish themselves, and to render their manners agreeable to the world around them. Of this case, there is, of course, nothing to be said, but that all complaint on the part of the indolent and negligent is totally unreasonable ; and, indeed, is not to be reasoned with ; but only to be rebuked.

Without dwelling upon this, therefore, I pass at once to the third, and, to most persons, probably, the hardest case of all: the case, I mean, in which the superiority of one to another is the gift of nature, or of circumstances. One inherits wealth ; another has beauty ; a third is endowed with high intellectual gifts. And from one or another of these causes, or from all of them combined, some are placed above you in the world, and, perhaps, far above you. They are sought as you are not sought ; they are admired and praised as you are not admired and praised. Attention, adulation, homage, are poured out in lavish abundance, at their feet ; their names are written in every newspaper, or mentioned in every drawing-room ; while you sit in silent places, beneath the shadow of the domestic roof, or by the humble way-side of life ; and the great world passes you by, without comment or inquiry. This, I say, is one of the great trials of society—this is, perhaps, the greatest trial in its utmost pressure—and I come now, again to the question, how is it to be met?

My answer to this question will relate, first to the distinction itself, and next to the state of mind with which it is to be regarded.

In the first place, the distinction is far less than it seems; I mean that it is far less to the successful aspirant, than it seems to the observer. Somebody is above *him*, as far as he is above you; and he is, perhaps, as little satisfied with his advancement, as you are with yours. He does not estimate his success as you do; and he is, probably, just as anxious to rise to some higher point, as you are to rise to his point. The same questions, it is likely, the same trials are passing in his mind that are passing in yours. Nay, how often is it the case, that the man, upon whose position you are looking with admiration, and almost with envy, whom you dare not approach, by whom you imagine that your attentions would be scorned—how often is he pining, in discontent, in loneliness, and under fancied neglect! The cup of successful ambition, I doubt not, is often drank in solitariness, and is dashed besides, with many a bitter ingredient.

But, in the next place, distinction is not only less than it seems, but it is, in another respect, of far less importance than it seems. It is so, I mean, in this respect; that it has no peculiar portion in the *love* of society. Admiration, praise, notice, it may have; but love is not the guerdon of success. That belongs to goodness, and to goodness alone. It is not talent, wealth or beauty that wins affection. No; let it not be thought that God has dealt so unequally with his earthly children, as to make the dearest boon of social existence, love, to depend on any factitious or arbitrary distinctions. He has thrown lighter toys among those children, to fall irregularly, and to be gathered unequally, and according to no strict rule of justice—fortunes and honors, stars and coronets, and crowns, has he thus disposed of, to be scrambled for—and often to be crushed and spoiled in the grasp which gains them; but so has he not disposed of the solid and enduring wealth of love. No, not to high birth nor haughty rank; not to beauty, proud of peerless charms; not to genius that stands aloft in misanthropic scorn—to none of these is love given. It is dispensed on a more rigorous condition. It is no chance prize, no "accident of an accident." It is taken *out* of the blind lottery of life. To goodness, and to goodness only, is true love given. And well, full well is that boon earned, and dearly, most dearly is it cherished, in ten thousand thousand dwellings, unadorned by wealth, unknown to fame, unvisited by the flaunting robes of worldly fashion. By those still waters of deep, pure love, let the multitudes of men sit down—of those silent fountains let them drink deep, and not disturb them, nor turn them into bitterness, by eager and angry struggles, for the lighter gifts of worldly distinction.

But I have admitted that these gifts have their value, and conceding this to them, I am to consider, in the second place, and finally, with what state of mind they are to be regarded.

And the first feeling which is called for in the circumstances, is one of profound submission to the will of God. Your neighbor holds a position above you, I have supposed, not merely by the aid of arts which you cannot practise, and do not envy; not alone by means of superior industry or study, to which you are bound in justice to give place; but by the force of talents, or other recommendations, which he owes to the sovereign Dispenser of every blessing. It is God, therefore, who has made you to differ. Was it for you to demand of the great Creator, what measure of abilities, what charms of person, what endowments of fortune, or what honors of parentage, he should bestow upon you? Even if you could perceive no good reasons, in the general economy of things, why one human being should differ from another; even if you thought it ever so desirable that all men, in natural advantages, should stand on a perfect level, it is enough for you to know, that disparity is the sovereign ordination of the infinite will. Thy neighbor's greatness, be it derived from original talent, from beauty, or high parentage, is the shrine of the Almighty Sovereignty. Before it thou shouldest stand in awe; in awe, I say, not of thy neighbor, but in awe of God. And the voice which comes from that shrine, to thy murmuring thought, is, "be still, and know that I am God!" Dost thou complain of this? As well mightest thou demand, that some higher world had been assigned thee for thy sphere! As well mightest thou demand, that thou hadst been made one of a loftier order of creatures—angel or archangel.

Here I might pause. But I would not leave the subject without pointing out some other states of mind, with which the trial, whether of real or supposed inferiority, is to be met. With this purpose in view, let us look at our own nature, and let us look around us, upon our fellow-men. To gain the end in view, it is

ON SOCIAL AMBITION. 205

needful that we look upon our fellow-men with love and confidence—upon our own nature, with devout gratitude and veneration.

Upon our fellow-men, I say, let us look with love, with confidence. To our peace of mind, this is essential. A man may think lightly of this advice; he may disdain to submit the high controversy with his rivals to a moral force; he may smile in derision, when we put forward the dictates of a gentle and loving spirit, to wrestle with the strong and stormy passions of human life; he may say, that it is as if we sent a child into the battle of armed men; yet let me tell that man, that this is the only thing—this child in the man's heart—this child-like love, this child-like confidence—is the only thing that can bring the poor and miserable strifes and envyings of the world to an end. Let him call it what he will—weak, poor-spirited, mean—it is the only thing that can help him. That emblem-child which our Saviour once set in the midst of his ambitious disciples, is here the only powerful teacher. Refuse that teaching, pursue the worldly course—refuse, in short, to stand in any relation to your fellow-beings, but that of strife for the precedence; and there is no help for you. It is not in heaven nor earth to help you. It is thus that the disinterested love of our kind is made a necessity; not to be dispensed with, but upon condition of giving up all true peace of mind. Thus stern and uncompromising is the language of Providence. If you had been called upon only to love and admire beings far above you, in some loftier sphere of existence, it had been easy. So had you been little tried. But you are placed side by side, with beings who, some of them, tower above you;

you are placed in this close pressure of social competition—and why? It is, I say, that every particle of mean selfishness and base envy, may be expelled from your bosom. Love, then—pure, confiding, generous, disinterested love—has become to you a necessity. You cannot do without it. You might have stood without it on some solitary and barren point, alone in the creation; but in the world, you cannot live, and be happy without it.

And how often have I seen, and surely was struck with observing it, that simple love, simple confidence, simple self-forgetfulness, makes its way in the world, makes its way to the heart, penetrates through all barriers—finding every where an open door, and good welcome and acceptance! I will not say that it was plain in person, poor in estate, or humble in condition; it might be so, or it might not; but this I mean to say, that in every sphere, disinterested goodness is the pre-eminent quality; happy in itself, and most likely, other things being equal, to be happy in the love of others. Yes, amidst all the selfishness and injustice of the world, this is true. And, therefore, would I send every complainer, every murmurer, every jealous or anxious or desponding person, that is ever thinking of himself—I would send him to the school of love—to the school of Christ. Thou mayest seek, restless, discontented one! many resources, many reliefs; but thou must come to Christ, if ever thou wouldst find rest to thy soul. This is no cant language, no language of the pulpit merely; it is the language of simple truth; the only language that applies to the simple, actual relations of being to being. Had there been *no* Bible—had there been *no* religion, it were true. Never canst thou look rightly upon thy neighbor, upon thy companion, soaring above thee, unless thou lookest upon him in a kindly and loving spirit. This only can compose the miserable strifes of society. Come down, celestial goodness!—as an angel, come down; and unseal the fountains of healing, and spread new life and beauty over the barrenness of an unkindly, envious and unhappy world!

One further consideration I have mentioned, and to that I would invite your attention for a moment in close. It is the consideration of our own nature.

Your neighbor is above you in the world's esteem, perhaps—above you, it may be, in fact; but what are *you?* You are a man; you are a rational and religious being; you are an immortal creature. Yes, a glad and glorious existence is yours; your eye is opened to the lovely and majestic vision of nature; the paths of knowledge are around you, and they stretch onward to eternity; and most of all, the glory of the infinite God, the all-perfect, all-wise, and all-beautiful, is unfolded to you. What now, compared with this, is a little worldly eclat? The treasures of infinity and of eternity are heaped upon thy laboring thought; can that thought be deeply occupied with questions of mortal prudence? It is as if a man were enriched by some generous benefactor, almost beyond measure, and should find nothing else to do, but to vex himself and complain, because another man was made a few thousands richer.

Where, unreasonable complainer! dost thou stand, and what is around thee? The world spreads before thee its sublime mysteries, where the thoughts of sages lose themselves in wonder; the ocean lifts up its eternal anthems to thine ear; the golden sun lights thy path; the wide heavens stretch themselves above thee, and worlds rise upon worlds, and systems beyond systems, to infinity: and dost thou stand in the centre of all this, to complain of thy lot and place? Pupil of that infinite teaching! minister at Nature's great altar! child of heaven's favor! ennobled being! redeemed creature! must thou pine in sullen and envious melancholy, amidst the plenitude of the whole creation?

"But thy neighbor is above thee," thou sayest. What then? What is that to thee? What, though the shout of millions rose around him? What is that, to the million-voiced nature that God has given *thee?* That shout dies away into the vacant air; it is not his: but thy *nature*—thy favored, sacred and glorious nature—is thine. It is the reality—to which praise is but a fleeting breath. Thou canst meditate the things. which applause but celebrates. In that thou art a man, thou art infinitely exalted above what any man can be, in that he is praised. I had rather *be* the humblest man in the world, than barely *be thought* greater than the greatest. The beggar is greater, as a man, than is the man, merely as a king. Not one of the crowds that listened to the eloquence of Demosthenes and Cicero—not one who has bent with admiration over the pages of Homer or Shakspeare—not one who followed in the train of Cesar or of Napoleon, would part with the humblest power of thought, for all the fame that is echoing over the world and through the ages.

Upon those mighty resources, then, upon those infinite benefactions of thy being, cast thyself and be satisfied. Thou canst read; thou canst think; thou canst feel; thou canst love—and be loved; thou canst love the infinitely lovely:—say, then, that it is enough! In that ocean of good, let poor and pitiful pride and ambition be swallowed up. Amidst an infinitude of blessings, let humble gratitude and boundless reverence, be the permament forms and characters of thy being.

DISCOURSE IX.

ON THE PLACE WHICH EDUCATION AND RELIGION MUST HAVE, IN THE IMPROVEMENT OF SOCIETY.

II. PETER I. 5—7. ADD TO YOUR FAITH VIRTUE; AND TO VIRTUE, KNOWLEDGR; AND TO KNOWLEDGE, TEMPERANCE; AND TO TEMPERANCE, PATIENCE; AND TO PATIENCE, GODLINESS; AND TO GODLINESS, BROTHERLY-KINDNESS; AND TO BROTHERLY-KINDNESS, CHARITY.

I HAVE thus far, in this series of discourses on society, been occupied chiefly with the consideration of evils and dangers. I shall in this discourse, invite your attention to remedial and conservative principles. It is not my intention, however, to apply them to the evils already stated, since it was natural to connect with the notice of them, some consideration of the proper remedies; and since there are other evils no less obvious and urgent. I may add here, that I aim at no completeness in this series of discourses; my plan is to notice only such topics, however isolated and disconnected, as justly press themselves upon our attention, in the moral views which we are taking of modern society.

The principles of improvement and safety which I propose now to examine, are education and religion. The space which I shall be able to give to these subjects, in a single discourse, must be, compared with their importance, very small; and, indeed, instead of attempting fully to discuss their social bearings, my purpose rather is, in accordance with the hint of my text, to suggest some things which need to be *added* to the popular views of them.

But let us consider, for a moment, the state of things on which these suggestions are to bear.

It is, doubtless, a very extraordinary state of things. Its distinctive feature, is a grand popular movement, slowly propagating itself through all civilized nations— a revolution of ideas, which is elevating the mass of mankind to importance and power ; and, in fact, to the eventual government of the world. It is a revolution which goes alike beyond all former examples in history, and principles in philosophy. The *education* of this age—that mass of sentiment and maxims which it has received from former ages—does not prepare it to understand itself. Though the noblest genius and philosophy of former times, have been distinguished by their generous recognition of the claims of humanity ; yet they have seldom descended to work out the great problem of human rights. They have shown more admiration for human nature, than confidence in it. Their speculations, indeed, have proceeded upon grounds widely different from the present state of facts. When Aristotle discoursed in such discouraging terms on the popular tendencies, he discoursed concerning a people that could not read ; that had no newspapers ; that were ignorant and brutal, compared with our educated and Christian communities. When Plato reasoned of his ideal republic, his ground was pure hypothesis ; his work pure fiction. The philosophy of modern politics, has not been written in past times ; it cannot be written now; that work, I believe, in its full perfection must be left to a future age. I do not pretend to say what it will be; the principle of intelligent, Christian freedom may develope results, that are out of the range of our present contemplation. But this, I think, is evident, that when the future philosopher and historiographer rises, that shall analyze and pourtray the stupendous revolution that is now passing in the civilized world, he will speak of a revolution having no precedent in history. None was ever so universal, so profound, or so fearful. All former revolutions have been local, occasional and sanguinary. In former days, when power has been wrested from its despotic possessor, it has been done only by a violent and bloody hand. But now, an influence, silent and irrisistible, is rising up from the mass of the people, and is stealing from thrones and princedoms and hierarchies their unjust prerogatives; and, at the same time, as if by some wonder-working magic, is making their incumbents helpless to resist, and even willing to obey. Potentates are learning a new lesson, and so are the people too. Before, revolutions have been violent and bloody, from the very weakness of those who have carried them on, from the very uncertainty whether they should succeed. Now, the people are reposing in calm security upon their undoubted strength. Assurance has made them moderate. Let no one mistake their moderation for apathy, or their quietness for defeat; for they are calm only in proportion as they are determined and sure.*

---

* Nothing surprised me more, four years ago in England, than what appeared at first sight, this apathy; this moderated

Such is, undoubtedly, the character of the present era, however we may regard the good or the evil involved in it. To me, I confess, it is far the most momentous and sublime era in the history of the world. The introduction of Christianity, and the discovery of printing—the two greatest events on record—are, in fact, now producing, for the first time, on the broad theatre of national fortunes, the very results which we are witnessing. They have given birth, if not to the free principles of modern times, at least, to their free action. Like the sun and the moon in heaven, they have penetrated by their influence the great deep of society. The effect produced, may well awaken that solemn and even religious emotion in the mind, of which a late distinguished writer has spoken. What is now presented to the attention of the world, is not, as formerly, kingdoms convulsed, or navies wrecked upon the shore, but that "tide in the affairs of men," that slow rising, and gradual swelling of the whole ocean of society, which is to bear every thing upon its bosom.

It is scarcely possible to speak of this great movement of modern society, without something like anxiety and apprehension. The very terms, in which our conceptions of it naturally clothe themselves, bear an aspect as of something portentous and fearful. And that there is actual danger in this revolution of opinions, I am so far from denying, that it is the very purpose of this discourse to discuss the only principles of safety.

tone of the most radical reformers; but how much more was I struck, to find, on closer observation, this deeper determination, this repose of conscious strength; the purpose to succeed not weakened, but only stronger in its calmness!

But, at the same time, I cannot take my place among the alarmists. I cannot believe, that the feeling of apprehension which is springing up all over the civilized world, is justified in its full extent. There are dangers, doubtless: what season of probation for high ends, ever failed to be a season of peril? To warn one another of that peril; to summon brave, honest and true hearts to meet it; to stand amidst the people as one of their brethren, and to lift up the voice of friendly admonition, is well. How well it is, to stand aloof from them, and to fling down discouragement and scorn upon the popular cause, I must leave others to determine. But this I must say, that if indeed that cause shall fail, if the future historian of this momentous period, must write its story in tears and blood, I shall ever believe it will be, in part, because the proper intellectual guides of the world, were not true to the solemn trust reposed in them. It is, indeed, an extraordinary fact—a fact reversing, in a striking manner, the usual course of things—that while opinion ordinarily propagates itself from the more educated to the more ignorant classes, the popular cause is now rising and swelling against the loudest remonstrances of so many superior minds, as if it were, indeed, an ocean-tide, against which nothing is destined to prevail.

This remonstrance, this alarm, seems to me, I have ventured to say, to be carried to an unwarrantable extent. Alarm, indeed, appears to be one of the epidemic diseases of the age. Every religious association, every little spiritual coterie, every school of sect, speculation and philanthrophy, is trembling for the fate of the world. *Now*, the philosophy of the world is going to ruin it; *then*, its extravagance, intemperance, licentiousness is to do the work ; then popery, heresy, infidelity, is elevated to this bad eminence in mischief. The danger from some of these quarters, I freely admit. But, it is really worth while to observe, through how many prophecies of ruin, through how many critical and doomed periods, the world has lived. Truly, one is sometimes tempted to say to these alarmists, " Good sirs, have a little patience ; the world is likely to last our time ; the purposes of Providence will stand, though you be disappointed in some of your favorite theories or projects."

It is one effect of this alarm, to turn the public attention too much to immediate and palpable resorts for safety, to the readiest instruments that come to hand, rather than to those deep and broad foundations which must be laid in the moral education, the cultivated and spiritualized mind of the community. Thus, if some Constitution can be preserved, if some House of Lords can be hedged about with impregnable defences, it seems to be thought, that the world will be saved. Thus, almost all the reforms of the day, are turning upon some palpable evil; as intemperance, licentiousness, pauperism. But important or otherwise, as any of these efforts may be, there is a work of redemption that must go deeper, must go down into the heart of the world, or it will *not* be saved, in the great crisis that is approaching. How easy were it to show, that there are evils lying beneath all palpable evils, and which, if the same universal attention were fixed upon them, would appear far greater. Intemperance, licentiousness, pauperism, and with these, popular violence, mobs and tumults, are all but indexes of deeper evils, symptoms of deeper maladies, that are seated in the very heart of society. Alas! the world is not well, is not happy in itself—the infinite wants of humanity are not provided for—else, would not the world break out, on every hand, for relief from those necessities and pains, that are preying upon its inmost bosom.

I must add, that even where the real conservative principles, education and religion, are resorted to, they are too often, I fear, but superficially regarded; and are, as they are used, but ready instruments, instead of being considered as deep principles and thorough remedies. If education with us, is a mere technical system, a mere teaching of the arts and sciences commonly learned in schools; if religion is a mere state-engine, or only a form or creed, or barely a charity to the poor and vicious, neither will exert the needed influence. It is striking to observe, that the whole strength of the Tory party in England, all its will, wish and thought about religion, seems to be occupied with the preservation of a visible Establishment. I may do injustice to this aim, but it seems to me, that it is, in the hands of many of its most earnest supporters, the mere worldly scheme of worldly men; and certain I am, that no such scheme will answer now. I maintain, on the contrary, that deeper views of education and religion must be added to those which now prevail; that to education must be added a moral influence, and to religion a deeper philosophy and a more thoroughly practical character, in order to make them the guardian powers that the present age requires. And these are the positions, of which it is now my further purpose, to attempt some illustration.

The first subject to be considered is education. From the earliest settlement of the country, this has engaged the earnest attention of our communities. We have set the first example in the world, of the instruction of the whole mass of the people. Education has ever been our watch-word, and our boast. No celebration of any public festival, no grave dissertation of the closet upon our institutions, ever omits the recognition of its importance. On every side, it is constantly represented, as the sheet-anchor of our liberty.

Well is it that we pay this homage to education; but have we sufficiently considered what it must be, to answer the end proposed? Have we not made it a mere watch-word—have we not regarded it as a mere talisman, and expected some magical effects from it, rather than entered into a deep consideration of its nature; of the qualities which adapt it to the preservation of the national order and security?

I beg attention to this inquiry. And for the purpose of awakening that attention, I wish to present to you one or two extraordinary facts bearing on this point, from the history of education in Europe. In Prussia, where, so far as mechanism is concerned, the most perfect system of public instruction ever known, has recently been adopted—in that kingdom, I say, education is considered as nothing without religion. "The first vocation of every school," says one of its ordinances, "is to train up the young in such a manner as to implant in their minds, a knowledge of the relation of man to God, and at the same time, to excite both the will and the strength, to govern their lives after the spirit and precepts of Christianity. Schools must early train children to piety, and, therefore, must strive to second and complete the early instructions of parents." Again, in France, which some while since sent one of her most distinguished philosophers* to inquire into the Prussian system of education, and where that system, but without its religious influence, has been partially adopted, we are presented with this extraordinary and astounding statement—viz., *that in the best educated departments, the greatest amount of crime has been found to exist.* This is not an observation made at hazard; it is absolutely a matter of *statistics.* Nakedly stated, the fact is this; *that education in France has produced crime.* This, at least, is what is admitted by the friends of education in France, and insisted upon by its enemies in England;† and with my views of the subject, I have no difficulty in admitting that it is true.

For this is the view which I take; that education, considered simply as instruction in reading, writing, arithmetic, &c.,—education, separate from any moral influence, does not necessarily tend to make any people better, and may be easily perverted, so as to make them worse. " Knowledge," it is often said, " is power;" but it is power, as capable of bad as of good uses. Thus, the knowledge of reading and writing communicated to a people, may only increase the number of forgers and counterfeiters: the knowledge of arithmetic may only multiply the chances of knavery in accounts. Thus, also, an acquaintance through newspapers, with the conduct of government or of obnoxious individuals, may urge a simple people to

* Cousin. See his Report on the Prussian System.
† See an article on Democracy, in Blackwood's Magazine, No. 225.

disaffection and treason, or hurry a quiet people into mobs and tumults. And, in the same way, *general* knowledge, into which no moral principles are infused, may lead men to ambition, discontent, envy and unhappiness, and by these means, to excess, extravagance and vice. But I am speaking mainly of that particular knowledge, which is commonly gained in schools. There is, indeed, a higher intelligence which is favorable to virtue, inasmuch as it sees all else but virtue, to be utter folly and mistake. But of knowledge, considered as a mere technical acquisition, I say, that it is a mere instrument, whose use and utility will depend on its moral direction.

It is upon these clear and indisputable grounds, that I maintain the necessity of adding to our knowledge, virtue; to our system of education, a moral and spiritual influence. Other things must be taught in our schools, besides the elements usually considered as belonging to them. Good morals and pious sentiments should be as anxiously and earnestly taught, as reading and writing.

But I must not be content on this vital point, with a general statement. Education, in the largest sense, is the preparation of the mind for the scene in which it is to act. What, then, should be the education of a free people—and, indeed, of human beings as such? I answer, that our youth should be taught, at some period before they leave the common schools, that they are to be electors, jurors, magistrates, and, perhaps, legislators; and thus, virtually, rulers of the country. They should be made to feel something of the weighty charge that is about to be devolved upon them. They should be made to understand the duties to their country and to their God, which are implied in the trust they are about to assume. Were this faithfully taught in all our schools, we might hope, ere long, to see a time, when the whole political action of the country should not run to passion and caprice and prejudice, and a mere contest for the mastery. Were this done, we might hope to see, ere long, an end of that pernicious distinction, which is now made between individual and party morality, between personal and official conscience ; and political confidence and public honor would no longer be heaped upon men, whose lives are stained with private vices. Again, an education of youth for the part they have to act in our communities, should enter deeply into their social relations, should imbue their minds with independence, magnanimity, candor and courtesy, should put them on their guard against ambitious aspirings and preying discontents, should moderate the strife for social precedence, should teach respect for the laws, should clothe the constitution of the country with an inviolable panoply, should arm the majesty of legal justice with the authority of conscience. In fine, an education for life, essentially involves the deepest principles of religion ; and though the family is the great school for this kind of education, yet no school should fail of recognising it, as a part of the nurture and discipline of youth. The weariness and ennui that are commonly witnessed in our schools, the indocility and insubordination of which there is so much complaint, arise, in a considerable measure, from the want of any perceived connection between them and the practical objects of life. The child does not well understand what all this study is for. Place, then, before him, the scene of life, make it a part of the regular business of instruction, to speak to him of the situations in which he will be placed, and of what will be a just and noble conduct in them; and then, as surely as human nature has any principles to be relied on, their attention and interest will be aroused. The ends of life, the principles of happiness, the art of living—physically, mentally and morally considered—the morals of business and pleasure, the occupations and callings of men, carried into detail—what they are, what are the instruments they work with, what is their utility, what are their duties—all these subjects, not in dry and abstract terms, such as I now use, but with vivid and almost dramatic representation, might be presented to our youth, and contribute to that intelligence and virtue, which are the basis of our national well-being and safety.

Education must rise among us, or the nation must sink. That it *will* advance, I cannot doubt, when I see the spirit that is manifested in various parts of the country. But there is one alarming fact, that ought to fix the attention of the country, till it is aroused to greater exertions than it has yet put forth. The progress of population in some of the states, is, at this moment, outstripping the progress of education. There was a time when scarcely a youth could be found in the whole nation, who was not taught the elements of learning. The number of the uninstructed, is now some hundreds of thousands, if it must not, indeed, be stated to be more than a million! I know not in what terms to dwell upon this fact, that shall present its full claims upon the public attention. If nations, as such, have ever any vocation, ours is to educate the people.

If Providence ever laid a weight of obligation like the weight of destiny, upon any people, it has laid that obligation upon us. If it ever spread before the eyes of any people, the yawning gulf of destruction, and distinctly warned them to beware of it, it has spread before us, in that character, the dark gulf of popular ignorance. Into it, the nation will inevitably descend, unless it is closed up. No single sacrifice, like the fabled sacrifice of the Roman Curtius, can avert the danger. The fearful chasm in our popular education, can be closed only by the united efforts of the whole people. A representative government represents the character of the people. And that government which represents prevailing ignorance, degradation, brutality and passion, has its fate as certainly sealed, as if, from the cloud that envelopes the future, a hand came forth, and wrote upon your mountain walls, the doom of utter perdition!

To avert such a doom, the next great power to which we appeal, is religion. Intelligence and religion are the two grand conservative principles of all society. And neither of them can be relied on, to the exclusion of the other. Religion is wanted to give to intelligence a right direction; and intelligence is equally wanted to make religion rational, sober and wise; to preserve it from superstition and fanaticism; from that fatal substitution, so common, of forms and fancies and articles of faith for practical virtue. I say, that neither of these great conservative principles can be dispensed with. Many political economists have insisted on the necessity of education, without seeming to be sensible of the necessity of religion. But I cannot understand upon what ground a man can believe in one, without believing in the other. Nay, if I *believed* in neither, if I looked upon the frame of society only with the eye of an artist, if I cared not what became of human governments, or the human character, or any thing else human, I should still be compelled to see and admit, that there is no basis for human welfare, individual, social or national, none conceivable or possible, none provided by the great Framer of the world, but intelligence and virtue.

But it is not my purpose in this discourse, to defend so large, and, I hope, so evident a proposition. It is my design rather, as I have stated it, to point out an extension of the great conservative principles, which, I apprehend is not equally admitted, or, at least, not equally considered. This design, so far as it relates to religion, contemplates that subject in two relations to the general welfare; first, to the poor and distressed classes of society, and secondly, to the whole body.

With regard to pauperism, and its consequent miseries and vices, the religious action of society has hitherto mostly contented itself with charities; with means and efforts directed to the relief of its palpable evils. I trust the time has now arrived, when a new principle is to be adopted. This principle is, to do the least possible for the body, and the utmost possible for the mind; to apply ourselves directly to the root of all evil, the soul's ignorance and debasement; to elevate the physical condition, through the improvement of the moral condition.

It has, at length, been found out, that general and indiscriminate charities only multiply the evils which they propose to relieve; that pauperism grows by what it thus feeds on. The history of English charities has shown this on a large scale, and our own experience, so far as we have followed that example, has brought out the same result. This treatment of pauperism constantly produces a two-fold effect; physical necessity and mental imbecility together, grow and thrive upon it. So certain is this, that beggary has become, to every reflecting man, who has looked into the subject, the index to the saddest combination of physical and moral evils. In Europe there is more apology for it. But I confess, that in *our* country, in *our* streets, it affects me to see a man or a woman stretch out the hand for alms. For I know, that in almost all cases, it is an indication just as clear as if a placard were presented by that hand, setting forth a story of indolence, improvidence, vice and degradation. And just as plainly would a true hand-writing show, that to give to such applicants, is, in almost every instance, only to increase all that debasement and misery. Nay, and I am inclined to think there is more suffering that is buried in silence, ay, and clothed in the decent garb of respectable poverty, than is indicated by the brazen beggary of the streets. Still, I admit, that such cases are to be attended to. But I maintain, that the only right attention is that which follows them to their homes. When it finds there, sickness, or helpless age, or urgent distress, which for the moment nothing else can meet, it is to give relief. But the grand principle of all wise charity is, that he who would benefit a poor family, must visit it, must make himself acquainted with its condition and character, and must apply himself to the removal of those mental and moral evils which lie at the foundation of all its wants and miseries.*

In fine, religion, when it addresses itself to the relief of indigence, must learn to respect the poor, and to feel for them. " To goodness we must add brotherly kindness." I fear we little know what a deep and almost terrific sentiment of hatred, is often engendered in the breasts of the poor, by the ordinary administration of charities. They feel themselves degraded rather than obliged, by this manner of giving. They become, in fact, enemies of their benefactors. They have their part to play as well as the philanthropists. They consider it a sort of contest between them; and *their* business is to get all they can; to deceive as much as possible; and to remunerate themselves, to the utmost, for the unhappy and degrading relation which they sustain to their superiors. This is human nature. And it is only by forgetting what human nature is, that we have been able to overlook this inevitable result. A *man* is not to be relieved as your horse or your dog may be. It must be done with a sentiment of respect. I would that a new mode of giving were introduced, more accordant with the humanity and gentleness of the Gospel. I would that a man should be pained by having a fellow-being approach him in the humble attitude of a beggar. I would that a flush of ingenuous and sympathizing shame, should overspread the brow of the giver. Alms are not to be a matter of business; and yet let it be

* On this head, I cannot do any thing so well, as to refer the reader to Mr. Arnold's last admirable Report. It is Mr. A.'s "Seventh Semi-annual Report of his service as Minister at large in New York."

considered whether all public and indiscriminate charities will not, without the greatest care, inevitably be of this character. They must not be conferred upon the poor with indifference, or flung to them with contempt.

Would you do good then to your poor brethren of the human family—respect them, love them, feel for them. Go forth, and commune with them. Lay aside your robes of pride; they will but entangle you. Go freely forth, and as you have opportunity, mingle with them; commune with them frankly; help them; comfort them; make them respect themselves; make them virtuous; make them happy. How can you hope to do the good you ought to do, to your poor brethren, till in deep sympathy you feel and act as one among them, and of them? They are not out of the pale of humanity. They *are* your brethren. You *are* of them. Before the great Giver, you are *all* poor. Where is the proud, strong, rich man, that stands aloof from his fellow-man, as if he were one of another species? To-morrow, perhaps, thou shalt lie down upon thy bed, to die—poor as the poorest—about to be stripped of every thing. *To-day*, thou oughtest to kneel down before thy God, and to say, "give me, O thou Supreme and ever Gracious One—not gold and silver—but that which is infinitely dearer, that which I infinitely more need than ever houseless outcast needed my alms— give me thy pardon, thy mercy, thine everlasting favor!"

Such, my friends, is the application of religion to the single relation in society of the rich to the poor; let us now consider it in its bearing on the welfare of the whole social body.

The simple and single question is, what kind of religion is adapted to the ends of our particular government and our peculiar social economy? If religion were to answer the purposes of a despotic government, it might be a mere political engine, a creature of the state. Such were most of the religions of antiquity. If it were to be the mere tool of a priesthood, or of an ecclesiastical state, it might be, to answer that purpose, a superstition and a bondage. Believing, acquiescing, submitting, might then be every thing, and practice, little or nothing. But if religion is to be the friend, the improver and guardian of a whole people, what must it then be?

I might answer in the very words of Scripture, and say, that it must be a religion " first, pure; then, peaceable; full of good fruits, without partiality, and without hypocrisy;" or in the words of my text, and say, "add to godliness, brotherly kindness, and to brotherly kindness, charity."

But let us enter into some detail; and looking beyond the narrow bounds of sectarian preference, let us consider upon broad and rational grounds, what the religion of a free people must be.

Surely, it must first of all, be pure. It must lay the axe at the root of every thing wrong in society. It must hold no compromise with the vices either of the rich or of the poor, of the high or of the low; of politicians or private men, of statesmen or citizens. All are to come under one grand law, and to be amenable to one rule. There is to be no saving clause for people of condition, for the great or rich, for prince or monarch. None are to be considered as above the restraints of religion, and none beneath its mercies.

But the main consideration on which I intend to insist is, that our religion must be practical. Solemn forms, and dark scholastic dogmas, might answer the purpose of producing an outward decency and an implicit acquiescence, but they will not be living powers, acting on the vital interests of society. Doctrines, that have been written in books, must be written in the heart. Creeds must not take the place of virtues, nor professions of principles. All substitutions that prevent religion from bearing directly upon the heart and the daily life, must be done away. Nor is the work to be done in this respect, a slight one. How much religion *is* kept from the hearts of the people by the common forms of its administration, is a serious question. In this view, I look with more than doubt, upon the peculiar constitution of the church in this country. We have not an establishment, and we bless ourselves in our exemption from it. But we have what I fear is worse in its effect upon the popular mind, an ecclesiastical oligarchy. In most other Christian countries, the people are regarded as the children of the church, and are freely invited to participate in its ordinances. Two or three sects among ourselves, the Catholics, the Episcopalians, and the Unitarians in some of their churches, follow the same rule. But with these exceptions, the churches of this country hold the grand characteristic ordinances of Christianity, in the power of their vote. And if religion, in its only embodied form, thus stands aloof from the people, if it surrounds itself with a barrier of exclusion, does it not so far cut itself off from free access to individual minds and hearts? In such a country as this, above all others, religion should be the liberal, generous and gracious protector and friend of the people. No otherwise can it be efficient and practical.

But there are other defects in its administration. If religion clothes itself with the cumbrous armor of the Middle Ages, with scholastic dogmas and disquisitions, it cannot worthily and manfully fight the battle for freedom. The great foes of our liberty, sin, vice, avarice, sensuality, luxury and social ambition, are not so to be vanquished. What care *they* for decrees, and substitutions, and imputations of righteousness, and the subtilties of creeds—paper shields and helmets of parchment, and solemn priestly robes—what, I repeat, do the rooting herds of worldliness and voluptousness, care for them? Religion must come to a closer contest with human wickedness, if it would ever gain the mastery. The pulpit must be unchained. The preacher must be free. No fastidious solemnity, no artificial sanctity, no superstitious dogmas of prevailing opinion about what is peculiarly spiritual or religious, must restrain him. He must go down freely into the midst of life, and nothing must escape him that seriously affects the virtue of society. The power which the preacher might exert on the public welfare, is as yet but little known. One day in seven given up to him; ten thousand pulpits in this land opened to him; so many posts in a country to hold it against its moral enemies—such an array of force, were it wisely exerted, might stand against all dangers, and ensure the national intelligence, virtue and piety.

But there is still another and more subtle foe to the practical efficiency of our religion; and that is found in the prevailing idea of its nature. The constitution of the church, the character of the pulpit, have their influence, and it is great. But there is, more deeply embedded in the very heart of society, the conception, that religion does not consist in the practical, every day virtues—justice, honesty, brotherly kindness, gentleness, candor and truth—but that it consists essentially in a certain peculiar state of the affections, an acquiescence of the heart in a particular plan of salvation, the consummation of a special process of experience, the result, in short, of a miraculous conversion. Other things, indeed, follow from religion; but this is religion itself. I have weighed every word I have now uttered, with unfeigned anxiety to do no injustice to the popular sentiment. And I do not object, let it be observed, that this process and these peculiarities should be considered as occasional appendages of real piety and goodness, but only that they should be regarded as its essence. And that they are so regarded, the answer of three persons out of every four you meet, will show you. If you question them as to their religious character, you will find that is made by them to depend on these points. The question with them will be about a time and a process, a despair and a hope, a conviction and a conversion. The main stress of their anxieties will rest upon these points. They will not ask themselves, whether they are now honest and upright, temperate and forbearing, kind-hearted and true; but whether at a particular time they have had a particular experience, and whether they have kept up the feeling of that experience all along till now.

I have entered farther than I intended into this distinction; but it is, indeed, most vital to the bearings of religion on society. For is it not perfectly evident, that in proportion as too much stress is laid upon the points just noticed, too little will be laid upon the virtues of social and private life ? This, I apprehend, is the grand defect of the religion of our country. There is much religion among us, and, I believe, that it is increasing. So far all is well, is cheering. Would that it were all sound, rational and true !

It is possible, in our religion, to give an undue prominence even to the purest spirituality and piety; and thus, to give too little space to the social virtues. There is one piece of sacred history that most emphatically teaches us on this point. David was a most devout man ; his writings show it ; and this, I suppose, is what is meant by his being called " a man after God's own heart." And yet he was guilty of some of the most heinous social offences on record. And this is not a solitary instance. Your own observation, perhaps, might furnish some sad examples of this tremendous error. Some of the most devout men that ever I have known—I say not that they were hypocrites—men, as I believe, of sincere though erring piety and prayer, were, in their social relations, some of the worst men that I ever knew. What does the whole history of religion, Pagan, Popish and Protestant, more clearly show, than this exposure ? Men have worshipped God, and, at the same time, hated, persecuted, cast out, crushed and destroyed their fellow-men. It was against this error that an apostle set himself, when he said, "he that loveth not his brother whom he hath seen, how doth he love God whom he hath not seen !"

For the improvement of society, then, we want a religion of society. We want a religion that comes home to the heart in all its affections; that touches all the relations of husbands and wives, parents and children, brothers and sisters, friends and associates. We want a religion for business and for amusement, for public office and private duty, for every social act that a man can perform—whether he gives his suffrage, or decides questions in a court of justice, or dispenses wealth in hospitality, or sits at the frugal board of humble poverty. We want a religion of kindness, and gentleness, and generosity, and candor, and modesty, and forbearance, and integrity, and self-respect, and mutual respect.

And let me add for my own defence, that we want a religion that will speak of all these things. I know very well, that some of the topics which I am discussing in this series of discourses, have fallen upon ears quite unaccustomed to hear such things from the pulpit. I know that some persons will consider many of these matters as having nothing to do with religion, and quite out of place in the pulpit. Most earnestly do I protest against this conclusion. What was the example of the great Master? Did he show any of this modern fastidiousness about preaching? How free and natural and various was his manner! how unrestrained his discourse! Though delivering words of inspiration, which were to be recorded for the instruction of all ages, though constantly engaged in the highest mission ever fulfilled on earth, though surrounded by the watchful eyes of jealous and formal Pharisees, yet there was no staid or affected solemnity in his discourse; he addressed himself to every case, availed himself of every incident around him; the homes of Judea rise before us as we read him; her rulers, her judges, her political condition, her social state, all have a place in his teachings and warnings;

there was not a topic within the range of moral influence to which he did not freely apply himself. Upon the authority of that great example, I claim a right here, in the Church of Christ, to speak of every thing that affects the moral, the vital welfare of the people. I have a contest here—with error, with sin and misery. I do not want any technical system of theology to tell me what they are. I know what they are. If I had never heard of any creed or system, I should just as well know what sin and misery are. I know what they are, and where they are. I see them, I feel them, all around me. And so seeing and feeling, I must have liberty to speak to them—to go where they are—to go wherever a free discourse upon them, will carry me; without stopping to inquire whether it is beyond the artificial pale of what is called a sermon. You may call the communication by whatsoever name it pleases you to characterize it. Say, if you choose, that it is *not* a sermon; call it an oration, a speech, an address; but if it answers its purpose, if it opens to you a wider range of duties, if it spreads the feeling of conscience over a larger field of life, I shall be satisfied. That heavy and dull word, *sermon*—with a thousand formal and lifeless pictures of association, stamped upon it—is, I fear, a shackle to many preachers—and a stone of stumbling to many hearers—and such an one as prevents many from hearing at all. Let it be a free, natural, manly address to the people, on their most vital interests; and it would be a different thing—different to many hearers—and very different with many preachers.

And such *is* the proper office of preaching. It *is* a simple address to the people, and upon their most vital interests. And in saying this, in defending the position which I now take, I am not wandering at all from the leading subject on which I am engaged—the influence of religion upon our social and national welfare. This is precisely what we want—that the preacher should come out from his set forms, his technical themes and monotonous tones, and speak freely of every thing—of every thing that morally concerns the people, as if he spoke for his life, or for the life of his friend. And it is for *more* than life that he speaks—for the welfare of a whole mighty people, and of unborn generations. For that welfare of the people never did, and never can, depend upon any thing but its virtue and piety. This is the only hope of future times. Yes, the presence of God must be among us—that pillar of cloud and pillar of fire must accompany the march of coming generations, or they will wander, and be lost—like the nations that have ceased to be.

My friends, our work on earth will soon be done. That mighty procession, ere long, will pass by our graves. What matter is it that we shall sleep in the dust, if our work is done and well done; if we have helped to raise up in those that come after us, a mighty host of the intelligent, the virtuous, the happy and free! This secured—and I see, in prospect, a land of peace and prosperity, a land of churches, and temples of science, and towers of strength; and the progress of the coming generations shows like a glorious triumph. Fair flowers shall be strewed in their path; bright omens shall cheer them on; they shall fulfil the prayers of the pious dead; they shall reward the tears and blood of martyred patriots; they shall accomplish the hopes of abased, broken, and prostrate humanity!

DISCOURSE X.

ON WAR.

ECCLESIASTES IX. 18. WISDOM IS BETTER THAN WEAPONS OF WAR.

MY subject this evening is war; and my purpose is to consider it as an immense social evil, and one which the rising spirit of modern society is likely to control. The connection between the two subjects is too obvious to be insisted on. But the system of war is connected with the great interests of society, in one way which, though less obvious, is, perhaps, more important than any other—I mean by the accumulation of national debts. War not only consumes the present possessions of mankind, but it uses up in advance, the property of future generations; it lays a burthen of taxes upon ages to come. How great this burthen is, and in how many ways it presses upon the social happiness and improvement of the world, are subjects, I think, which have not yet been sufficiently considered.

But before I enter upon the general subject of the social evils produced by war, let me undertake briefly to state the ground I take with regard to it.

I do not say then, in the first place, that war, under all circumstances, is wrong. A war, strictly defensive, I hold, is right. But very few wars, I believe, will be found to possess this character. Yet when such a case does occur, I do not believe that any nation is obliged to sit still, and see its fields ravaged and its homes violated, without lifting an arm in resistance. The right which nature gives us of personal self-defence, extends, I conceive, to the relations of states and kingdoms. If I may break the arm of a ruffian who lifts a club to destroy me, I may go farther, if necessary—I may break both his arms; and so long as he has a limb or a sense which can aid him to inflict upon me the evil he meditates, I may disable it; and thus I may go on defending myself, till the assailant himself is destroyed. So also may I defend others, whose life is committed to my protection. I should be a monster and not a man, if I could sit still, and see a savage enter my doors and murder my family before my eyes. But that savage or that ruffian, is precisely the representative of an invading army.

Nor do the Scriptures, justly construed, speak any other language. They command us indeed—but it is with the evident language of strong hyperbole—they command us, when smitten on one cheek, to turn the other, when robbed of our coat, to give our cloak, when compelled to go a mile, to go twain; and, in fine, not resist evil, but to return good for evil; the sum of which is, that we are not to *retaliate* evil. No reasonable person can suppose it to be literally meant, that we are to resist not at all; that when a rude assailant thrusts his hand in our face, we should not endeavor to put it aside; nay, that we should help him and give him every facility, to work his brutal will upon us. Angry retaliation is forbidden, not mild and manly self-defence; and this distinction applies alike to public wars and private conflicts.

In the next place, I do not deny, that war has sometimes developed powerful energies and heroic virtues. They furnish, indeed, but a slight compensation to humanity, for the sufferings of its slaughtered millions, they yield but a poor argument for war; yet their existence is not to be denied. The advocates of peace. I must think, have been too anxious to brand with dishonor, every thing connected with national conflicts. Let mere mercenary soldiership, let the rage of brutal passions in a battle, let the ordinary principles of martial ambition, be given up to their reprobation. But let not him who draws the sword for justice, when nothing else can secure justice, who offers his life for the freedom of a people, when no meaner sacrifice on its altar will suffice—let not him be denied the virtue of heroism. Let not him who firmly takes his station before an invading foe; who stands forward, and offers his breast a shield for helpless age and infancy, and the sanctity of a nation's homes—let not him be denied the praise of magnanimity. Of those, indeed, who make war their trade and boast and pleasure, a different judgment is to be formed.

But if a hostile army were landed on our shores, and I saw the youth of a peaceful village hurrying from their homes to prepare for the dread encounter of arms; if I saw them mustering on some green spot, which they had trodden lightly on many a gay and peaceful holiday, but which they now trod with the step of brave and beautiful manhood—abjuring all softness, all fondness—girding on the armor of battle— and sadly but sternly resolved to sacrifice that young life in its first freshness, to save their household altars from violation—if I saw them stand there, as they have stood in the valleys of Switzerland and on the plains of America, resolute and firm, with flushed cheek and unflinching brow, ready to do what God and their country should demand of them, I should feel that I looked upon a noble spectacle. And when that goodly band returned from the conflict, broken, alas! and shattered—loud and grateful should be a nation's welcome; and green should be the sod and wet with patriot tears, that covered the fallen; and high should rise the monument to tell to other days, of brave men who feared not to die for justice and freedom! Life indeed is dear, and the probation of human souls is not to be lightly shortened; but we are not to forget that that probation may sometimes be wrought out through blood, and that there are things dearer than life— things, to which life may be well sacrificed, whether in labors of philanthropy, in the fires of martyrdom, or in the strife of battle!

These are qualifications which I think we ought to make in considering the subject of war. It is not of a war of self-defence, or for the defence of freedom, that I am about to speak; but of war in its ordinary character, where the impulse is mutual national hatred or jealousy, and the object something far short of the freedom, safety or essential welfare of any people. The qualifications I have made, therefore, will very little affect the general estimate.

To that estimate, I now proceed, and particularly with reference to its bearing upon the social welfare of mankind.

But I wish to invite your attention, in the first place,

to the peculiar, the extraordinary character of this terrific dispensation of misery. The history of the human race presents us with many things to wonder at, with things that bear the character of extravagance, absurdity, and almost of insanity; but it presents us with nothing so amazing as the system of war.

It appears, sometimes, in surveying this part of history, as if the most settled and established principles were failing us; and we are tempted to ask—Is human happiness worth the price at which it is commonly estimated? Is it, in fact, worth any thing?

If it is, what are we to think of a vast and portentous science and system ordained for its destruction? Other calamities come upon us by means that are indirect and unforeseen, and often irresistible. They lie in wait for us, and smite us unawares; or they follow us at a distance, and overtake us at an hour when we think not. They steal upon the path of indolence; they rush upon the footsteps of improvidence; they overwhelm the victim of indulgence in the very house, the guarded home of his pleasures. But what destroying power, what angel of death, besides war, has gone forth in the sight of all men, and marked and measured out the field of destruction, and bared the human breast, shrinking, as it naturally does, from every wound—bared it to a shock like that of battle?

Other evils there are, and enough of them, to which the human race must submit. They lurk in the tainted breeze and in the most secret channels of life, in pains which no weapon inflicts, and in sufferings which no sympathy can relieve. But war is like none of these.

And even of those calamities which men bring upon themselves, not one, in the treatment of it, bears any comparison with this. The cup of excess has, indeed, slain as many as the sword of violence. But when was ever a *system* devised, to facilitate and extend the ravages of intemperance? When was ever a book written, when did human ingenuity ever deliberately set itself to plan the means by which intemperance could kill the greatest number; by which it could inflict a yet more insufferable degradation; by which it would widen and deepen the tide of misery? Nay, and even in those cases where mischief and misery have been reduced to a system and trade, the system has been taught, and the trade has been carried on, silently and secretly. Gaming-houses, and houses of yet darker ignominy, have been builded, it is true, and books have been written, to teach the desperate practice of the one, or to lure to the deadly haunts of the other; but over all these works of darkness, a veil like that of midnight has been drawn, to hide them from the public eye.

But there is one theatre, where death stands unveiled, and "destruction has no covering;" where they do their fearful work, not only designedly but openly; and with such credit, too, that that theatre is called the field of honor. There, men are not only destroyed in troops, in battalions and armies, but they are destroyed by system, and killed by science. Yes, and for this field, weapons are skilfully prepared, and actors are adroitly trained; and that, too, at establishments which, even in a time of peace, cost tenfold more than all the universities and hospitals and beneficent asylums in the world. War, in fact, is among the recognized arts that engage the attention of mankind. But while, of all other arts, the design is, to save and to bless, to improve and to delight; this is emphatically the art of destruction; to crush and to kill, to lay waste kingdoms, to spread havoc and distress among nations—this is its chosen work. Were the art brought to still greater perfection, to that horrible perfection indicated by some late experiments, and were some machinery, some "infernal engine" invented, by whose tremendous discharge a whole army might be destroyed in a moment, success in tactics like this, might open the eyes of the world to the enormity of the martial principle. Then might war, at last, after having for ages ranged through the earth, desolating empires and destroying generations, become its own destroyer.

But no such fortunate catastrophe has yet come. Still war rages, with a violence only too impotent either to satisfy the passions of men on the one hand, or, on the other, to destroy itself. If we must judge from the history of the last fifty years, civilization has not weakened its power. If it has done something to tame the fierceness of anger and revenge, it has more than balanced the account by the invention of deadlier engines. Europe never saw such bloody fields of battle, as within the last fifty years.

But let us further and more distinctly, contemplate the immediate evils and sufferings produced by war. The great difficulty about this subject is, that no such contemplation is likely to be given to it. Nobody seems to stand in the relation to it which is necessary to a fair and full estimate. From those engaged in war, blinded or absorbed by it, its true character is hidden; and to those in the bosom of peace, the contemplation of bloody conflicts and routed armies is scarcely more affecting, than to behold the dashing clouds and broken fragments of a dispersing storm in the sky; it is far off, and belongs to another element. But let a man bring home to him one single instance from that awful and uncounted aggregate of horrors, and how can he be unmoved by it! Death! come when and where it may, be it on the bed of down, or on the supporting bosom of affection—it is an awful visitation. The agonies and shudderings of nature proclaim it to be the great trial-hour of human destiny. But that hour, in the hot assault, or amidst the lingering agonies of the battle-field, or where the groans of the crowded hospital are its harbingers—how does it come? No pillow of down, no supporting arms are there, to receive the victim; no kind voice speaks to him; no noiseless step of affection approaches, nor looks of love hang over him, like a pitying angel's countenance; but he goes down—man as he is, with all a man's sensibility, it may be—with all a man's ties to earthly home and love—he goes down amidst groans and execrations and horrors, darker than the shadow of death that is passing over him. This is but one death, such as war visits upon the human race, and yet it would not be in human nature actually to witness one such instance, without the most agonizing desire to afford relief. But now what facts are those, which the history of war unfolds to us! The single campaign of Bonaparte in Russia, carried death, and such death, not to one thousand, nor to five thousand, nor to fifty thousand, but to five hundred thousand human beings. Alexander and Cesar, it is computed, caused, each of them, the death of two millions of the human race; and the wars of Bonaparte bring up the whole number of victims sacrificed to the ambition of THREE

MEN, to six millions! Let us look at it. Six millions of human beings!—the aged, the young, the manly and strong, the fair and lovely, the imploring mother, the innocent child—and death, dealt to each one, without discrimination and without mercy! Six millions!—a number equal to half the population of this whole country. Strike off, then, half of the territory and people of this fair and happy land, and suppose them to be sacrificed one by one, their possessions, their goods and their lives, with every species of cruelty and insult, and with the perpetration of every nameless horror; and to whom sacrificed? To but three ministers in the dark kingdom of war! But this is only an item, a single passage in the history of its fearful dominion. There have been in Christendom, since the reign of Constantine, nearly *three hundred wars!** What a mass of calamities, of rapine and violence, of crime and misery, is included within the brief description of these three words—what waste of the treasures of nations, what wo in the abodes of millions, it passes all human power to calculate. But all this, nevertheless, has been experienced, though it cannot be calculated or imagined. *Human hearts have felt it all.* Not one drop of this ocean of ills, but has fallen, a burning drop, upon nerves and fibres that have quivered with agony at its touch. Fourteen centuries of war, and thousands of bloody battles, recorded in that brief description, are but the record of human, of individual sorrows and tears and groans.

I wish it were possible for me to make the case more apparent and palpable. That beings, possessed

* See Third Report of the Committee of Inquiry instituted by the Massachusetts Peace Society.

with the most exquisite sensibility to grief and pain, should be able to look on, calmly or patiently, while such things are done and suffered, only proves that the reality of the evil is lost to them in its vastness. Any wound inflicted in our sight, any pain depicted in the countenance of another, " any annoyance" in any " precious sense," fills us with solicitude and sympathy. The mother, in the midnight hour, steals to the couch of her child, if but a harder breathing invade " the innocent sleep." The child hangs over the couch of infirm and reverend age, with a filial piety that counts every pain, as an holy thing. The friend sits through the live-long night, with watchful eye and ear, to anticipate the slightest want of a sick and suffering associate. These are but the dictates of humanity. Where are those dictates, when a system is fostered and honored in the world, which tears shrieking children from their arms to be murdered by a brutal soldiery, which tramples the aged and venerable head beneath the feet of lawless strangers, and from whose wide theatre are for ever rising groans that are unpitied, and cries that bring no aid. " On one side," says an eye-witness to the horrors of the sack of Moscow, in 1812, " on one side, we saw a son carrying a sick father; on the other, women who poured the torrent of their tears on the infants whom they clasped in their arms. Old men overwhelmed by grief still more than by years, weeping for the ruin of their country, lay down to die, near the houses where they were born. No respect was paid to the nobility of blood, to the innocence of youth, or to the tears of beauty."*—" It is impossible," says another eye-witness, one who saw the wounded in the

* Labaume, p. 209 and 213.

hospitals after the battle of Waterloo, " it is impossible to conceive of their sufferings. Turn which way I might, I encountered every form of entreaty from those, whose condition left no need of words, to stir compassion. I know not," he says, " what notions my feeling countrymen have of thirty thousand wounded men, thrown into a town and its environs. They still their compassionate emotions, by subscriptions; but what avails this to those, who would exchange gold for a bit of rag to bind up their smarting wounds. My heart sickens at the contemplation," he says in conclusion, " and I am obliged to turn away from this picture of human misery, caused by pride, ambition, a love of military glory, and the folly of mankind in paying adoration to their destroyers. Would not angels weep at such a scene as this? But is this all? Ah! no. Each of these dead or wounded soldiers had a mother, who had watched over his cradle, and had attended him in his sickness, and shed over him the tears of maternal solicitude. Many had wives and lovers, to whom they were dearer than the light of the sun. Many had children, who looked to them for support and protection. We may rationally suppose, that for every man who was killed or wounded in this deadly conflict, the hearts of at least ten persons—parents, wives, children, brothers and sisters—were lacerated. Oh! what hecatombs of sacrifices on the bloody altar of Moloch! How long will mankind continue to be accessary to such crimes, by bestowing praises upon their perpetrators! How long will it be, ere every human being will deem it his imperious and solemn duty, to disseminate the principles of Peace and extend her empire!"*

* Charles Bell.

But let us pass now from immediate evils to those which, although more remote, are not less destructive to the welfare of society.

In contemplating the progress of civilization, there is one fact, which deserves more attention, I apprehend, than it has yet received ; and that is the severity of human labor. The advancement of society from a state of barbarism is, of course, marked by growing and more regular industry. To a certain extent, this is, doubtless, natural, and accordant with the designs of Providence and the general welfare of men. But there is a point beyond which labor is not good and ought not to be necessary ; and that the condition of multitudes, both in Europe and America, is far beyond this point, cannot, I think, be doubted. It has been maintained, on a careful calculation, that all the conveniences of civilized life might be produced, if society would divide the labor equally among its members, by each individual being employed in labor two hours during the day.* I will not undertake to say whether this estimate is correct ; but I am certain that ten, twelve and fourteen hours, each day, of hard work, cannot be necessary to the proper ends of society, in its natural and healthful state. Yet this is what is required of the mass not only of adult laborers, but of their children too, in many cases, barely to support life. The effects, especially, in the manufacturing districts of Europe, are most deplorable. The evidence on this point, before the British parliament, three or four years since, presented a picture of desolating and crushing toil, and especially of children, pale, emacia-

---

* Goodwin's Political Justice.

ted, trembling from exhaustion, and bereft of every trait of childhood, and almost of humanity, that was enough to make the heart sick with the contemplation; and all the mitigation that the wisdom and generosity of a great people could devise for these helpless and miserable beings, cursed—I had almost said—cursed with existence, was, that they should not be compelled under the age of sixteen, to work more than ten hours a day. But the evil of excessive toil, is not confined to the manufactories. No one can travel through the agricultural districts of Europe generally, without seeing that it is not only in "the sweat of his brow," but in the sadness of his brow, that man earns his bread. The pressure is, doubtless, lighter in this country, but still, I believe, it is too hard. I concern myself here with no questions about combinations of laborers, to diminish the hours of work; I do not undertake to say, what may be necessary or right, in the existing state of things; but speaking in general, of what I conceive to be the intentions of Providence and the capacities of man, I aver with confidence, that there is more hard labor in this country, than consists with the true welfare and improvement of society.

If this could be doubted, it would be sufficient to say, and this is the point to which I wish to come, that there are causes in operation enhancing human toil, which are immense, which are unnatural, and which never ought to have existed. Passing by others, my business now is, to consider a single cause—the burthen of debt, that is to say, which past wars have accumulated upon the present generation, and upon many, we may add, that are to come after it.

War subtracts from the amount of productive labor.

the strength of all who are engaged in its actual service, and of all who are engaged in providing arms and munitions for it. In barbarous ages, when nations fought out their own battles and so finished the account, this was only a loss to the nation and to the world, for the time being. But in process of time, men found that they could not fight enough on their own account, and they brought in the resources of after times to assist them. It was left for the progress of civilization, to fall upon the expedient of creating national debts ; that is, of hiring out the labor of posterity to pay the price of blood. Some idea of the extent of this tremendous assessment, may be formed from a single item. The wars which grew out of the French Revolution, commencing in 1793 and ending in 1815, cost Great Britain alone, eleven hundred millions of pounds sterling;* and a large proportion of this stupendous amount now exists in the form of a national debt, and the interest of it is annually levied upon the entire industry of the kingdom. In addition to this, England and all Europe are supporting immense standing armies. Go where you will, and the soldier presents himself—a cormorant that is eating up the substance of the land, and adding nothing to its resources. There he stands, idly leaning against some bastion or gate-way, while the farmer in the neighboring field, must redouble his labors to support him. I complain not of the soldier, who is, after all, the most miserable of these parties ; insomuch, that I have heard it stated, as the opinion of a distinguished military commander in Europe, that war itself is not so

* Lowe's Present State of England.

fatal to life as peace—that ennui destroys more men than the sword; I do not complain, then, of the soldier who is the creature of the state; I do not complain of the state which is, perhaps, obliged thus to stand on its defence; but I charge the system, the war-system, which taxes and tasks the industry of one part of the world for the purpose of destroying the other, with stupendous injustice and folly.

Let us dwell a moment longer, on the extent and nature of this taxation.

War appears to be far off from us; and it is far off from most men; for the field of actual military operations, in almost any country, is comparatively small. A battle is fought at a distance, and the groan that it sends through the world soon dies away; and men think of it no more, but as a matter of history—a matter with which they have no concern. They forget that the war, the battle, comes to them in another shape, in the form of burthensome imposts; that it comes and writes its account on every threshold, and on every table whether rich or poor, in the civilized world. For every article, whether of convenience or luxury, which is produced in Europe, the consumer, *of whatever country*, is obliged not only to remunerate the labor employed upon it, but to pay a heavy additional per cent in taxes; and far the largest portion of these taxes are levied by the military system. The language of every military government, not only to its own citizens, but to all the world is this; "you must not only pay the industrious among us, but you must help to support our idle and expensive soldiery;" that is to say, "you must work harder, because we have a great many among us who do not work, and then, too, they must have arms and munitions and fortifications, which is another heavy item in the account." "Does this taxation do us any good?" the world asks. And the answer is, "none at all." It contributes not to the manufacture of any necessaries or comforts or luxuries of life, but only to the fabrication of warlike weapons—of "cold and bare steel"—of that which gives you nothing to eat nor to drink, nor to wear, nor to employ for any useful purpose. And again, it contributes nothing to the support of any useful class—of learned men, or instructors of the people, or artists to delight them; but only to the training of an order of men, who for your pains may, any day, be turned upon you like tigers and bloodhounds, to rend and tear you in pieces. And now look at the pressure of this system. It is a burthen upon every thing to which men can attach value. It is a tax upon all the possessions and pleasures of life, upon food and raiment, upon every element of nature, upon the very light of heaven. It presses upon you, and upon me. But for this, our labors might contribute in much greater measure to our comfort and independence; in a measure very seriously and sensibly affecting the happiness of our lives. It is a burthen which presses heavily on the rich; it is a burthen which crushes the poor. It is urging universal toil to excess; it is grinding thousands and millions down to the dust: and in this way, perhaps, it has occasioned more of the extraordinary intemperance of modern times, than any other cause. If this tax were direct and specific, if it were not covered up under the names of excise and impost and revenue; if it were, in so many words, a war-tax, it would speak a language to which the world could not be indifferent. It would be a voice of blood crying from the earth and air, from sea and land, to which men could not close their ears.

But consider for one moment longer, I beseech you, the nature of this assessment. In the name of heaven, I solemnly ask, what are its conditions? What is the tenor of the bond, that is to settle up the account of an expensive war? A mighty debt is incurred; and it presses upon the already hard and exhausting labor of thousands and ten thousands, with vexatious and wearing importunity. What is the valuable consideration which is to reconcile to their lot, the worn and weary victims of this toil and poverty? What is the language to them of the war-system? It says to them—this is what it says—" I will raze to the ground your pleasant habitations; I will slay your sons in battle; I will give up your daughters to accursed violation; I will spare no store of your gains, no treasure of your hearts, no delight of your eyes; and when I have done all this, you shall pay me for what I have done; and to satisfy the debt, you shall come under bondage to me, for a portion of every day, during the remainder of your lives. Nay, and more than this shall you give; more than the toil of your weary limbs and the sweat of your aching brow. The light from your window, and the pottage from your cold hearth; the sorrow of your suffering wives and children, the tears of your half-clad and starving families, shall you give to pay the mighty debt."

It is sometimes asked, whether wars can ever be done away. I would ask in return, if the very argument I have now used does not show that they can, and must, and shall be done away.

There is, I know, a vague and dreamy notion possessing some minds, that war, somehow or other, is a matter of necessity, that it results from the ordination of nature, that the law of force is the law of the whole creation, and must be submitted to. Among animals, they say, the stronger destroys the weaker, and man but conforms to the principle. But the instance of animal natures comes far short of supporting this argument. The animal destroys when and where, he has need of food; and when he destroys without this motive, he is accounted mad. But what should we think, if the animals of one whole country were banded in battle array against those of another? The world would stand aghast at such madness, seizing the tribes of irrational creatures. And yet, what in them, would be a horrible madness, is, in man, honor, courage, skill; nay more, and is held to be among the necessary and irresistible tendencies of his nature.

"But," it may be said, "whether natural and necessary or not, war has always existed; it has been in the world, since the creation; it has become the habit of the world; and it cannot be done away. There will always be national controversies; there will always be selfish and vindictive passions at work in the human breast; and, in short, while man is man, there will always be war."

Do we live in an age, when the antiquity of an evil is held to be a good argument for its perpetuity? Arbitrary rule, despotism, in one form or another, is as old as the world. The slave-trade has existed for ages. The most ancient histories, are histories of ignorance and barbarism. Does the world sit down, and quietly acquiesce in the conclusion that these things must exist for ever? Civilization itself must have been held in check, by such a fatal concession to antiquity.

Civilization is advancing ; it has as yet, by no means, reached its limit. Is not this a sufficient answer to the whole argument? One barbarous custom after another has yielded to the progress of knowledge ; why may not war, like the tournament and the ordeal by fire, cease to engage the respect of mankind? The habits of the world are not too strong to be controverted and corrected. But there is another point on which I intended especially to insist. There is *one habit* of the world, signalizing more than any other the present age, which, if it continues to gain strength, is almost certain to effect, sooner or later, the abolition of war. And that is the habit, which the people of all civilized countries are now acquiring, *of looking soberly and steadfastly to their own real interests.* Let them look at these, and resolutely pursue them, and they must ere long banish the horrible custom which, every century, costs the lives of millions, and brings distress and anguish upon millions more. War may be the interest of ambitious rulers, but it never can be the interest of the body of the people.

In connection with this point, let it be distinctly considered, that public opinion is becoming the grand and paramount law of nations. It has always had great force. It has had great force even in the most despotic states. But what distinguishes the present crisis is, that public opinion is becoming the absolute and universal law. The aim of all liberal minds, every where, is to make government the very expression of an enlightened public opinion. So it ought to be.

They ought to be represented by a government, their feelings and wishes ought to be respected, whose interests, whose life and property and happiness, are intrusted to that government to be benefited or injured by it. They ought to judge, their opinion ought to prevail, who are themselves the parties interested. But, now, what is public opinion? Not the opinion of rulers, not the opinion of military men, nor the opinion of a few whose interest it might be, or rather who might think it their interest, to plunge a nation into war; but it is the collected opinion of the whole mass of a people; it is an opinion to which both sexes contribute an influence, which springs from all the relations and endearments of society; it is an opinion, whose dwelling is the happy home, whose altar is the domestic hearth-stone. And is it possible, when this public opinion arrives at its proper ascendancy, that nations shall wish to lay open their peaceful villages and their happy homes to the invasion of fire and sword, and all the horrors of war? Is it possible, that they will choose to suffer all this to gratify an insane, unnatural and merciless ambition—which builds itself up upon their destruction; whose monuments are heaps of the slain; whose tower of pride is built of human bones, and cemented with the blood of brethren and the tears of widows and orphans; whose shrine of glory, like that of Moloch, for ever demands human—none but human victims? Can men, when once they begin to think, bear all this, and above all can they bear it, when they see that it answers no useful purpose, when they find that negociation is just as necessary after the conflict as it was before, when they find that nothing is gained for abstract justice, and every thing is lost to social life, to vital prosperity, to domestic happiness. Look at two nations dwelling in amity with each other; each land filled with cities and temples, with smiling villages and peaceful dwellings, the homes of centuries. Behold the thousand paths of industry and enjoyment, whether upon the hill-side or upon the gliding river's bosom, thronged with the prosperous and happy. Hear the song of the reaper in the harvest-field answering joyously to the call of the herdsman in the pasture; and if a sigh ariseth by the way-side, mark the ready ear of the kind and gentle to listen to it. Survey, in short, the lot, and be it, that it is the mingled lot of life, joyous or sad, but ever dear and holy. Trace, in fine, the invisible bond of sympathy, that binds home to home and heart to heart, and gaze upon the broad land and its many shores, where the light of Peace falls upon every field and every wave to hallow it, as it were, with the serenest and the sweetest smile of heaven. Now, I ask, if, for a controversy about a tract of land, or a contested right in a fishery, or an affront offered to an ambassador, the people of these countries—not their rulers as independent of them—but if the people, expressing their will through governments of their own choice, can be disposed to enter into war; to drive the ploughshare of ruin, through all these peaceful and happy scenes; to turn the joyous songs of ten thousand dwellings into sighing and wailing; to plant the bloody step on every green turf, and to thrust the violating hand into the retreats of every domestic sanctuary. It cannot be. Men cannot be for ever so insane, as to treat their dearest interests in this manner. At any rate, if the tendencies of public sentiment, at this day, hold out any warrant, if the hopes of philanthropy and piety are not mere illusions, if the ways of God's providence are not darkened with a cloud that is never to clear up, the time must come, the time will come, when wars will cease.

As certainly as popular governments are to rise in the world, wars are to decline. And they are to rise: I say not in what form, but in some form by which they shall express the will of the people. If there ever was a tendency in human affairs, the tendency of all opinion, of all moral action, of all instruments and agencies in the world, is to this result. And when it is obtained, it may be relied on for the establishment of some new and more rational mode of settling national controversies. I say not what it may be in form. It may be by arbitration, by resorting to umpires, or by creating a Court of Nations. But whatever be the mode, I look to an intelligent and moral public opinion for the fulfilment of that great prophecy, that men " shall beat their swords into ploughshares, and their spears into pruning-hooks, that nation shall not lift up sword against nation, and they shall learn war no more."

DISCOURSE XI.

ON POLITICAL MORALITY.

PROVERBS XIV. 34. Righteousness exalteth a nation, but sin is a reproach to any people.

There is a branch of morality, seldom discussed in the pulpit, too seldom discussed out of it, which I shall propose for your consideration this evening; it is political morality. It will not be thought, I trust, that any apology is due from the pulpit for taking up this subject. If the duty which one man owes to another, then the duty which each man owes to a whole country, is worthy of the most religious consideration: and the more so, because it is not only an important but a neglected subject.

Indeed, one is tempted to ask—scarcely with irony—is there any such subject, any such thing, as political morality? There is a law of nations, binding them to perform certain duties to each other. There is a law of the land, binding upon the citizens of each particular nation. There is a law of morality, penetrating deeper into the life and heart, than judicial law can go. But is there any thing of this, or any thing like this, applicable to politics? On the contrary, are not political relations entirely severed from the obligations of conscience? Into almost every part of a man's life conscience may look, ay, and with an eye of authority; but with the part which he acts as a politician, is it not true, that conscience has no business whatever? As a *man*, he is bound to be a good man; and in that character, he is amenable to the judgment of God. As a *man*, he is bound to be honest, candid, high-minded and true; but would it not be quite preposterous to demand this of him, as a president, a governor, a diplomatist, a party-man, an opposition man? In a party conclave, you can easily conceive that questions may be discussed on grounds of *policy;* but would it not be quite surprising, if not ridiculous, for a man to get up and say, "is this right?—is it conscientious?—is it a high-minded course?" Would not the look of silent astonishment, in such a conclave say, as plainly as any thing can say—"that is *another* question?" "Speak not evil one of another," is a holy precept; but can it be that it has any relation to newspapers? Especially in a warm party contest, as in a battle, are not all laws of mutual forbearance and kindness, abrogated; and is not the only consideration then, how to strike down an adversary? May not a man do things and avow principles then, which would disgrace him in the ordinary walks of life? May he not violate the law, by bringing minors and non-residents to vote? May he not give and take bribes? Nay, may he not lift his hand to heaven, and perjure himself in such a cause? In fine, will not the end sanctify the means? It is a very bad principle every where else; but will it not do in politics?

The great modern master of dramatic representation shows his nice observation of human nature, when in a case of false swearing, he makes a man say, "I will swear to any thing: all is fair when it comes to an oath *ad litem.*" That technical, and to him, unmeaning phrase, is probably introduced by the writer, as serving the purpose of a salvo to his conscience; as helping to blind him to the iniquity of the transaction. And so it is with the technical word, politics. And men say, or act as if they said, " all is fair when it comes to politics." Even in case of the oath, wherewith a man perjures himself at the ballot—what is it, that he says to himself, or that the partisan tempter, says to him? "Oh! it is nothing but an electioneering oath!" In other words, *all is fair when it comes to politics.*

A part of the reason here involved, doubtless—that is to say, a part of the reason why politics possess this morally loose character, lies in the vagueness of the term. The words, trade, bargain—or the words, charity, philanthropy—have a definite meaning affixed to them. But men cannot so readily *tell* what they mean by the word, politics; and to this subject, therefore, it is less easy to apply the principle, of morality.

Another reason, having a similar tendency to blind the mind to the necessary moral discriminations in politics, is to be found in the unusual modes and forms devised, for the expression of public opinion. If a man is false to his thought, when he professes to convey his thought in conversation, he at once feels that he is dishonest. He sees at once the contradiction between what he says and what he thinks. But when he gives his vote at the ballot-box, or causes it to be recorded in a legislative assembly, it is comparatively an artificial act, and he does not so clearly perceive its character and relations. He does, indeed, in that act, profess to declare an opinion—he does profess to declare his mind—but what is it, in *form*, to him? It is a vote, not an averment; it is saying, " yea" or " nay," not saying, " I believe," or " I do not believe."

There is another consideration to be stated, of the same general and dangerous tendency. The action of men in masses always lessens the sense of individual responsibility. Thus, a mob will do things, which no individual of that mob would ever think of doing alone: and this, not because he *could* not do it alone; for any man can break windows, or shoot down his adversary in the streets; the truth is, the man loses in the crowd the sense of personal responsibility. And so it is with political combinations. A private man, a merchant or a lawyer, would feel degraded, if he should offer a bribe to induce his neighbor to express a favorable opinion of him personally, or, if he should threaten him with a loss of business for failing to do so; but he will resort to either of these methods, for procuring the same expression of opinion towards some public man—some politician, or party-man.

I have thus been lead, briefly to state some of the causes of that separation of morality from politics, which obtains to a fearful extent in the public mind. No more than a bare statement of them is necessary to show, that they lack all proper grounds of justification for the result which they have produced. The way is open, therefore, for an attempt to settle some principles in the science of political morality.

Political morality may be considered in relation, first, to particular actions which it enjoins or forbids, and secondly, to the general principles which it sanctions or disclaims.

Under the first head is to be ranked, the duty of giving a vote at the elections. I hold, that it is the duty of every legally qualified person in the country to vote. And let it not be thought, that this point is any ways well settled in the public mind. Expedient it may have been thought, in some party emergency, that every citizen should vote; and at such a crisis, that expediency may have been much talked of; but all this is a very different thing from a sense of duty, which pervades all times. The emergency passes, and this shallow feeling of expediency passes away with it. It is the bond of duty to which I appeal.

There are reasons for it, founded in the very nature and meaning of the action. Suffrage is the very basis of our government. The government in this country is committed to the whole people. Every man has a share in it. Every man exerts an influence upon it, either by his action or by his neglect. Can this be a case, then, in which a man is allowed to stand neutral?

In theory, the government here represents the whole people. The practice should conform to that theory. To every man among us, a certain political trust is committed. Every man should quit himself of that trust. If the administration of our affairs is corrupt or incompetent, the people is to blame—the whole people. The blame is to be shared among them all. But especially does it attach to those who say that the government is bad, and will do nothing to make it better. "Why stand ye idle, all the day?" may it well be said to such. Why stand ye idle all the election-day? When, on such a day, ye see the thousand and the million contributions that are made to swell the mighty stream of public opinion and government, why stand ye idly gazing upon it, as if it did not concern you? As well might ye stand idly gazing upon the streams collecting in the hills above your dwelling, which at any moment may come down, and sweep its foundations from beneath you.

If it be said that that is unlikely to happen, then let me say in turn, and to keep the figure for a moment, that those streams *will* come down, either to fertilize or to waste the land; and they *shall* be the power, either good or bad, to grind the very corn that feeds your families and your neighborhoods. If government does not make the corn *grow*, yet it touches every thing that affects its value—labor, price, manufacture—yes, it touches the very staff of life; and that by many means, by many statutes, besides "corn-laws." Government, then, is something that comes near to us. We greatly err, if we suppose, as many seem to do, that it is something factitious and far off. It comes near to us—to our warehouses and our firesides, to our granaries and our kneading-troughs. Revenues and tariffs, banking-laws and the monetary system—these terms may sound like a strange speech to the mass of the people; but they represent, and they vitally affect, their daily and home-bred interests.

And these interests, I say again, are committed to the whole people. They are directly affected by legislation certainly; and legislation comes from the whole people. It is not with us as if our rulers were hereditary. Then we might fold our arms, and say, "it is none of our concern." And why? Because in that case, we should *not* be the governors. But now we *are* the governors of the country. And if any portion of us—if, for instance, a tenth part of our population refuse to give due attention to this duty, it is as if the chosen governors of the country should withhold a tenth part of the talent or of the time due to their office.

I do not demand of any one, that he should be an eager and noisy politician. I only demand that he should vote; that he should, no matter how quietly, thus express his interest and take his share in the common weal—thus assume, what he professes to prize so highly, the privilege and duty of self-government. But I am obliged to say, and I hardly know whether it is with greater mortification or the more profound concern, that the very persons among us who are most apt to neglect this duty, are the very persons most of all bound to fulfil it—I mean the rich and the educated. It is a statement most fearful in its bearing on the prospects of the country, but it is true. I do not deny, that many of both classes are found at their posts, when their country calls upon them. But there are rich men, who are too much engrossed with their business to give their vote—too much engrossed with gain to attend to their duty; or who, perchance, are too fastidious, to expose their persons amidst the throng at the polls. And there are educated men, who are so much disgusted with party strifes, that they will have nothing to do with them. They give them up, as they scornfully say, to demagogues and brawlers. And so very simple are these sensible and refined persons, that they do not seem to perceive when they say this, that they are giving up their *country* to demagogues and brawlers. Yes, their *country!* And here it is, too, on the very side where it most needs support, that its legitimate defenders on that side, are opening their ranks to the onset and the rushing crowd of popular ignorance and party violence. " Fools and blind !"—would it be said, should they be overwhelmed by that crowd—"that did not perceive that they too had interests at stake—that very property, that very repose, which they so much valued. For when the crowd came, what did it find ? Not good and manly citizens at their post ; but only certain money-changers in their counting-houses, or silken loungers in drawing-rooms, or certain learned monks in their cloisters !" I do not fear any such violent and vandal incursion of popular ignorance and passion ; and yet, *if* any thing is to overwhelm the country, it will be this. If there is any one thing more to be feared than any other—any one overshadowing peril to our political institutions, it is, that *numerical force* will overbalance the *intellectual and moral strength* of the country. I say again, that I do not fear it—except with that fear which bringeth safety. I do not fear it, because I trust that events are teaching intelligent and educated men their duties ; and because I believe, that into the numerical force, otherwise so much to be dreaded, there is a constantly increasing, and will be a still larger, infusion of intelligence.* But if it shall be otherwise ; if population is to outstrip education ; if *numbers*, and not *principles*, are to be the watch-words and war-cries of party, and the governing powers of the state, the dreaded result is inevitable.

In connection with this topic, there is a question often raised concerning a certain educated class in the

---

* Not in cities perhaps, from temporary causes; but in the country at large.

country, to which I shall give a moment's attention. This question is—ought the clergy to vote? And to this question, I firmly answer, yes; always and every where. This is a right which they ought never to suffer to be drawn into debate. It is enough that they are, by public opinion, nearly disfranchised, and that absurdly enough, of their natural right to hold offices under the government.* We hear much of freedom, and invasions of freedom, in this country. What would any other respectable class of citizens say, if they were excluded from all active share and interest in the government? They would fill the country with their complaints, and the world would be called upon to look at this monstrous anomaly, in our free institutions. I shall be at no pains here to say, that the clergy probably do not desire public employment. Whether they do or not, is not the question. I say that they have a right to it, as much as any other class. And the frequent language of reproach and satire heard, on every assumption of this right, I hold to be disgraceful to a free press and people. But the question now is about suffrage. And on this point, I maintain, that for the clergy to cast their vote with the rest of their fellow-citizens, at the elections, is not only their right, but their bounden duty. Nor should their congregations, in manly candor, ever desire to deprive them of this right, or to dictate to them in regard to the discharge of this duty. This is not a country—a republican government is the last in the world, that can afford to part with the influence of a large and intelligent body of its citizens.

* They are so by law in some of the States.

I have dwelt longer than I intended upon this first and foundation principle of our political morality—that which requires every legally qualified citizen to give his vote at the elections. There is another duty coincident with this, which is too obvious to call for much argument, and yet too often violated, to be passed over in silence; and that is the duty of giving an *honest* vote.

Every citizen in this primary act that gives its being and character to the government, is bound to express his honest conviction. The vote demands the contribution of his mind, of his judgment, of his patriotism and fidelity to the common weal. The citizen is the real governor. And if the elected ruler is forbidden, by every just principle, to swerve from an honest purpose towards the public good, so is the ruling elector. And he who surrenders his judgment or conscience to private interest, or the mere dictation of a party; he who accepts a bribe or offers one; he who, in the ballot, smothers his own conviction, or attempts to coerce anothers, is perjured in the holiest rites with which he swears upon his country's altar.

The familiarity with which certain transactions at the polls are spoken of—yes, palpable infractions of the law with regard to the age, residence, and where a property qualification is required, the property of voters—the freedom with which parties charge these practices upon each other after an election—are facts of evil omen. And the common defence set up for them is, if possible, worse than the things themselves. The country, we are constantly told, is in danger; every nerve must be strained, every means used, to carry certain measures; the opposite party leave no means, however flagitious and desperate, untried, and we must meet them on their own ground—must fight them with their own weapons. Admirable doctrine! that goes around the whole circuit of parties, and lends a handle to each one, wherewith to push on the cumulative argument for dishonesty and intrigue! The country in danger!—and to be saved by corruption! by bribery, false swearing and the violated law! The nation sick and prostrate by the tampering of some ignorant administration with its health and vigor—and how to be cured? By the canker and the gangrene that are eating out its very vitals!

Away with such paltering and paltry arguments for the expedient against the right! If it must be so, I had rather my country were destroyed by truth, than saved by falsehood. I would rather it were ruined by virtue, than redeemed by corruption. But do not the very terms of this statement show, that it is not so? No; "honesty is the best policy," for man or nation, for individual or party. But if honesty is any where to be demanded or expected, it is in the first act that gives its character to the government—the *elections*. Admit any false principle there, and what, in consistency, can you look for, but a corrupt government? Will you poison the fountain-head, and expect the streams to be pure?

I insist, then, that the elector shall be honest. He should no more dare to be false to his own mind, false to his conscience, in giving his vote, than he would in giving his word. His vote *is* his word; and the only word, perhaps, that he *can* speak in the great ear of the nation. If that word is a lie, he sacrifices, as far as in him is, the right government and rectitude of the country.

We have now attended to one branch of our specific political duties, the morality of elections—binding every citizen to vote, and every citizen to vote honestly. The other department of specific morality, embraces the duties of the elected—of legislators and magistrates.

And here I must confess, that the tone of public sentiment on this subject—the admission almost universal, that legislators and magistrates when elected will act, and must be expected to act, for sinister ends—is one at which I tremble. If this charge were the offspring of mere party recrimination, I could understand it, and could look upon it with comparative indifference. But the truth is, that the charge has been bandied about, between parties, till it has become resolved into a general maxim, or a maxim, at least, of frightful prevalence among the people. If the allegation were only, that every administration is liable to be corrupt, and does sometimes lean to party ends—against such a fact, arising from the weakness of human nature, I could bear up. But when, by four out of five of all the men you meet, of all parties, it is sapiently or carelessly said, that " all is corrupt in the government ;" that " in Congress, of course, every thing is decided by party ;" that " the Capitol is but a scene of intrigue and corruption ;" then is public virtue not only shaken, but it is sapped to the very foundation. And if something does not arrest this tendency of public sentiment, it is not too much to fear, that it will whelm the whole fabric in ruins. If virtue in a public man, is a thing altogether out of the calculation of his constituents ; if he is allowed to look upon his place only as a sphere of personal and party selfishness ; if single-minded principle, if single-hearted truth for the country, is thus mocked at by the people, and its possessor is lead to regard himself, as a prodigy or a fool for his honesty, what is to save the state—all the barriers of virtue broken down—from overwhelming corruption?

Is this general proscription of public men, just? I deny that it is. If it were, then indeed, I should have nothing to say, but that which I shall directly attempt to say, in discharge of *my* conscience with regard to such high and heaven-daring iniquity. But I deny that the common, the too easy allegation against public men, is true. It may suit the impatience of disappointed partisans, or the envy of inferior men, or the vanity of the all-knowing ones, or the too deep and habitual distrust of the national mind, to bring these sweeping accusations; but I am persuaded, that there are men in our high places that ought to stand acquitted of them—men to whom they are a heinous and cruel injustice. I know that all are *not* corrupt; that all are *not* gone out of the way. Mistaken they may be; prejudiced they may be; it is but human, to err; but they are not all to be set down as dishonest men. I know this as well as I can know any fact of such a nature. I know it, because I know the men; or because, I know the character they have sustained, and still sustain, among their friends and neighbors. It is obviously, a most arbitrary and unwarrantable proceeding, to charge upon public men as such, a worse character than upon the communities they represent; to hold them, in virtue of their elevation, to be bad men; to convert the shield of a goodly reputation, the moment the insignia of office are stamped upon it, into a target for universal abuse and opprobrium.

But, on the other hand, when this treatment is deserved, when a man is false to the high trusts of magistracy and legislation, when he makes of the greater trust only the greater argument for infidelity to the common weal, there is no language of reprobation too strong to visit upon him. Called by a whole district, perhaps, a whole country, to guard and promote its welfare—presiding, alone or jointly, over the affairs and destinies of a whole people—each one's interest involved, each one's interest dear—and the interests of thousands, perhaps, of millions, uniting to lay upon him the bond of his great office—if he can shake it from him easily, if he can snap it asunder as tow, and cast it aside as the rubbish of old and out-worn morality, I would he might know, in what tone the outraged conscience of a nation can speak. I would that the public bosom were taught to heave, and the public eye to flash upon him, with withering and crushing indignation.

It may be thought a light thing, and to little purpose, to say to the man, high in office, " you are bound by the laws of morality and honor, to act faithfully for the country—yes, and above all men bound." There may be some men of lofty station, and more than one such, who would smile at the simplicity of the appeal, and would imagine that it must come from some child, or from some scholastic and retired person, sadly ignorant of the world. And if, yet more, the nobleness of his function were insisted on; if he were admonished, that nothing on earth can approach so near to the beneficent Divinity as a just and good government, watching over a great people, ministering to the security, comfort and virtue of millions—he might regard it as a picture drawn by some visionary dreamer. *Is* it so? Is the adjuration of subject millions, appealing to their rulers—is the good or the evil flowing down from them, through all the dwellings of a whole country—is the sighing and the crying that goes up from nations, asking—ever asking for truth and justice in the high places of the world—is all this to pass for visionary dreaming? Not so! Forbid it heaven! Forbid it earth! That profane trifling with the sanctitude of power—that accommodating, detestable morality, that allows greatness to be a shield for injustice, and office an exemption from duty—let all the world rise to forbid. That humble ignorance should err, that burdened weakness should falter, that crushed poverty should swerve, may find some apology with man, some indulgence with heaven : but lofty power—but commanding intellect—but proud independence of the low wants of life—these, if any thing, shall be held amenable to the moral judgment of mankind—these, if any thing, shall stand confronted with the most awful accusations of human guilt, before the just and dread tribunal of God!

I am sensible, that the discussion in which I have now engaged, of specific political duties, has already gone to the usual length of a public discourse ; but I must venture to beg your indulgence to a few closing remarks, of a more general character. For, I am not willing to leave the subject without showing, in the first place, that there is a lawful and useful sphere for those powers and principles, which are involved in the political action of a people ; or without pointing out, in the second place, the evil of pressing them beyond the bounds of a just morality.

In the first place, then, there is a lawful sphere for political and party action. Parties, as such, are not to be deprecated. Oppositions are not to be deprecated. Newspapers devoted to the maintainance of particular views, newspaper arguments, public speeches—speeches in caucus—are not to be deprecated. They are all to be welcomed, they are all good, in their place.

What is their place? Let us consider it.

Parties then, properly regarded, are founded on the different views that are unavoidably taken of public measures and public men. All men cannot think alike. Differences of opinion are inevitable. Parties then, are necessary. And they are useful. It is for the public advantage, that all questions touching the common weal, should be freely discussed. The legitimate action of parties is, the embodied manifestation and advocacy of their respective views of the public policy. This is their proper sphere; and this is their proper limit. It is no part of their business to malign the motives of each other, or to use immoral means for the advancement of their respective ends. And not only so, but it is peculiarly incumbent on these political combinations, if they would act an honorable part, to guard themselves from prejudice, passion and violence, from slander, intrigue and oppression. This may be accounted no better, I am sensible, than "the foolishness of preaching." It is the grave voice of political morality, and not of faction. But I cannot admit, that it is out of place here. I cannot believe, that all high principle is for ever to be excluded from politics. I have in my mind still, the *beau ideal* of a party-man, differ as it may from the common example. He is not a man to whom all opinions are indifferent; and, *there-*

fore, he is a party-man. He is a man who adopts an opinion and defends it. But then he is a man who stands up manfully and nobly to defend his opinion—courageously and courteously to defend it—honestly and candidly to defend it; and he spurns the idea of misrepresenting either the argument or the character of his adversary. He cares more to be true to his own mind and conscience, than to any thing else. He guards his liberty from all party invasion; for he will not be a machine. He takes care not to add to his own natural selfishness, the selfishness of ten thousand other persons—for he will not be a blind leader of the blind. He is for his party, indeed; but yet more for his country; and for God above all. " God and my right," is the motto engraven on the arms of a king; but upon his living bosom, is stamped the impress of a nobler motto—" God, and my country!"

There is also a theory of opposition to the government—the beau-ideal of an opposition-man, which, it were to be wished, were more considered than it is. To pull down and destroy, is not in ordinary circumstances, the legitimate end of an opposition. But it is to limit, to control, to correct, and thus ultimately to assist. It is not to look upon the government, as a hostile power that has made a lodgment in the country, and is to be expelled by a party war; but as a lawfully constituted power, that is to be watched, restrained, and kept from going wrong. Still, it is the government of our country, and is to be respected. Still, it is the government of our country, and is to be regarded with a candid, and I had almost said, a filial spirit. Its officers are not to be assailed with scurrilous abuse, nor its departments to be degraded by vile epithets. There is a certain consideration and dignity to be preserved by an opposition. If not, if its spirit is altogether factious and fault-finding, if it rejoices over the errors of an administration, it so far loses all respectability: it shows, that it is not so anxious for a good government, as to be itself the government.

Oppositions, then—parties, party arguments and measures, all have their legitimate sphere. But now I say, in the second place, that when they transcend their sphere, when they overleap the bounds of morality, they become engines of evil and peril to the country.

The only sound and safe principle, I must continually insist, is that which binds morals and politics in indissoluble union; which admits of no compromise, exception or question; which will hear of nothing as expedient, that is at variance with truth and justice. Politics are to have no scale of morality, graduated to their exigencies. That which is wrong every where else, is wrong here. That which is wrong for every other body of men, is wrong for a party. A bad man, in every other relation, is a bad man for the country. He may, indeed, chance to espouse some right measure. But he who is devoid of all principle in private life, can give no satisfactory pledge, that he will be governed by any principle in public life.

The evils of forsaking the moral guidance in political affairs, are various and vast, and they demand the most serious consideration. They more deeply concern the country, than any peril to its visible prosperity. They are such, that they demand our most solemn meditation in our holiest hours and places.

The tendency of political action, when set free from

moral restraint, is to break down all personal independence in the country. Parties, then, demand, not honesty but service, of their votaries. Governments strengthen themselves by bribery and corruption. Oppositions take the same arms, and, in their hour of success, retort the same measures. Abuses become precedents, and precedents multiply abuses. Every new administration, every generation of politicians becomes, not wiser, but worse than their predecessors, their fathers. The tendency of things, without moral restraint, is ever downwards. Already have we arrived at that stage of deterioration, when you will find many respectable and honest men in the country, blinded by reasonings like these—" Why should not an administration, they say, reward its friends and supporters? What is it, but righting the wrongs done by a previous administration? What is it, in fact, but choosing its friends, rather than its enemies, to help it carry on the government?" I will grant, that this must be done, in regard to its immediate council—its Cabinet. But when it extends beyond this to subordinate officers, what is it but a system of favoritism and proscription, fatal to all public virtue? Honesty then becomes a discarded and persecuted virtue; and mere, blind, unscrupulous party zeal becomes the only passport to honors and emoluments. Honorable citizenship is sunk in base partisanship. The entire national dignity, so far as it is connected with its political action—freedom, franchise, patriotism, self-respect—all is merged in a vile scramble for office. The national conscience is sold in the market. The national honor is all bowed down to the worship of interest. The corrupted nation sets up a golden calf, in place of the

Divinity of pristine and holy truth; and not the Israelites, at the footstool of God's manifested presence, were more debased and sacrilegious idolaters.

The destruction of mutual confidence and respect, is another evil connected with our party strifes, and to me, it is one of the most painful.

Pass through the different party circles of the country, and what shall you hear? In the course of a single day, you shall hear every public man in the country, charged with a total want of principle. You shall hear this constantly, from men of the greatest sobriety and weight of character. Not one man in public life, high enough to be a mark for observation, shall escape this tremendous proscription. If you open the newspapers, in the hope, by some patient reading and investigation, to ascertain what the truth is, you find yourself immediately launched upon a sea of doubts. Every fact, every measure, every man, is represented in such different lights, that you are totally at a loss, so far as that testimony goes, what to believe. You are in a worse condition than a juror, vexed by contrary pleadings. You have no judge to help you, and the whole country is filled with party pleadings, without law or precedent, without rule or restraint. You soon come to feel, as if nothing less than the devotion of a whole life, can enable you thoroughly to understand the questions that are brought before you: but you have no life to give—you have something else to do. There is, indeed, one way to find relief; and it is the common way. It is to believe every thing that one party says, and nothing that another says. But he must altogether abjure his reason, who believes that this is the way to come at the truth. And yet, this is the course usually adopted; and men are reading their favorite journals the year round, not to get their minds enlightened and their judgments corrected, but only to have their passions inflamed, and their prejudices confirmed.

Thus, the grand instrument of public opinion is broken. A sound and virtuous public opinion is the only safeguard of the country, and yet men lay their hands upon it as recklessly, as if it were given them to practice upon, and to pervert and poison at their pleasure—as if this great surrounding atmosphere of thought, which invests and sustains the people, were but a laboratory for the experiments of ingenuity and tricks of legerdemain.

Thus, I say, confidence is fallen, and with it is fallen mutual respect. What respect can there be between parties, who are constantly accusing one another of fraud and perjury, of the worst practices and the basest ends? What respect between editors of journals, who are daily charging each other with intrigue, malignity and wilful falsehood? *Can* any honorable mind desire this state of things? Can nothing be done to introduce a new morality, a new courtesy into our discussions? Must our conflicts always be of this bad and brutal character? Is it not the inevitable tendency of this fierce and blasting recrimination, to blunt the sense of honor? Instead of feeling "a stain like a wound," a man is likely to come out of such conflicts seared and scaled all over, as with the mail of leviathan. I confess, that I look with more respect upon the gentle courtesy of the old chivalry, upon the mad sense of honor defended in the tournament, upon the bloody battling of national pride and jealousy, than upon the abusive and outrageous language of our party strifes.

All this, too, in a time of peace! All this for difference of opinion, on grave and difficult questions, upon which men may lawfully and honestly differ! Opponents for such cause, treating one another like ruffians! Reputation—the life, the more than life of a man, stabbed and slain in the shambles of this political butchery! Tell us not, men of the world! of our *religious* disputes. Talk not of our *odium theologicum.* Say nothing of the contentions of professional men, or of the quarrels of authors. Their sound is scarcely heard now, nor is it likely any more to be audible in this land; for it is all lost in the loud strife and fierce battle of politics, that is every year and every month, rising and raging around us.

And the tendency of all this, in fine, is to debase and brutalize the country. Personal independence beaten down; mutual confidence and respect prostrated; moral deterioration follows as a natural consequence. I do not forget to limit the observation. I know that political action is not the whole action of the country. I do not say, that the national character is all sunk to the point of its political derelictions: by no means. But this I say, that immorality in politics, so far as it can take effect, tends to debase and brutalize the country. It tends to corrupt the public sentiment, and to degrade private virtue. No man is so pure, but he is vilified without mercy, by the opposite party. No man is so base so vicious and criminal, but he is sustained without conscience, by his own. It tends to divest the franchise of all dignity, and the government of all venerableness. Let politics be separated from principle, from a high and commanding morality, and instead of the calm majesty of a free people at the polls, we shall see the brawls of a vulgar election; and instead of a magnanimous and self-poised government, a miserable, time-serving, place-keeping faction!

But I must check myself. I ought not, for your patience' sake, to enlarge on this topic, though, alas! it were too easy to do so. Is it not possible, I have said, to introduce a new morality, a new courtesy into our political disputes? And little as you may imagine that this question is thought of, yet I am persuaded, that there are thousands of lofty minds that ask it, with eagerness it may be, with sighing, and almost, with despair. But I am persuaded that it is possible. Even if the pulpit would do its duty, I persuade myself, that much would be accomplished. If, leaving barren polemics and useless abstractions, it would address itself to this momentous theme of the nation's moral wellbeing—if, among the duties which men owe to men, it would solemnly and emphatically place the duties they owe to their country, it could not be without some effect. Sad and lamentable, that in a country like this, the pulpit should be wanting to such a trust! Yes, it *is* possible to do something—to do every thing. Possible, did I say? How easy were it? It is but for every writer and speaker to the country, to charge himself to speak and write with fairness, candor and courtesy; for every citizen to vote honestly; for every legislator and ruler, to act as one who has sworn at the altar of truth, in the sight of Heaven. Oh! come, holy truth, easier than falsehood! primeval virtue, better than victory!—and that which the sages of the world, the prophets of human hope, looking over the ages, have sighed to behold, shall appear—a free and happy community—a free, lofty and self-governed people!

DISCOURSE XII.

THE BLESSING OF FREEDOM.

(Delivered on the Thanksgiving Anniversary in 1837.)

JEREMIAH XXX. 21. AND THEIR NOBLES SHALL BE OF THEMSELVES, AND THEIR GOVERNORS SHALL PROCEED FROM THE MIDST OF THEM.

THE subject on which I am about to address you, is the blessing of freedom; the advantages of that political condition in which we are placed.

There are various causes in operation, which tend to lessen in us, the due sense of these advantages. Extravagance of praise—asserting too much with regard to any principle—overdrawn statements of its nature, and perpetual boasting of its effects, are likely in all cases, sooner or later, to bring about a reaction. I think we are now witnessing something of this reaction. The abuses of the principle of liberty also, the outbreakings of popular violence, mobs and tumults prostrating the law under foot, and the tyranny, moreover, of legal majorities, and withal, the bitter animosities of party strife, and the consequent incessant fluctuations of public policy, constantly deranging the business of the country—all these things are leading some to say, but with more haste and rashness than wisdom,

I must think, that even political oppression and injustice, which should make all strong and firm and permanent, would be better than that state of things in which we live. Add to all this, that the blessings which are common, like the air we breathe and the light of day—blessings which are invested with the familiar livery of our earliest and most constant experience—are apt to pass by us unregarded; while the evils of life, calamities and concussions of the elements, shipwrecks and storms and earthquakes, rise into portentous and heart-thrilling significance; and we see another and final reason why the advantages of our political condition are liable to be undervalued. We have departed just far enough from those days in which the battle for freedom was fought, to substitute indifference and complaint, for the old enthusiasm and devotion.

Indeed, it appears to me, that the time has come, not only in this country, but on the theatre of the world's public opinion, when the merits of popular representative government are to be thoroughly examined. In fact, they were never brought into such controversy all over the world, as they are at this moment. Nay, even in this country, strange as it may seem, there is, in some minds at least, such a controversy. But, in England, the question about giving supreme dominion to the public will, is the great, the ultimate and vital question of the day. That question, too, is penetrating into France and Germany; and it will yet make its way into Italy, and Russia, and the Ottoman Empire itself.

The first step which I shall take in defending the ground which we as a nation have taken, will be carefully to define it. What then is the ground which we have taken? What is the principle of a democratic or representative government? It is, that no restraints, disabilities or penalties shall be laid upon any person, and that no immunities, privileges or charters shall be conferred on any person or any class of persons, *but such as tend to promote the general welfare.* This exception, be it remembered, is an essential part of our theory. Our principle is *not*, as I conceive, that *no* privileges shall be granted to one person more than to another. If bank charters, for instance, can be proved to be advantageous to the community, our principle must allow them. It is upon the same principle, that we grant acts of incorporation to the governors of colleges, academies and hospitals, and to many other benevolent and literary societies: it is upon the ground that they benefit the public. And what is government itself, but a corporation possessing and exercising certain exclusive powers for the general weal. The President of the United States is, by our will, the most privileged person in the country; he holds, for the time being, an absolute monopoly of certain extraordinary powers. Will any man say, then, that no person shall enjoy any privileges which he does not enjoy? There may, doubtless, be monopolies and immunities which are wrong, unjust and injurious. But when the popular cry is, "down with all monopolies! down with all corporations and charters!" I hold, that it is a senseless cry. It is a senseless cry, because it is suicidal; because it is fatal to all government.

Again, I maintain, that our democratic principle is not that the people are always right. It is this rather; that although the people may sometimes be wrong, yet that they are not so likely to be wrong and to do wrong as irresponsible, hereditary magistrates and legislators; that it is safer to trust the many with the keeping of their own interests, than it is to trust the few to keep those interests for them. The people are *not* always right; they are often wrong. They must be so, from the very magnitude, difficulty and complication of the questions that are submitted to them. I am amazed, that thinking men, conversant with these questions, should address such gross flattery and monstrous absurdity to the people, as to be constantly telling them, that *they* will put all these questions right at the ballot-box. And I am no less amazed, that a sensible people should suffer such folly to be spoken to them. Is it possible that the people believe it? Is it possible that the majority itself of any people, can be so infatuated as to hold, that in virtue of its being a majority, it is always right? Alas! for truth, if it is to depend on votes! *Has* the majority always been right in religion or in philosophy? But the science of politics involves questions no less intricate and difficult. And on these questions, there are grave and solemn decisions to be made by the people; great State problems are submitted to them; such, for instance, as concerning internal improvements, the tariff, the currency, banking, and the nicest points of construction; which cost even the wisest men much study; and what the people require for the solution of these questions, is *not* rash haste, boastful confidence, furious anger and mad strife, but sobriety, calmness, modesty—qualities, indeed, that would go far to abate the violence of our parties, and to hush the brawls of our elections. I do not deny, that questions of deep national concern, may justly awaken great zeal and earnestness; but I do deny, that the public mind should be bolstered up with the pride of supposing itself to possess any complete, much less, any suddenly acquired knowledge of them. I am willing to take my fellow-citizens for my governors, with all their errors; I prefer their will, legally signified, to any other government; but to say or imply, that they do not err and often err, is a doctrine alike preposterous in general theory, and pernicious in its effects upon themselves.

A popular government, then, is not to be represented as an unerring government, but only as less likely to err, less likely to oppress and wrong the people, than any other.

Errors there are, indeed, and enough of them, to make the people unfeignedly cautious and modest, in the great attempt to govern themselves. The violence and immorality of party strifes, the prostration of all social order beneath the feet of infuriated mobs, the taking of life without the forms of law, murder, indeed, in the open day, and with more than the impunity of ordinary concealment—these things fill us at times, with alternate disgust and despair. Let the weight of public reprobation rest upon them. I would not lift one finger of the heavy hand which ought to lie upon them, and which ultimately must lie upon them. But let it not be thought, that strifes and tumults are the peculiar results of republican institutions. Will any one say that, during the period of our national existence, we have suffered more from the turbulence of the people, than other nations under different forms of government? Have we forgotten the riots, the burning of hay-ricks and destruction of machinery in England; the horrors of the successive revolutions in France; the tumults and secret societies of Germany; the Ottoman throne swaying to and fro to the pushing pike-staffs of lawless Janizaries; the atrocities of Russian despotism in Poland; the *gentle* tyranny of Austria, not so blood-thirsty—no, but only burying alive her noblest subjects in the graves of Spielburg and Venice—have we forgotten these things, that we are willing to exchange for such fortunes, the peaceful order of these free and happy States?

It is true, indeed, and lamentable as true, that this peaceful order is sometimes broken. It is true and lamentable, that some of our citizens have strangely forgotten the very principle on which our institutions are based—freedom—freedom of speech, freedom of publication, freedom of trial by jury as the only condition on which life, liberty or property in this country shall be ever touched. My blood runs cold in my veins, and I tremble as I look upon my children, to think—that my house or yours, may yet be surrounded by an armed mob, that you or I may be shot down, without remorse, on our own threshold, simply for asserting our honest opinion. But, I thank God, that this is yet a country, and I trust in God, always will be a country, in which I can express my indignation alike against the despotism of a government, and the despotism of a populace. When it ceases to be such, be it no longer my country! Give me any tyranny, rather than that most monstrous of all the tyrannies ever heard of—the bloody violence of a lawless people, with liberty on their lips and murder in their hearts. Let this body of mine sink under the Turkish bow-string or the Russian knout, rather than be trodden out of life under the heels of a brutal populace. I am not an abolitionist, in the technical sense of that word, and I say it now, only that I may give my words the greater force. For if I thought every abolitionist in the country worthy of death, I should still say that the hand which inflicted it, without the forms of law, was the hand of a murderer. And wo and shame to the country, if such deeds can go unpunished!

I have said that I am not an abolitionist, but let it not be supposed, on the other hand, that I am a friend to the system of slavery. With what face could I enter upon a defence of the doctrine of liberty, if I were so? The very despot could defend liberty upon that plan—that is, "liberty for me," he would say, "and bondage for you." Slavery is, undoubtedly, an anomaly in our free institutions. And when I defend and eulogise our freedom, that, of course, must be set aside, as a lamentable, though I trust, that it is to be a temporary exception.

Let me now proceed to speak of liberty as a blessing, and the highest blessing that can appertain to the condition of a people. This, you know, is denied. It is maintained, on the contrary, that liberty is a curse. I do not say that such a proposition is openly maintained in *this* country. But in other countries, it is maintained, with a zeal to which we must, at least, allow the credit of sincerity, that the liberty we contend for, is a curse; that it is not only a dream of enthusiasts, but a wild and dangerous dream, which must sooner or later, wake to the fearful realities of disorder, anarchy and bloodshed. We are called upon, therefore, with equal earnestness to defend the ground, which we as a people, have taken. This defence, I will humbly, in my place, attempt.

And in the first place, I value our political constitution, because it is the only system that accords with the truth of things, the only system that recognises the great claims and inalienable rights of humanity. There may be nations who are not prepared to assert these claims, and to enjoy these rights. I speak not for *them.* But for me it is a happiness that I live under a political system, that is not based upon error, that involves no gross and palpable violation of the great and manifest rights of humanity. I might feel, in Austria or in Prussia, that I was no sufferer from the political system under which I lived ; nay, I might be one of the favorites of that system ; but I would not desire to be the favorite of a system, which would be a constant reproach to my reason and my conscience. Why, I must naturally desire that even the machinery of a manufactory, were I engaged in one, should be the best—should exhibit the fittest adjustment of part to part ;—how much more must I desire this, concerning the machinery of that political constitution, which involves not only interests, but rights and duties.

There *is* not, and there cannot be, any true system of political morality, which does not consult the greatest happiness of the greatest number. And no splendor of a nobility, no magnificence of a throne, can atone for the want of that principle. No sentiment of loyalty, however honorable and graceful it may seem, can stand in place of the dignity of justice.

And what is that justice—the justice of a social system? What is the tenor of the law under which all men evidently hold life, and all the blessings of life, from the great Creator? Is it that one man's will shall reign, a despotic sovereign, over the welfare of millions ? Is it that any one class shall be raised to perpetual honor and power, while all other classes shall be proportionably depressed? Is this justice? I am not saying now what temporary expediency may be ; but, I say, is this justice ? How, is it manifestly the will of heaven, that men, its children, should regard and treat one another? Must we quote written texts, to prove that the great Being who reigns over all is no respecter of persons ? Must we solemnly appeal to the universal sense of right in the human breast, to show that according to the will of God, the dispensation of wealth, happiness, honor and all the blessings of existence should come the nearest possible to the measure of distributive justice—the nearest possible to being the reward of merit? That it cannot come precisely to this point, is true ; but is that any argument for failing to come the nearest possible to it? Can any honorable and generous mind willingly consent to live—can it live happily, with monstrous social injustice all around it—with monstrous social injustice as the very basis of its distinction ;—and that injustice capable of a remedy? And *is* there not injustice in the social, the semifeudal system of Europe—a system of immemorial preferences in church and state, in political employments and social honors ? What is it but to run a race, in which certain hereditary competitors have all the advantage ! Would you send your sons so to run a race even in a May-day game ? But what is this to the race of life, the race for happiness which all men are running? Would you put out your children to an apprenticeship, or into a school, where certain of their fellows, by no merit of their own, were placed so far above them, that they could only by gracious permission, raise their eyes to them? But what would this be, to the great discipline and school of life? These are not mere figures. They represent facts. They point to grievous burthens, heavy to be borne. Is it not a burthen to the Dissenter, that all the ecclesiastical revenues of a kingdom, should be garnered up for a privileged church? Is it not a burthen to the commoner, that so many of the powers and honors of a state, should be lavished upon a hereditary class? Is it not a burthen to the laborer or artisan, that so large a portion of the capital of a country, should be for ever sequestrated from their reach, for the ease and aggrandisement of a few? The capital of a country consists mainly in its soil, its mines, its woods and waters. And, now, to take the most prosperous example of feudal institutions in the world—who, I ask, who own almost half of the soil and mines, the woods and waters of England? Her nobles. And by law, they are permitted to hold them, in perpetual entail, in their own families, for their own advantage, and even free from attachment for debt! And, in addition to this, by the custom and courtesy, should I not rather say, the discourtesy of society, they are permitted to look down upon the whole surrounding world.

I thank heaven, that I live in a country of more equal institutions. I do not pretend here to judge of English reforms. Whether they are too rapid or too slow, I am not qualified to decide. But I may, at least, thank heaven, that we do not need them. Perhaps I have a hearer, to whom even these candid allusions to England may not be agreeable. It may not be without some degree of irritation, that he will ask, why I should say any thing in disparagement of England?

the most glorious country, he may say, in the world. He may say this, and I shall not refuse to agree with him: but the glory of England is the work of time and position, and of a noble race of men, and not, I trust, of the inequality of her political constitution. Why, then, do I speak as I do, even of the fairest and most modified example of feudal institutions? I will answer. It is because I stand up for justice, as the dearest immunity of a civilized state. It is because I stand up for humanity, as the noblest claim in the world. It is because I contend for a dignity, higher than that of kings and nobles—the dignity of truth. It is, in fine, because I am willing, and I wish to stand on earth as a man—beneath the equal and even canopy of heaven—in presence of the impartial justice and lovingkindness that reign in that heaven—there to discharge my lot, and to work out my welfare as a man. It offends me, to think that I or any other man should be bolstered up with hereditary advantages, or with social or religious immunities, that are denied to mine equals, my brethren, in the sight of God. That is my feeling, be it called quixotism, or whatever else any one may call it. I have, in this matter, an unfortunate and strange way of thinking of others, as if they possessed my own nature; and I cannot patiently bear, that the children of one common Father, should be treated with a partiality that would revolt me, if it were introduced among the children of an earthly parentage. It is monstrous in the eye of reason; it is treason to gentle humanity; it is as truly unjust, as if it were the oppression of bonds and burthens; and the time will come, when it will be so regarded. The dignity of the English mind, I am certain, will not always bear it. In the mean time, I say it again, I thank heaven, that I am made no party, either better or worse, to the injustice of such a system.

II. In the next place, I value our liberty, and deem it a just cause of thankfulness to heaven, because it fosters and developes all the intellectual and moral powers of the country.

Freedom is the natural school of energy and enterprize. Freedom is the appropriate sphere of talent and virtue. The soul was not made to walk in fetters. To act powerfully, it must act freely; and it must act, too, under all the fair incentives of an honest and honorable ambition. This applies, especially, to the mass of the people. There may be minds, and there are, which find a sufficient incentive to exertion, in the love of knowledge and improvement, in the single aim at perfection. But this is not, and cannot be, the condition of the mass of minds. They need other impulses. Open then, I say, freely and widely to every individual, the way to wealth, to honor, to social respect and to public office, and you put life into any people. Impart that principle to a nation of Turks, or even of Hindoos, and it will be as a resurrection from the dead. The sluggish spirit will be aroused; the languid nerve will be strung to new energy; there will be a stir of action and a spring to industry all over the country, because there will be a motive. Alas! how many poor toilers in the world are obliged to labor, without reward, without hope, almost without motive! Like the machinery amidst which they labor, and of which they are scarcely more than a part, they are moved by the impulse of blind necessity. The single hope of bettering their condition, which now, alas!

never visits them, would regenerate them to a new life.

Now, it is with such life, that this whole nation is inspired. It is freedom that has breathed the breath of life into this people. I know that there are perils attending this intense action and competition of society. But I see, nevertheless, a principle that is carrying forward this country with a progress, altogether unprecedented in the history of the world. Invention, internal improvement, and accumulation among us, are taking strides before unheard of. More school-houses, colleges and churches have been builded, in this country, within the last twenty years; more canals and railroads have been constructed; more fortunes have been acquired, and, what is better, more poor men have risen to competence; and, in fine, more enterprizes and works of social and religious beneficence have been achieved, than ever were done, take them all together, in an equal time, by an equal population, under heaven. For these things, I love and honour my country. For these things, I am thankful to heaven, that my lot is cast in it. And this I say, not in the spirit of boasting, but because I think the time has come when it needs to be said; because I believe that many of us are insensible to our advantages; because the eyes of the world are fixed upon us for inquisition and for reproach, and incessant foreign criticism is liable to cool the fervor of our patriotism.

Nay, I will go further, and confess the secret hope I have long entertained, that the liberty wherewith, as I believe, God has made us free, that the equal justice, the impartial rewards which encourage individual enterprize in this country, will produce yet more glorious and signal results; results that will proclaim to all the world, that political equity is the best pledge for national dignity, strength and honor; results which will, effectually and for ever break down the pernicious maxim, that a certain measure of political injustice and favoritism, is necessary to the order and security of the social state. As I believe in a righteous Providence, I do not believe in this maxim; and I trust in God, that it will receive its final and annihilating blow in this very country. It is not that I challange for our people any natural superiority to other people. It is not to the shrine of national pride that I bring the homage of this lofty hope, but to the footstool of divine goodness. It is to our signal advantages, and especially to the equal justice of our institutions, that I look for the accomplishment of this great hope. I believe that *freedom*—free action—free enterprize—free competition—will be found to be the best of auspices for every kind of human success. I believe that our citizens will be found to act more effectively, and more generously, and more nobly, for being free; that our citizen soldiers will, if called upon, fight more valiantly for being free; that our laborers will toil more cheerfully for being free; that our merchants will trade more successfully; nay, and little as it may be expected, that our preachers and orators will discourse more eloquently, and that our authors will write more powerfully, for the spirit of freedom that is among us. The future, indeed, must tell us whether this is a dream of enthusiastic patriotism. But I would fain have the most generous of principles for once laid at the heart of a great people, and see what it will do. Alas! for humanity—never yet has it been treated with the confidence of simple justice. Never yet has any voice effectually said to man, " God has made thee to be as happy and as glorious if thou wilt, as thy most envied fellow." When that voice does address the heart of the multitude, will it not arouse itself to loftier efforts, to nobler sacrifices, to higher aspirations, and more generous virtues, than were ever seen to be the offspring of any unequal and ungenerous system that ever man has devised? God grant that the hope may be realized, and the vision accomplished! It were enough to make one say, "now let me depart in peace, for mine eyes have seen thy salvation!"

III. In the third place, I value political liberty, because, of that which a free and unfettered energy obtains, it gives the freest and amplest use.

What is the effect, nay, what is the design of a despotic government, but to deprive the people of the largest amount that it can, or dare, of the proceeds of their honest industry and laudable enterprize? Under its grossest forms, it levies direct contributions; in its more plausible administration, it levies taxes; but in either case, its end is the same—to feed and batten a few, at the expense of the many. In order the more effectually to accomplish this purpose, such governments require standing armies, or to speak more exactly, a military force to act at home. That is to say, a part of the citizens, one of each family, perhaps, must be armed and trained, in order to coerce and control the labor, the toil, the entire labor of the rest.

Such then, more or less strongly marked, is the condition of labor in every part of the world, with the exception of our own favored country. The people must work till they are weary, for the supply of their *own* wants. So far the law of labor is healthful, and every way useful. But after that, they must work a while longer—one or two hours every day—to support a home military force. And then, when the yoke is fairly fixed upon their necks, they must work as much longer as their masters please, to gorge the almost insatiable appetite of a luxurious court, and a herd of idle courtiers and sycophants beside. And the reward they get, is two-fold; perpetual poverty, and an utter contempt of their grovelling employments.

Let me not be told, that differences in the form of government are mere matters of speculation; that they have very little to do with our private welfare; that a man may be as happy under one form as another. I think it was on occasion of our Revolution, that Dr. Johnson put forth some such oracle as this. But it is not true. It may pass for good nature, or for smooth philosophy, if any one pleases so to call it, but it is not true. What more obvious interest of human life is there, than that a man's labor shall produce for him, the greatest possible amount of comfort; that he should enjoy, as far as is compatible with the support of civil order, the proceeds of his toil! Labor, honorable and useful as it is, is not so very agreeable, that a man should recklessly give it for that which is not bread. And *that*, he emphatically does, who gives it for pensions, sinecures and monopolies, and establishments and wars, which benefit him not at all. What real interest have the people had in four-fifths of the wars that have devastated Europe, and burthened all her governments with enormous debts? It is strange, indeed, when the laboring hand is so near the suffering heart, that men do not feel this. But the reason is, that the exactions of selfish and unjust governments come upon them in the indirect form of taxation—of impost and revenue, and excise, and the hundred minor and contemptible contrivances that have been invented, to hide from them the fact. Let them be told, let them see, that of their ten hour's toil each day, four or five hours only are for themselves or their families, while the remainder are for other families and other children than their own, and they would think it intolerable. But this, more or less, always is, and always must be, the condition of the people, where governments do not represent its expressed and supreme will. For it is not in human nature, lawfully and justly to use unlawful and unlimited power. I only wish to know that governments *have* the power to oppress the people, to know that they use it. And the very definition of such a power is—*a power not emanating from themselves.* Tell your neighbor, ay, or your friend, that he may govern you, not as much as you please, but just as much as he pleases, and you know very well what the consequence will be. You would not trust your dearest friend, nor scarcely an angel in heaven, to have such a power over you. I thank heaven, that there is no such power, and nothing approaching to it, in this country. And in order to make out a clear case of superior advantages, on our part, it is not necessary that I should go into details, (for which, indeed, I have not space;) it is not necessary, that I should now particularize and say, that this government possesses such a power, and that government a certain other power, which bear hard upon the people; for every government not emanating from them, is sure to present a case of such hardship. But one fact, I will mention in this connection, which may stand in place of all other facts, and that is, the eternal enmity which exists in every other country between the government and the people. That enmity, as old as the creation, has never been brought so completely to an end as here. I know that we hear sometimes of measures of an administration, as having an unfriendly bearing upon particular interests; but it is certain, that the government with us, can never stand up in permanent hostility to that people, of which it is the creature. But when we turn our eyes abroad, what do we see? Every where the people are demanding constitutions, charters, immunities, changes, which their respective governments will not concede to them. So far as the satisfaction of a people with its institutions is concerned, we are, after all that is said about popular disturbances among us, in a state of singular, of enviable, I may say, of profound tranquillity. And well do I know, if I know the spirit of this people, that that tranquillity would be effectually disturbed, were a tithe of the resistance and refusal to which every other nation must submit, to lay its intolerable grievance on us. The very cup of blessings with us, would be a cup of wrath and indignation.

I have offered some reasons to show that our freedom is a blessing. It is founded in rectitude as a principle; it fosters the intellectual and moral growth of a country; and it favors the amplest enjoyment of all the blessings of existence. These are reasons. But I should not exhaust the subject, even in this most general view of it, if I did not add one further consideration in behalf of freedom; a consideration that is higher and stronger than any reason; I mean the *intrinsic desirableness* of this condition to every human being. In this respect, freedom is like virtue, like happiness; we value it for its own sake. God has stamped upon our very humanity this impress of freedom. It is the unchartered prerogative of human nature. A soul ceases to be a soul, in proportion as it ceases to be free. Strip it of this, and you strip it of one of its essential and characteristic attributes. It is this that draws the footsteps of the wild Indian to his wide and boundless desert-paths, and makes him prefer them to the gay saloons and soft carpets of sumptuous palaces. It is this that makes it so difficult to bring him within the pale of artificial civilization. Our roving tribes are perishing—a sad and solemn sacrifice upon the altar of their wild freedom. They come among us, and look with childish wonder upon the perfection of our arts, and the splendor of our habitations; they submit with ennui and weariness, for a few days, to our burthensome forms and restraints; and then turn their faces to their forest homes, and resolve to push those homes onward till they sink in the Pacific waves, rather than not be free.

It is thus that every people is attached to its country, just in proportion as it is free. No matter if that country be in the rocky fastnesses of Switzerland, amidst the snows of Tartary, or on the most barren and lonely Island-shore; no matter if that country be so poor, as to force away its children to other and richer lands, for employment and sustenance; yet when the songs of those free homes chance to fall upon the exile's ear, no soft and ravishing airs that wait upon the timed feastings of Asiatic opulence, ever thrilled the heart with such mingled rapture and agony, as those simple tones. Sad mementoes might they be of poverty and want and toil; yet it was enough that they were mementoes of happy freedom. And more than once has it been necessary to forbid by military orders, in the armies of the Swiss mercenaries, the singing of their native songs.

And such an attachment, do I believe, is found in our own people, to their native country. It is the country of the free; and that single consideration compensates for the want of many advantages, which other countries possess over us. And glad am I, that it opens wide its hospitable gates, to many a noble but persecuted citizen, from the dungeons of Austria and Italy, and the imprisoning castles and citadels of Poland. Here may they find rest, as they surely find sympathy, though it is saddened with many bitter remembrances!

Yes, let me be free; let me go and come at my own will; let me do business and make journeys, without a vexatious police or insolent soldiery, to watch my steps; let me think, and do, and speak, what I please, subject to no limit but that which is set by the common weal; subject to no law but that which conscience binds upon me; and I will bless my country, and love its most rugged rocks and its most barren soil.

I have seen my countrymen, and have been with them a fellow-wanderer, in other lands; and little did I see or feel to warrant the apprehension, sometimes expressed, that foreign travel would weaken our patriotic attachments. One sigh for home—home, arose from all hearts. And why, from palaces and courts—why, from galleries of the arts, where the marble softens into life, and painting sheds an almost living presence of beauty around it—why, from the mountain's awful brow, and the lovely valleys and lakes touched with the sunset hues of old romance—why, from those venerable and touching ruins to which our very heart grows—why, from all these scenes, were they looking beyond the swellings of the Atlantic wave, to a dearer and holier spot of earth—their own, own country? Doubtless, it was in part, because it *is* their country. But it was also, as every one's experience will testify, because they knew that *there* was no oppression, no pitiful exaction of petty tyranny; because that *there*, they knew, was no accredited and irresistible religious domination; because that *there*, they knew, they should not meet the odious soldier at every corner, nor swarms of imploring beggars, the victims of misrule; that *there*, no curse causeless did fall, and no blight, worse than plague and pestilence, did descend amidst the pure dews of heaven; because, in fine, that *there*, they knew, was liberty—upon all the green hills, and amidst all the peaceful valleys—liberty, the wall of fire around the humblest home; the crown of glory, studded with her ever-blazing stars, upon the proudest mansion!

My friends, upon our own homes, that blessing rests, that guardian care and glorious crown; and when we return to those homes, and so long as we dwell in them —so long as no oppressor's foot invades their thresholds, let us bless them, and hallow them as the homes of freedom! Let us make them, too, the homes of a nobler freedom—of freedom from vice, from evil, from passion—from every corrupting bondage of the soul.